Faith and Money
How Religion Contributes to Wealth and Poverty

For those who own it, wealth can have extraordinary advantages. High levels of wealth can enhance educational attainment, create occupational opportunities, generate social influence, and provide a buffer against financial emergencies. Even a small amount of savings can improve security, mitigate the effects of job loss and other financial setbacks, and improve well-being dramatically. Although the benefits of wealth are significant, they are not enjoyed uniformly throughout the United States.

In the United States, because religion is an important part of cultural orientation, religious beliefs should affect material well-being. This book explores the way religious orientations and beliefs affect Americans' incomes, savings, and net worth.

Lisa A. Keister is Professor of Sociology and Director of the Markets and Management Program at Duke University. She conducts research on wealth inequality, asset accumulation, and the causes of each. She is the author of *Getting Rich: America's New Rich and How They Got There* (Cambridge, 2005) and *Wealth in America* (Cambridge, 2000). Her research on Chinese corporations and the country's economic transition appeared in her book, *Chinese Business Groups* (2000), as well as various articles.

Faith and Money

How Religion Contributes to Wealth and Poverty

LISA A. KEISTER
Duke University

CAMBRIDGE
UNIVERSITY PRESS

CAMBRIDGE UNIVERSITY PRESS
Cambridge, New York, Melbourne, Madrid, Cape Town,
Singapore, São Paulo, Delhi, Tokyo, Mexico City

Cambridge University Press
32 Avenue of the Americas, New York, NY 10013–2473, USA

www.cambridge.org
Information on this title: www.cambridge.org/9780521721103

First published 2011

Printed in the United States of America

A catalog record for this publication is available from the British Library.

Library of Congress Cataloging in Publication data
Keister, Lisa A., 1968–
Faith and money : how religious belief contributes to wealth and poverty / Lisa A. Keister.
p. cm.
Includes bibliographical references and index.
ISBN 978-0-521-89651-1 (hardback) – ISBN 978-0-521-72110-3 (paperback)
1. Wealth – Religious aspects. 2. Wealth – United States. 3. Money – Religious aspects.
4. Money – United States. 5. United States – Religion. I. Title.
BL65.W42K45 2011
201'.73–dc22 2011015744

ISBN 978-0-521-89651-1 Hardback
ISBN 978-0-521-72110-3 Paperback

To JWM

Contents

Figure and Tables

Figure

Tables

Acknowledgments

My gratitude to the people who assisted me with this book and to the organizations that facilitated my work is deep. I received extremely helpful comments at various stages of the project from a large number of people including Jimi Adams, John Bartkowski, Jackie Brooks, James Cavendish, Mark Chaves, Barry Chiswisk, Christopher Ellison, William Form, Robert Hummer, Evelyn Lehrer, Katherine Meyer, James Moody, Christian Smith, and four anonymous reviewers for Cambridge University Press. Innumerable comments at seminars were also indispensible, including from people who attended talks at Duke University, the University of Chicago, Cornell University, the Center for Advanced Study in the Behavioral Studies at Stanford University, Yale University, Ohio State University, UC Irvine, UC Santa Barbara, the American Sociological Association, and the Religion, Economics, and Culture/Society for the Scientific Study of Religion.

A grant from the National Institutes of Health program on Intergenerational Family Resource Allocation (funded by the National Institutes of Child Health and Human Development and the National Institute on Aging) supported early portions of this research, and a grant from the National Science Foundation, Sociology Program (SES 0848653) helped me complete it. The Center for Advanced Study in the Behavioral Sciences and Duke University provided space to write the book, and a host of graduate students provided excellent research assistance at various stages of the project. Most notably, E. Paige Borelli, David Eagle, Steven Foy, Brad Fulton, Andrew Miles, Matthew Painter, and Alexis Yamokoski assisted in preparing data and tables. Laura Tesch provided editing assistance.

Some pieces of this book were originally published in journal articles. Chapter 6 contains portions of a paper originally published as Keister, Lisa A. 2007. "Upward Wealth Mobility: Exploring the Roman Catholic Advantage." *Social Forces* 85:1195–226, and Keister, Lisa A. 2008. "Conservative Protestants and Wealth: How Religion Perpetuates Asset Poverty." *American Journal of Sociology* 113:1237–71.

I

Religion and Wealth

Wealth ownership is essential to financial security and general well-being. *Wealth*, or net worth, is total household assets less total liabilities. Wealth is relatively enduring – both within and across generations – and is related in some way to most other measures of achievement. For those who own it, wealth can have extraordinary advantages. It can enhance educational attainment, occupational opportunities, political power, and social influence. It provides a buffer against income interruptions, medical emergencies, and other crises such as accidents and natural disasters. Wealth can create more wealth when it is reinvested, and it can generate income in the form of interest or dividends. At high levels of wealth, the income it generates can make paid employment unnecessary. Yet even a small amount of savings can improve security, mitigate the effect of job loss and other financial shocks, and improve well-being dramatically. There are, of course, disadvantages of owning wealth as well, but most people agree that having wealth is more desirable than not having it.

Although the benefits of wealth are significant, they are not enjoyed uniformly in the United States because asset ownership is highly concentrated (Keister 2000b, 2005; Wolff 2004). Between 1995 and 2004, mean net worth increased 72 percent to $448,000, whereas the median net worth increased only 31 percent to $93,000. Between 2004 and 2007, the period in which a financial and housing bubble developed, mean net worth grew to a remarkably high $506,000, and median net worth increased to $109,000. Consistent with this growth, in 2004, the top 1 percent of households owned 33 percent of net worth, and the top 10 percent owned 70 percent of net worth. At the same time, 16 percent of households had zero or negative net worth.[1] Financial wealth – net worth less net equity in owner-occupied housing – is a measure of relatively liquid resources. In 2001, the top 1 percent of households owned 40 percent of financial wealth, and 26 percent of households had zero or negative financial assets. Throughout the years leading up to the recession, these values – not surprisingly – became even more extreme (Bucks et al. 2009). Prior to the twentieth century, wealth mobility was extremely unusual, and even today, the majority of people do not change positions in the wealth distribution compared with their parents or during their adult lives (Keister 2005). Economic downturns tend to reduce wealth inequality as the wealth of those at the top of the distribution of wealth tends to drop. The recession of 2008–2009 was typical in its effect on wealth ownership: As stocks and many other financial assets lost value, the net worth of wealthy households declined, leading to a slightly more equal distribution of wealth. However, in that recession, as in many recessions, wealth inequality remained quite high, and those who owned some wealth typically were better prepared than those without assets to weather the crisis (Bucks et al. 2009). As the economy improves, the wealthy also appear to be rebounding comparatively quickly.

Although we know a great deal about the distribution of wealth, we still know very little about the individual and family processes that contribute to that distribution. It seems logical that a person's general approach to the world – their cultural orientation – would be related in predictable ways to their wealth. After all, the things we consider important and our operating assumptions about how the world *does* work and how it *should* work are certain to affect the goals we pursue, our decisions about critical life events, and, ultimately, how well off we are. In the United States, because religion is an important part of cultural orientation, it follows that religious beliefs should affect material well-being. Yet this relationship has proven to be much more difficult to study effectively than it might appear at first, resulting in decades of intense debate among social scientists and other observers. A growing body of research has recently begun to provide compelling evidence that religion affects outcomes such as education, income, and work. Yet what is missing is a comprehensive study of how religion is related to one of the most critical indicators of well-being: wealth ownership.

---

[1] All values are 2004 dollars. Author's estimates from the Survey of Consumer Finances; consistent with other estimates from these data (Bucks et al. 2009).

This book fills this gap by asking how religion and wealth are related. That is, I explore how people's religious affiliations are associated with their educational attainment, family processes, incomes, savings, and, ultimately, their accumulation of net worth. My focus is on total wealth, but my interest is in both those who are wealthy and those who are wealth-poor. Most of what I do is describe empirical patterns, but I do so with a realization that most readers will want to understand why these patterns exist. When I can, I provide explanations based on contemporary theory and empirical evidence. For example, I ask why it is that conservative Protestants have tended to have much lower wealth than mainline Protestants. There is some evidence that certain conservative Protestant groups are gaining financial ground, but for much of recent history, members of conservative Protestant religious groups have been relatively poor. How do conservative and mainline church members compare today and why? Have conservative Protestant churches simply attracted those with few resources, or is there something about the teachings of these churches that affects how people work, spend, and save? Similarly, why have white Roman Catholics been upwardly mobile in recent decades? In other words, why do contemporary white Catholics resemble mainline Protestants in their worldly success more than they did in prior generations? How do Catholics from other ethnic origins compare to white Catholics? What other groups are upwardly mobile?

In this book, I answer these questions and more. I study a range of contemporary American religious groups and show that there are distinct patterns across groups in asset ownership, debt, saving, and overall wealth. I explore the degree to which these patterns reflect the indirect effect of religion on wealth via other behaviors and processes such as educational attainment, marriage and family patterns, job and career processes, and income. I also propose that there is an important connection between religion and orientations toward work and money, and I explore how this connection potentially creates a direct association between religion and wealth. The ideas I propose and examine in this book are designed to provide a plausible explanation of very strong empirical patterns. This is not a definitive statement but rather a first account designed to encourage others to continue to explore and improve our understanding of the important relationships that are involved here. I do not have a stake in a particular answer or ranking of religious groups. I do not have an agenda or an axe to grind. On the contrary, I am deeply committed to understanding the sources of wealth inequality. By studying the relationship between religion and wealth, I hope to shed light on the factors that account for the complex relationship between cultural orientation and material well-being, one of the most crucial questions in the social sciences.

A Challenging Question

I recognize that the relationship between religion and material well-being is a topic with a long history in the social sciences, and I know that it is a very difficult issue to address effectively. However, both the relevant questions and the landscape have been changing in ways that make this topic both important and timely, and contemporary data and methods make it possible to provide empirical evidence that sheds new light on the topic. Sociologists have debated the material consequences of religious beliefs, affiliation, and practices for a large part of the twentieth century (Mathews 1896; Wuthnow and Scott 1997). Weber (1930 [1905]), Sombart (1911), and others have related religion and aggregate outcomes. Weber, for instance, famously linked religion to economic development and the rise of capitalism, arguing that otherworldly asceticism among European Protestants (Calvinists, Pietists, Methodists, and others) fueled the rise of capitalism in Europe. These arguments have been controversial because, among many other reasons, they propose individual- and family-level processes for aggregate outcomes without adequately addressing these processes empirically (Coleman 1990). Of course, Weber did not have access to the data available today. If he did, perhaps he would have approached the issue differently. More recently, Collins (1997) related religion to the rise of capitalism via entrepreneurship, using Japan as a case study. Kuran (2003) drew a connection between Islam and economic development (a negative relationship in this case), arguing that avoidance of usury prevented the development of financial markets and banking institutions.

More closely related to my objective is the contested literature from the 1960s and 1970s linking religion to status attainment. Lenski's *Religious Factor* (1961) ignited the debates by proposing that American religious groups differed from one another in their levels of social and economic attainment because of the values inherent in the religious beliefs. This proposal fueled heated intellectual exchange – but few convincing answers – before waning by the 1980s (Demereth 1965; Glenn and Hyland 1967; Jones and Westoff 1979; Roof and McKinney 1987). Research in this area virtually disappeared for at least two reasons. First, there was a growing realization that it was not sufficient simply to compare Catholics and Protestants, as scholars found themselves doing. It became increasingly apparent that Catholics from different ethnic groups and Protestants from different denominations could not always be grouped neatly. Unfortunately, limitations in both data and research methods made it difficult to explore more fine-tuned group differences that might have resolved some of the controversies. Second, it also became clear that family background was another important factor mediating the relationship between religion and socioeconomic status. However, empirical data at the time were not adequate to allow researchers to parse the relative importance of family background, childhood religion, and adult religion.[2]

In recent years, interest in the material consequences of religion has begun to experience a revival, and improved data and methods allow researchers to isolate and answer questions that eluded prior generations of scholars (Edgell 2006; Ellison and Bartkowski 2002; Glass and Jacobs 2005; Lehrer 2009; Sherkat and Ellison 1999; Smith and Faris 2005). Moreover, as Wuthnow (2004) pointed out, there are some elements of Lenski's *Religious Factor* that are worthy of reconsideration, particularly given modern data and methods that might adjudicate his claims.[3] The relationship between religion and wealth is particularly important now, given changes in patterns of both wealth accumulation and the American religious landscape (Keister 2003b, 2005, 2007, 2008). Wealth and poverty are no longer about shifts in the mode of production, but instead reflect group and individual commitments to human capital, savings, and entrepreneurship. The religious landscape is also different. The diversity of Protestant traditions, the changing position of Catholics, and the growth of groups such as Muslims and the Church of Jesus Christ of Latter-day Saints (Mormon/LDS) would be unrecognizable to early scholars, and yet these changes provide just the contrasting experiences that allow the testing of ideas about religion and wealth attainment.

My objective is to provide a comprehensive, contemporary, empirically grounded discussion of how religion, various individual and household processes, and wealth outcomes are related. In doing so, I extend a growing body of superb contemporary research that shows that religious

[2] Sherkat (2006) provides an excellent summary of literature relating religion and status attainment.
[3] Wuthnow (2004) identifies four elements of Lenski's proposal that are worthy of reconsideration, including his religious classifications and his proposals regarding differentiation among socioreligious groups. I address these issues in more detail as they become relevant throughout this book.

orientation influences education, income, female labor force participation, careers, and many other important individual and family outcomes (Chiswick 1993; Sherkat and Ellison 1999; Ellison and Bartkowski 2002; Lehrer 2004a; Glass and Jacobs 2005; Smith and Faris 2005). I discuss the complex interactions among various individual- and household-level processes, explore how these are related to overall wealth and the components of total wealth, and include a large number of religious groups. My results paint a picture of a complex, nuanced process because the relationship between religion and wealth is just that: complex and nuanced.

Although I attempt to be comprehensive, there are many issues I cannot address in a single book. One important question that I do not tackle here is how religion relates to economic development. Wuthnow and Scott (1997) provide an excellent summary and evaluation of the literature on this relationship, but such a summary is beyond the scope of this book. Similarly, I do not address other aggregate outcomes, including inequalities in well-being among groups. My findings are suggestive of important aggregate outcomes; for example, when I show that members of a religious group tend to have low wealth, I am also saying something about the distribution of wealth across religious groups. However, as Coleman (1990) and others have shown, there is more to the aggregation of individual and household outcomes than a simple summation. Elsewhere (Keister 2009), I addressed the multilevel processes that relate religion, micro-outcomes (e.g., wealth), and aggregate outcomes (e.g., inequality), but I do not incorporate that work here because it is not possible given today's data to adequately explore these processes empirically. I also do not address issues related to the reasons people hold certain beliefs, although there is a sizable literature identifying important factors that precede religious affiliation. Rather, I accept affiliation and stated beliefs as given and explore their consequences. Similarly, I do not address how and why religious groups conflict with each other on important doctrinal and political issues, nor do I address political action, social justice, or related issues. Related to the origin of religious belief is the issue of religious tolerance and clashes in religious ideas. There has historically been an ethos of tolerance for a range of religious ideas in the United States, which affects the nature of individuals' belief systems. Religious tolerance is an important issue, but the topic is beyond the scope of this work. Finally, I restrict my discussion to the United States. There are important benefits that could be gained from including cross-cultural analyses, but I have opted to err on the side of a thorough discussion of processes in the

United States – already complex enough – rather than include multiple countries in my discussion. Future research will certainly fill this gap.

In the remainder of this chapter, I provide a preliminary portrait of the relationship between religion and wealth. I propose that religion is important for understanding wealth and that the effect is both indirect (through other processes) and direct. I describe the theoretical foundations of the approach I use, provide details about data and terminology, and present an overview of the American religious landscape. My goal is to clarify who I am talking about when I refer to various religious groups and to identify the size and other traits of these groups that will become relevant throughout the remainder of the book. In Chapters 2 and 3, I discuss how religious affiliation is associated with behaviors and processes that are known to affect wealth. In Chapter 2, I explore how religion is related to family processes and human capital acquisition; and in Chapter 3, I study the relationship between religious affiliation and work, occupation, and income, including how religion is related to orientations toward work and money.

I then look directly at the relationship between religion and wealth. In Chapters 4 and 5, I provide detailed empirical evidence of the relationship between religion, asset ownership, and debt acquisition, focusing first on real (or tangible) assets and then on financial assets and liabilities. In Chapter 6, I focus on wealth mobility, or changes in wealth over time. I showcase three groups that are (or may be) in different stages of mobility. I describe the upward mobility of white Roman Catholics, a transition that occurred in recent decades. I then speculate about the potential mobility of conservative Protestants and Hispanic Catholics. In Chapter 7, I focus on other groups that have been unique in their wealth-accumulation trends, including mainline Protestants and MP subgroups, Jews, and Mormons/LDS.

Chapter 8 is a unique chapter. Modern data is superb and allows me to study relationships that would have been unheard of even a couple decades ago. However, there are still many questions about the relationship between religion and wealth accumulation that we can only answer moderately well with current data. These issues (e.g., how do social networks intercede between religion and wealth ownership?) are important and supported relatively well in some cases by current data. However, there are still many gaps in our understanding of the issues, most of which derive from inadequate data. I describe these behaviors and processes in Chapter 8 and speculate about how future research might be better able to provide definitive information and answers to these questions. I conclude the book with a chapter called "How Much Is Enough?" This is a question that is ultimately impossible to answer, but I nonetheless attempt to do so. If there is any source for an answer to this question, it might well come from religion.

Does Religion Matter?

There are, indeed, reasons to anticipate that religious affiliation and religious beliefs shape wealth ownership. In this section, I propose a causal model that provides a plausible explanation for a connection between religion and wealth. Adult wealth ownership is an outcome that reflects behaviors and processes that begin early in life and that interact and change in complex ways over the life course. Religion is likely to influence wealth outcomes both indirectly and directly. Religion likely affects saving, asset accumulation, and wealth *indirectly* through its effect on orientations toward education and educational attainment, marriage behavior, fertility, and the timing and ordering of education, marriage, fertility, job, and career behaviors. Life course processes are extremely complex, involving interrelated pathways about major life decisions, which condition the needs and capacities to save. Moreover, religious beliefs affect these processes in unmistakable ways. For example, there are marked differences by religion in family background and the context in which people are raised. There are also religious differences in attitudes toward educational attainment, the importance of education by gender, and returns to education. Education, in turn, is one of the strongest predictors of wealth accumulation. Thus, we would expect that those affiliated with religions that encourage educational advancement are likely to have an advantage in wealth accumulation over those affiliated with a religion that either does not incorporate ideas about education or is skeptical of or overtly hostile toward secular education.

Similarly, family formation, family dissolution, and other processes interact with one another and with educational processes in complex ways that affect wealth, and religion plays a critical role here as well. For instance, fertility behaviors – the onset of sexual behavior, the age at which a person first has children, the number of children born – and other processes related to family formation all affect saving, accumulation, and wealth. Because there are important variations in family formation across faiths and even denominations within a single faith, religion is certain to shape wealth ownership. Likewise, the timing of marriage, marital strength, divorce, and related processes affect saving and wealth, and there is evidence that marriage processes differ by religious affiliation. Similar arguments can be made regarding the relationship between religion and work behaviors, gender roles in the family and the labor market, income, nonwage work benefits, willingness to sacrifice career outcomes for family, entrepreneurship, and other processes that influence wealth ownership. To the extent that religion affects these processes – and mounting evidence suggests that religion is an important determinant of each of these processes – religion will affect wealth ownership.

Religion may also affect wealth *directly*. A person's orientation toward work, saving, investing, and related issues is critical to wealth accumulation, and these can be affected by religious beliefs. Orientations or values toward work and money refer to the general approach that a person takes to selecting among available jobs or careers, deciding whether and what kinds of loans to take, and determining how to save and invest, when possible. For example, investing in high-risk, high-return financial assets, as opposed to relatively conservative instruments such as certificates of deposit, can have dramatic effects on total wealth accumulated over the life course (Keister 2000b). Likewise, the timing and ordering of financial decisions can shape wealth accumulation in important ways. Beginning to save in early adulthood can have significant advantages over postponing saving until later. Because there is a degree of path dependence built into saving and consumption decisions, people tend to follow paths through their lives that influence in important ways the amount of wealth they accumulate over time. For example, a traditional trajectory might involve first buying a house and investing in financial assets only later in life.

Orientations toward work and money, saving, consumption, portfolio composition, and risk begin to develop early in life. The behaviors that result from these patterns also start to emerge early in life, and the implications of both orientations and behaviors cumulate over time. Children learn how to save from their families and other acquaintances. They learn about whether it is desirable to start a business, to invest in the stock market, to buy expensive consumer goods, or to accumulate debt. They learn detailed strategies within each of these general issues: for example, what kind of business to start, if any; how much risk is too much; and whether debt ever can be good or is always a problem. Children and young adults test these strategies, hone them, and personalize them, often through trial and error. A child who learns that investing in the stock market is desirable but then has a bad experience losing money in the market as a young adult might develop a lower risk tolerance as a result. Alternatively, a child who learns that most risk is bad but then interacts with people in college who have learned to invest and use risk to their advantage might develop a slightly higher risk tolerance. Adults draw on these early experiences, on the financial literacy they have accumulated through formal and informal training, and on other experiences to develop a strategy for saving, spending, and accumulating wealth.

What is most important here is that orientations toward work and money, saving, consumption, portfolio composition, and risk can be influenced by religion. Religion shapes values and priorities, affects decisions about which goals are worth pursuing, and contributes to the set of competencies from which actions such as saving behavior are constructed (Swidler 1986; Keister 2003a). Nearly all churches and related religious organizations offer some guidance for living, often including specific tips for money management such as household budgeting, desirable expenditures, and saving strategies. Religious beliefs attribute value to working for certain organizations and in some occupations. Religious beliefs also attribute value to saving, sacrificial giving, and other behaviors that directly involve money. The value associated with particular work and financial behaviors vary dramatically by religious beliefs, but there is little question that money is meaningful, that values and finances are intimately connected, and that Americans recognize this connection (Zelizer 1978, 1989; Wuthnow 1994).

Religion might also affect wealth ownership directly through social connections. As I mentioned earlier, we are not born knowing how to save or with a particular orientation toward work and money. Rather people learn how to deal with money from their parents and others they encounter as children and young adults (Chiteji and Stafford 2000). Strategies for saving, avoiding debt, and work behaviors that facilitate saving are largely learned. Not surprisingly, people who learn to save and invest typically find that their wealth accumulates, whereas those who do not learn these skills tend to be at a disadvantage in accumulating wealth. If people learn some of what they know about work, money, and saving from social contacts, and if they are members of churches (either as children or adults) where people save and invest, they are more likely to pick up those skills and use them. Religion and membership in religious organizations may also provide social contacts who can furnish information (e.g., about business opportunities) or capital (e.g., for investing) that facilitates wealth ownership. I address these ideas throughout the book, as in Chapters 2 and 4, where I discuss how orientations and perspectives can be reinforced in complex ways by the people we encounter over the life course. Testing any of the ideas about the role of social networks is extremely difficult because it requires a considerable amount of specialized data that simply do not exist. I will address data issues in more depth in the next section.

Finally, religion is likely to affect wealth directly through important intergenerational processes. That is, because parents usually transfer both their wealth and their religion to their children, there are powerful intergenerational processes that intensify the relationship between faith and money. Class background affects the values parents use to raise their children. In addition, parents with wealth bequeath their assets to their children, and the saving behavior of prior generations will determine inheritance size: Those raised in faiths whose members have little savings will inherit less than those in faiths whose members have higher savings. Parents also transfer their religious beliefs to their children. Most Americans remain affiliated with the religions in which they were raised, and many marry partners who were raised in a similar faith. Adults who remain affiliated with their childhood religion do not expand the group from which they can draw lessons and assistance. This is advantageous to high-wealth groups but can exacerbate asset poverty. Adult religious affiliation intensifies and reinforces the approaches and orientations (e.g., toward work and money) learned during childhood, especially when both partners in a relationship were raised in the same faith. Alternatively, the process by which partners who were raised in different faiths or who are members of different religions prior to marriage negotiate financial relations after marriage can be informative about the relationship between religion and wealth. I address this issue in greater detail in Chapter 9.

Formative Studies and Theoretical Foundations

Figure 1.1 organizes the ideas that I introduce in this section and that guide the remainder of this book. It provides a general map of the way background, adult family, education, work, and other processes relate to each other and to wealth ownership. The figure provides more detail than I discuss here; I will address the specifics of the components of the process and the relationships among the components in detail in subsequent chapters.

Sociologists will recognize that models I use draws on ideas from the status attainment and life course traditions in social research. I do not adhere strictly to either approach, and more importantly, the work that I do here moves beyond either system of thought by merging the two,

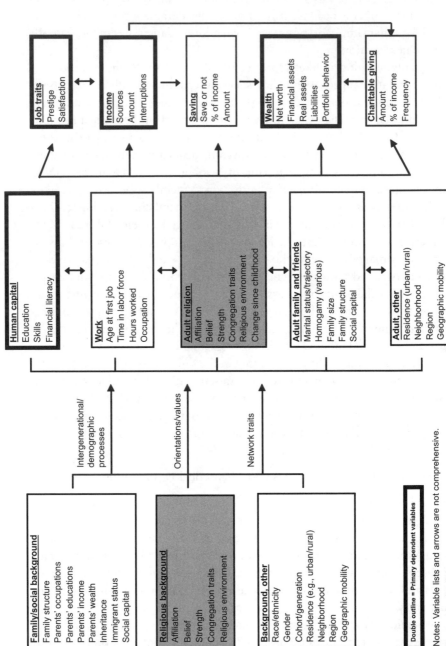

Family/social background
Family structure
Parents' occupations
Parents' educations
Parents' income
Parents' wealth
Inheritance
Immigrant status
Social capital

Religious background
Affiliation
Belief
Strength
Congregation traits
Religious environment

Background, other
Race/ethnicity
Gender
Cohort/generation
Residence (e.g., urban/rural)
Neighborhood
Region
Geographic mobility

Intergenerational/
demographic
processes

Orientations/values

Network traits

Human capital
Education
Skills
Financial literacy

Work
Age at first job
Time in labor force
Hours worked
Occupation

Adult religion
Affiliation
Belief
Strength
Congregation traits
Religious environment
Change since childhood

Adult family and friends
Marital status/trajectory
Homogamy (various)
Family size
Family structure
Social capital

Adult, other
Residence (urban/rural)
Neighborhood
Region
Geographic mobility

Job traits
Prestige
Satisfaction

Income
Sources
Amount
Interruptions

Saving
Save or not
% of income
Amount

Wealth
Net worth
Financial assets
Real assets
Liabilities
Portfolio behavior

Charitable giving
Amount
% of income
Frequency

Double outline = Primary dependent variables

Notes: Variable lists and arrows are not comprehensive.
See text for details.

FIGURE 1.1. Conceptual Model

introducing more complex relationships, focusing on an element of culture (religion), and studying a still relatively neglected outcome. Yet, to clarify my starting point for understanding how religion and wealth are related, it is useful to begin by discussing these two traditions. Status attainment refers to the process by which individuals arrive at socioeconomic standing over their lives, and the status attainment approach has become one of the most widely used theoretical perspectives in sociological research on social and economic well-being. The theoretical foundation of this approach is Blau and Duncan's (1967) seminal research on occupational attainment. This groundbreaking work demonstrated that achieved status (i.e., education and prior occupational prestige) was the most important determinant of attainment (i.e., occupational prestige) even controlling for ascribed status (i.e., parents' status). An extensive literature has subsequently extended the basic status attainment model to explain educational attainment, income, wealth, and other measures of well-being (Campbell and Henretta 1980; Looker and Pineo 1983; Otto and Haller 1979; Sewell, Haller, and Ohlendorf 1970; Sewell and Hauser 1975; Sewell, Hauser, and Wolf 1980). Researchers have also broadened the scope of the basic Blau and Duncan model by adding many explanatory variables including various other background traits, adult family behaviors and processes, psychological and social psychological indicators, structural characteristics (e.g., social relations and social capital) and positions, and characteristics of country of residence (Hauser, Sheridan, and Warren 1999; Hout and Morgan 1975; Lin and Yauger 1975; Ruef and Fletcher 2003; Stolzenberg 1975; Warren 2001).

Several traits of the status attainment approach make it a logical foundation for a synthetic model relating religion and wealth. Research in the status attainment tradition has identified many of the key concepts essential to a model of socioeconomic status (SES), including wealth ownership, and the mechanisms through which those concepts are connected to each other and to important outcomes. The status attainment model also allows for interactions between the central behaviors and practices, effectively describes how both childhood and adult family behaviors and processes affect adult outcomes, and correctly represents the chronological order in which processes are related to each other over time (e.g., family background affects education, which affects adult occupation). Moreover, although status attainment research has not paid explicit attention to the role of religion in creating SES, this model is consistent with the growing body of related empirical evidence relating religion and the various components of SES. One weakness of the status attainment model is that it does not adequately capture the degree to which individual lives are linked by key events that create coherent trajectories across time (Warren 2001; Warren, Hauser, and Sheridan 2002). Drawing simultaneously on ideas from status attainment and life course research resolves this issue.

The life course perspective is the standard approach used by sociologists to understand changes that occur in individual lives over time. Research using this approach was originally a reaction to Marxist approaches to SES and, to some extent, the systems approach made popular by Parsons and his colleagues (Mayer and Schoepflin 1989). Glen Elder and Matilda White Riley are often credited with popularizing the approach and with providing the initial articulation of its basic tenets (Elder, Elder, and Elder 1974; Elder 1975; Elder 1985; Riley 1973; Riley 1974), although this approach is less easily dated to a single seminal piece of research than status attainment research. Life course studies tend to have at least two important elements in common. First, research in this tradition typically approaches the individual life course as a coherent entity with multiple antecedent-consequent linkages that give it shape and substance (Kerckhoff 1993: 3). This starting point leads life course researchers to talk about trajectories or pathways over the lives of individuals and to mark these trajectories or pathways by the individuals' ages at key turning points (O'Rand 1996; Sampson and Laub 1996; Warren, Hauser, and Sheridan 2002). Second, life course research usually assumes that there are patterns or regularities across individual life courses that can be identified, explained, and used to understand other outcomes (Kerckhoff 1993). Events and roles do not occur at the same time or in the same order for all individuals, but there is enough similarity across the sum of individual experiences to explain sequences.

The concept of a turning point is central to this approach, and life course research seeks to identify important turning points for individuals and cohorts and to identify common trajectories that those turning points produce. Turning points are conditions or incidents that notably affect or redirect the individual trajectory or pathway and that ultimately bear strong influence over the trajectory's direction. Early work focused on particular events as turning points (e.g., World War II or the Great Depression), but later research extended the model to include turning points that either cannot be narrowed to a particular event or that vary across individuals. Research has focused on age groups, life phases, and domains such as family/fertility cycles, careers and employment histories, migration, and income/consumption trajectories. Turning points often operate by increasing a person's susceptibility to change. There has been some effort to use status attainment and life course models together, perhaps most notably by Hauser, Warren, and their colleagues who have effectively studied outcomes such as occupational attainment over the age-differentiated individual life course (Warren 2001; Warren and Hauser 1997; Warren, Hauser, and Sheridan 2002).

Although religion has not been a central concept in either status attainment or life course research, ideas from these perspectives have the potential to contribute to understanding the religion-SES connection. The strength of the status attainment approach for studying how individuals arrive at socioeconomic well-being makes it a logical starting point. Understanding how religion affects status also requires knowledge of the role that many standard components of the status attainment model play. Family background, education, adult family behaviors and processes, and structural traits are all antecedents of status attainment, and these are also all related to religion. Religion is also a critical component of family background itself. Given the importance of religion in the United States, a family's religious affiliation and practices tend to be important contributors to the identity of the family members. This is true even for families who are characterized by their lack of affiliation. The notion of a life course captures the nuances and shape of the trajectory within which religion influences status. Religious beliefs are dynamic and can either create or result from important turning points, and ideas from life course research have the potential to capture patterns in the resulting paths. In the following chapters, I elaborate on these processes.

A Note on Data and Definitions

Data Sources

I use four survey data sources in this book: the General Social Survey, the National Longitudinal Survey of Youth, the Health and Retirement Survey, and the Economic Values Survey. Incorporating information from multiple data sources allows me to provide a comprehensive discussion of the religion-wealth relationship and to take advantage of the rich information available in contemporary data. First, I use the General Social Survey (GSS), a representative cross-sectional survey conducted annually by the National Opinion Research Center since 1972. I use the 2006 data to provide an up-to-date snapshot of the American religious landscape and patterns in work and financial orientations by religion. The GSS contains information about socioeconomic status, social mobility, family, race, work, earnings, and other material outcomes that are useful for understanding basic patterns by religious group.

Second, I use the National Longitudinal Survey of Youth 1979 (NLSY) to relate religion in childhood, religion in adulthood, and adult wealth. The NLSY also allows me to observe how wealth ownership changes over time for a very large sample of Americans. The NLSY is a nationally representative longitudinal survey that was administered twenty times between 1979 and 2008 by the Bureau of Labor Statistics (BLS). The initial NLSY sample included 12,686 individuals aged 14 to 22 in 1979. The sample had three components: a nationally representative sample; a supplemental sample of poor white, black, and Hispanic youth; and a supplemental sample of military members. An extensive battery of wealth questions was added to the NLSY in 1985, when the youngest respondents were twenty years old. I use data from each survey year to understand how wealth accumulation and related processes occur for this sample. Early years of data are useful for understanding the role of family background and early educational processes in wealth attainment. I am able to draw on data for wealth and other measures of achievement at various points in the life course by using income, work, and wealth measures provided in each survey year.

The NLSY is ideal for answering questions about family background and adult wealth because it combines broad longitudinal coverage of a large sample with detailed information about wealth holdings, family background, life transitions, and adult status. In each survey year beginning in 1985, respondents reported whether they owned any of a comprehensive list of assets and debts and the value of each asset or debt if they owned it. Other sources of survey data on wealth ownership include more wealthy individuals, those who own the most assets. The Survey of Consumer Finances (SCF), for example, is a panel data set that oversamples high-income households to more accurately estimate wealth distribution (Kennickell, Starr-McCluer, and Sunden 1997; Wolff 1995). Because the NLSY does not oversample wealthy households, it may underestimate wealth concentration (Juster and Kuester 1991; Juster, Smith, and Stafford 1999). However, my objective is to estimate longitudinal patterns rather than cross-sectional levels of inequality, and the NLSY data are consistent longitudinally with estimates from similar surveys and other data sources (Keister 2000b). Moreover, the NLSY has been successfully used to estimate long-term family processes because it contains detailed information about family structure and processes during childhood, life transitions, and adult behaviors and socioeconomic status (Sandefur and Wells 1999). I use sample weights when reporting NLSY descriptive statistics for single years, but I do not use weights for multivariate longitudinal analyses. As a result, most of my descriptive statistics show less extreme patterns than are evident in the unweighted data.

Third, I use the Health and Retirement Study (HRS), 1992–2006, to explore how religion and wealth are related later in life. The NLSY provides excellent information about wealth for a large cohort through middle age. To understand how the process continues, I use the HRS, a survey of more than 22,000 Americans over the age of 50 conducted every two years since 1992 by the University of Michigan and the National Institute on Aging. More precisely, the target population for the 1992 HRS was all U.S. (contiguous states) adults born between 1931 and 1941 who resided in households. The sample was the household, and non-age-eligible people were included in the sample if they were a spouse of an age-eligible respondent. As a result, the HRS includes rich data on households and people for a range of ages, although it is not a probability sample of people born between 1931 and 1941. Indeed, the surviving sample in 2006 is ages 40–89 (averaging approximately age 68). The objective of the survey is to provide information about health and well-being for retired adults and those approaching retirement, but the survey also contains detailed demographic information, including religion. The survey includes information on labor market status, earnings, homeownership, other assets, insurance, and retirement planning. Most importantly, the HRS is an authoritative source of information about these processes for older adults. Again, I use sample weights when reporting HRS descriptive statistics for single years, but I do not use weights for multivariate longitudinal analyses. As with NLSY results, most of my descriptive statistics show less extreme patterns than are evident in the unweighted data.

Finally, I use the Economic Values Survey (EVS) to provide information about how religion is related to approaches to work and money. The EVS is a national survey of 2,013 adults conducted in 1992 by Robert Wuthnow and the Gallup Organization. Wuthnow consulted with more than one hundred religion scholars to design the survey, which collected detailed information about religious affiliation and job characteristics, work behavior, material well-being, and orientations to work, money, saving, and related outcomes. I use the EVS data to provide detailed estimates of the relationship between religion and a broad range of orientations and values in a single year. The EVS data contain detailed information about why people save or do not save, their perspectives on the role of religion and God in financial and work decisions, their ideas about the importance of work and family relative to religion, and related topics that underlie the mechanisms relating religion and wealth. Moreover, because the EVS data were collected in 1992, they represent patterns that were typical when the NLSY and HRS samples were at critical points in their life courses. All members of these samples had reached their working years and potentially could have been working, saving, and investing. Using these three data sets together provides a unique insight into broad patterns of wealth ownership by religion (from the NLSY and HRS) and details about the reasons underlying those patterns (from the EVS).

An Important Note about Current Data

I have very consciously chosen to use wealth data that is slightly older than the most up-to-date data available. I use data from 2004 (NLSY) and 2006 (HRS) because these years precede the most extreme part of the financial and housing bubble that preceded the recent recession. Using more current versions of either data set would mean that I report values from the height of the bubble. Preliminary investigations suggest that the differences across groups – including religious groups – before and during the bubble are negligible. However the values (e.g., mean and median net worth, mean and median values of the components of net worth such as housing and stocks) during the bubble are wildly high in some cases. During the recession, it is very likely that these values fell to levels very similar to the 2004/2006 data I use, as the economy corrected itself. Unfortunately, data for very recent years are not yet available. After considerable deliberation, I concluded that the versions of the data I use provide much more accurate reflections of the relationships between religion and wealth that I study in this book. Because I have chosen to use 2004/2006 NLSY and HRS wealth data, I use 2006 GSS data to describe the American religious landscape. More current GSS data are also available and show that the distribution of people across religious groups has not changed notably since 2006.

Definitions and Reporting

The majority of the results I present are descriptive statistics to ensure that the findings are transparent and easily interpreted. In Chapters 5 and 6, I include multivariate regression results to demonstrate how the findings withstand controlling for other factors that affect the wealth outcomes I study. The Appendix provides details for the regression models.

In each data set that I use, I draw on responses to questions about childhood and adult religious affiliation to create my religion measures. Separating Roman Catholics, Protestants, and Jews has been standard for decades, and I follow that tradition. For Roman Catholics (referred to simply as *Catholics* from here on forward), I include separate estimates for white and Hispanic Catholics because there is considerable research showing that white, Hispanic, and other Catholics are unique in important ways that are relevant to wealth ownership (Keister 2007). I do not have sufficient data to include separate estimates for black Catholics except in my initial portrait of religious groupings. There is also reason to believe that there are denominational differences for Jews that would be important for my analyses (Burstein 2007; Chiswick 1986; Hollinger 2004; Waxman 2001). However, small sample sizes prevent me from including separate estimates for Jewish denominations except in my initial portrait of religious groups (e.g., Orthodox, Conservative, Reform).

Classifying Protestants into denominational groups is complicated. The results I present reflect years of coding respondents, validating coding decisions with the research of those with considerable expertise in understanding the complexity of denominational distinctions, and assessing the robustness (i.e., sensitivity) of results to these coding decisions. My approach to classifying Protestants is consistent with the approach commonly used to study Protestants today, and perhaps more important, my results are very resilient to alternative coding strategies. Survey questions about Protestant denominational affiliation generate hundreds of specific religious groups, and most researchers use one of two strategies for determining denominational type. Smith (1990) provided an initial classification into fundamentalist, moderate, and liberal based on Bible interpretation, acceptance of Jesus Christ as Lord and savior, and evangelical practices. Steensland, et al. (2000) updated the earlier classification and added some categories.

I draw on both approaches to create my Protestant categories. I follow Smith (1990) quite closely but find Steensland et al.'s (2000) updates useful as well. My strategy is also nearly identical to that used by Greeley and Hout (2006). In particular, I classify Protestants as conservative Protestants (CP), mainline Protestants (MP), and black Protestants (BP). My CPs are Smith's fundamentalists minus the African American respondents. My MPs are Smith's moderates and liberals less the African Americans, Catholics, and Jews. I include respondents who identify as "Christian" or "nondenominational" as CPs consistent, with Greeley and Hout (2006). CPs include Southern Baptists, conservative

Lutherans (e.g., Missouri or Wisconsin Synod), Pentecostals, and others. MPs include United Methodists, moderate and liberal Lutherans and Presbyterians, Episcopalians, and others. BPs include multiple Baptist traditions (including respondents who are African American and Baptist but cannot identify a denomination), and others. In the very small number of cases in which a white or African American respondent clearly identifies with a denomination that is otherwise largely populated by people of the opposite race, I accept the respondent's response as accurate. This decision affected an extremely small portion of the sample and does not affect the substance of my findings.

Many readers will want to know if my findings differ by more specific Protestant groups. That is, do members of some conservative denominations behave notably differently from members of other conservative denominations? What about differences within mainline and black Protestant groups? Again, I have spent years exploring more detailed patterns. There are some, but they are rare and minimal. By and large, the members of these groups have family, educational, work, and wealth patterns that are quite similar to others in the same Protestant group. I initially explored provided additional detail, but the results quickly become cumbersome, and the benefit is negligible. In Chapter 7, I provide detail for mainline Protestants because there is some worthwhile information in the detail.

The American Religious Landscape

Before talking more about how religion is associated with wealth ownership, it is useful to consider what the American religious landscape looks like today. Indeed, the landscape is different from the one earlier generations of social scientists saw when they debated questions about religion. Of course, religious affiliation patterns and the beliefs and practices of religious groups are constantly in flux, but the traits I describe here provide a good sense of current patterns. To begin, consider the general patterns of affiliation included in Table 1.1. This table shows the percentage of Americans affiliated with broad religious categories; percentages in the table refer to the percentage of the total sample affiliated with that faith, even for subcategories of a larger group (e.g., 28.7 percent of the total GSS sample reported affiliation with a white CP denomination). Table 1.1 shows that more than half of respondents consider themselves Protestant, about one-quarter are Catholic, and slightly less than 2 percent are Jewish. Consistent with evidence that religious diversity in America is

TABLE 1.1. *Denominational Distribution*

	%
Protestant	53.0
Conservative Protestant (CP)	28.7
Black Protestant (BP)	8.1
Mainline Protestant (MP)	13.9
Other	2.3
Catholic	24.7
White	16.4
Hispanic	6.3
Other race/ethnicity	2.0
Jewish	1.7
Mormon/LDS	1.6
Other	2.6
No Religious Preference	16.4
Missing	0.06

Notes: Data are from the 2006 GSS. Sample size = 4,510.

increasing (Smith 2002), slightly more than 2 percent of the respondents are affiliated with other religions, such as Buddhism, Hinduism, Islam, and Native American religions.

Although there has been a good deal of consistency in the size of religious groups in recent years, the percentage of people within these broad groups by denomination and race has changed in notable ways. One important change is that a growing percentage of Protestants belong to CP denominations and fewer belong to MP denominations. Table 1.1 shows that nearly a third of all respondents are now associated with white CP denominations and another 8 percent are affiliated with BP denominations. In contrast, only 14 percent are affiliated with MP denominations. This differs notably from patterns evident a decade ago. In the 1998 GSS, about 27 percent of respondents reported that they were CP, and more than 20 percent were affiliated with MP churches. Hout, Greeley, and Wilde (2001) explored this change and showed that it can be accounted for mostly by demographic patterns. In particular, they showed that higher fertility rates and earlier childbearing among women from CP denominations accounted for most of this trend (Hout, Greeley, and Wilde 2001). CP denominations have grown from within. Perhaps more interestingly, Hout, Greeley, and Wilde (2001) found no evidence for other potential causes of this pattern. In particular, they found no evidence of increased conversion from MP to CP denominations, an explanation that others have suggested might be responsible. Likewise, they found no evidence that the relative rate at which people are leaving either MP or CP denominations or the relative rate of inflow from other non-Protestant groups is responsible. Decline in MP membership is likely to have slowed in recent years, but a reduction in conversions from conservative to mainline denominations contributed to further mainline decline. Hout, Greeley, and Wilde (2001: 498) concluded by pointing out that, although predicting the future is precarious, their "evidence suggests that trends underlying mainline decline may be nearing their end."

Another important change that has occurred in recent years is an increase in the percentage of Americans claiming no religious preference. Table 1.1 shows that 16 percent of respondents in the 2006 GSS reported no religious affiliation. This is a continuation of a trend that began in the 1990s: between 1991 and 2000, the percentage of adults with no religious preference grew from 7 percent to 14 percent (Hout and Fischer 2002). Hout and Fischer (2002) explored the reasons underlying this pattern, and although they used slightly earlier data than I am using, their conclusions are still relevant. Hout and Fischer showed that a combination of factors underlie this pattern. One important demographic contributor is an increase in the percentage of adults who were raised with no religious preference. Religious affiliation tends to follow a predictable pattern over the life cycle: People leave organized religion when they separate from their family of origin and reengage with religion when they have their own children (Greeley and Hout 1988; Sherkat and Ellison 1999). As less religious people have replaced more religious ones from previous generations, the percentage of adults with no religious preference has grown. A rise in the percentage of people who are delaying marriage and childhood has exacerbated this change. Contrary to the popular interpretation of the trend, Hout and Fischer found no evidence that growing religious skepticism has been a contributing factor. Indeed, they found that most people who claim no religious preference have conventional religious beliefs but are simply not members of organized churches (Hout and Fischer call them unchurched believers). Finally, they demonstrated that there is a political factor involved as well. The increase in religious nonaffiliation occurred primarily among political liberals and moderates, whereas political conservatives did not change. Hout and Fischer interpreted this as a reaction to the Religious Right. When possible, I include those who claim no religious preference as a separate category in my analyses.

Although it is useful to start with a discussion of broad religious categories, it is important not to lose sight of the fact that many denominations

TABLE 1.2. *Denominational Distribution: White Conservative Protestants (CPs) and Black Conservative Protestants (BPs)*

Conservative Protestants (n = 1,294)	%	Black Protestants (n = 369)	%
Southern Baptist	19.3	Southern Baptist[b]	20.1
Baptist, other[a]	21.8	American Baptist[b]	9.0
Pentecostal	7.3	National Baptist[b]	7.5
Church of Christ	3.7	Baptist, other[b]	43.1
Lutheran Church, Missouri or Wisconsin Synod	5.1	Holiness	3.8
Other conservative/evangelical	42.8	Other black Protestant	16.5

Notes: Data are from the 2006 GSS. Sample size = 4,510. Percentages are the percentage of total CPs or BPs. In subsequent analyses, I exclude respondents who are nondenominational or Christian but who attend services less than once per year (n = 74). This changes the number of CPs to 1,220.

[a] Included only when race is not black.
[b] Included only when race is black.

are included within these broad groups. Table 1.2 shows the distribution of CP and BP denominations and underscores the remarkable diversity of Protestant traditions that now characterizes religion in America. In this table, percentages refer to the percentage of all CPs or all BPs. The single largest CP denomination is Southern Baptist Convention, followed by other Baptists. The single largest response for BPs is also Southern Baptist, with a large number of BPs affiliated with other Baptist churches.

Table 1.3 shows that there is also considerable diversity in MP traditions. Again, percentages refer to the percentage of all MPs. The table shows that United Methodist, Presbyterian, and Lutheran are among the largest groups. Recall that only moderate to liberal Presbyterians

TABLE 1.3. *Denominational Distribution: Mainline Protestants*

Mainline Protestants (n = 627)	%
United Methodist	35.0
Methodist, other mainline denominations	7.2
Lutheran, other than Missouri and Wisconsin Synod	18.0
Episcopal	12.4
Presbyterian, all mainline denominations	14.8
United Church of Christ	1.9
Other mainline	10.7

Notes: Data are from the 2006 GSS. Sample size = 4,510. Percentages are the percentage of all mainline Protestants.

TABLE 1.4. *Catholic and Jewish Religious Subgroups*

Catholic (n = 1,114)	%	Jewish (n = 78)	%
White	66.3	Orthodox	42.3
Hispanic	25.7	Conservative	24.3
Black	3.4	Reform	18.0
Asian	2.9	None	12.8
Other	1.7	No answer	2.6

Notes: Data are from the 2006 GSS. Sample size = 4,510. Percentages are the percentage of all Catholics or Jews.

and Lutherans are included here. Table 1.4 provides subgroup details for Catholics and Jews. Once again, the percentages refer to the percentage of Catholics or Jews in each category. For Catholics, the relevant subgroups are racial and ethnic. As the table illustrates, the majority of Catholics are white, but more than a quarter are Hispanic. Black, Asian, and other Catholics compose much smaller percentages of total Catholics. For Jews, the relevant subgroups are denominational. The majority of respondents are Orthodox and Conservative, consistent with other research.

Strength of religious conviction is an important dimension on which American religious groups differ. Table 1.5 illustrates this by comparing

TABLE 1.5. *Strength of Religious Conviction (%)*

	Strong	Somewhat	Not strong
White Conservative Protestant (CP)	50.9	11.4	37.1
Southern Baptist	55.2	6.4	38.0
Pentecostal	57.9	10.5	31.6
Church of Christ	50.0	16.7	33.3
Black Conservative Protestant (BP)	59.4	11.11	28.7
Southern Baptist	58.1	9.5	32.4
Mainline/Liberal Protestant (MP)	35.1	11.2	53.8
United Methodist	36.1	13.7	50.2
Episcopal	34.6	9.0	56.4
Lutheran	41.2	11.8	47.1
Catholic	30.4	16.5	53.0
White	35.2	13.7	51.1
Hispanic	17.8	24.8	57.3
Jewish	39.7	15.4	43.6
Mormon/LDS	67.6	8.5	23.9
All Respondents	35.8	10.7	36.2

Notes: Data are from the 2006 GSS. Sample size = 4,510. Rows do not sum to 100% because these categories are not comprehensive of response options. Those with no religious preference do not have valid data on these variables, so I exclude them from the table.

self-reported strength of religious conviction for select groups. I included only groups for which there are significant respondents in the GSS, and I included only a sample of possible measures of strength. The estimates in this table demonstrate the important differences that have distinguished CPs, BPs, and MPs for decades. For instance, more than half of CPs and BPs, including the subgroups that I include, claimed to have strong religious convictions. Less than 40 percent of these groups reported that their religious convictions are not strong. By contrast, the patterns are virtually reversed for MPs: 35–41 percent reported strong convictions, and about half responded that their convictions are not strong. Greeley and Hout (2006) more thoroughly documented the beliefs held by various religious groups in the United States, with a focus on Protestants. They ultimately concluded that CPs are not very different from other groups on political perspectives, but their results show that CPs, BPs, and MPs hold distinctive religious beliefs.

Recent scholarship shows that white Catholics tend to be similar to MPs on a range of outcomes, including religiosity, whereas Hispanic Catholics are fairly unique (D'Antonio, et al. 2001; Keister 2007). The estimates for religious conviction included in Table 1.5 underscore this difference. Non-Hispanic white Catholics are much more similar to MPs today than they were in previous generations. Recall that much of the debate in the religion literature in the 1960s and 1970s centered on explaining Catholic-Protestant differences. There are still very important differences between white Catholics and conservative Protestants, as the table indicates. Moreover, it is not possible to group all Catholics together. White Catholics are largely descendents of Irish, Italian, German, and Polish immigrants who arrived in the United States starting in the 1840s and 1850s and initially settled in ethnic communities in medium-sized to large cities in the Northeast (Alba 1981). Hispanic Catholics are, of course, more recent immigrants whose assimilation trajectory is, at the very least, behind that of white Catholics and is potentially quite different than that of the latter. Differences in religiosity, religious participation, and religious beliefs shown in this chapter provide the basis for socioeconomic differences that become evident in the remainder of this book.

Tables 1.6 and 1.7 illustrate other aspects of religion that both define the groups I study in subsequent chapters and demonstrate the unique traits of these groups. Table 1.6 separates respondents by their participation in religious services. The responses I include (i.e., never, twice per year or less, weekly, several times per week) are not comprehensive because I excluded some possible responses. Yet the patterns here do

TABLE 1.6. *Religious Participation (%)*

	Never	Twice Per year or Less	Weekly	Several Times per Week
White Conservative Protestant (CP)	13.0	12.0	5.9	14.3
Southern Baptist	9.2	12.4	6.0	17.6
Pentecostal	11.6	4.2	5.3	30.5
Church of Christ	4.2	4.2	12.5	22.9
Black Conservative Protestant (BP)	7.6	6.0	7.3	13.8
Southern Baptist	16.2	0.0	4.1	10.8
Mainline/Liberal Protestant (MP)	14.7	15.0	6.2	2.7
United Methodist	15.6	11.9	6.3	2.7
Episcopal	16.7	20.5	5.1	1.3
Lutheran	14.7	8.8	2.9	0.0
Catholic	14.8	13.8	6.7	3.4
White	14.2	14.4	6.2	3.9
Hispanic	13.3	14.3	8.4	2.1
Jewish	21.8	16.7	1.3	6.4
Mormon/LDS	7.0	9.9	8.4	9.9
All Respondents	22.6	12.7	5.3	7.3

Notes: Data are from the 2006 GSS. Sample size = 4,510. Rows do not sum to 100% because these categories are not comprehensive of response options. Those with no religious preference do not have valid data on these variables, so I exclude them from the table.

underscore group differences. For instance, attending services multiple times per week is somewhat common among some conservative denominations but relatively rare for mainline groups and Catholics. White, Hispanic, and black Catholics are more similar in their participation than they are on other traits – a reflection of Catholic religious doctrine that the groups share. Table 1.7 illustrates patterns in three reported religious beliefs: the Bible is the actual Word of God, the Bible is the inspired Word of God, and there is an afterlife. As one would expect, differences between CPs and MPs are dramatic on Bible interpretation, and these patterns provide additional evidence that the broad groups (i.e., CP, BP, and MP) are highly internally similar. Indeed, these patterns are consistent with findings that although people who are affiliated with different religious traditions may think they have unique beliefs, the substance of those beliefs is quite similar within groups (Wolfe 1998).

What about relatively small religious groups? Small groups can often provide important clues about how religion and religious beliefs affect wealth ownership. Groups such as Mormon/LDS, Jehovah's Witnesses, various Orthodox groups, Muslims (a small group in the United States), and Chaldeans (Arab Catholics) receive very little research attention

TABLE 1.7. *Religious Beliefs (%)*

	Bible Actual Word of God	Bible Inspired Word of God	There is an Afterlife
White, Conservative Protestant (CP)	34.2	24.8	55.3
Southern Baptist	38.8	24.7	52.3
Pentecostal	47.4	16.8	54.7
Church of Christ	41.7	27.1	60.4
Black, Conservative Protestant (BP)	44.7	17.1	50.1
Southern Baptist	39.2	27.0	55.4
Mainline/Liberal Protestant (MP)	16.9	42.6	33.4
United Methodist	18.7	43.4	58.9
Episcopal	6.4	41.0	46.2
Lutheran	17.7	26.5	38.2
Catholic	15.8	40.7	47.6
White	11.0	46.5	51.5
Hispanic	26.9	27.3	36.0
Jewish	9.0	35.9	37.2
Mormon/LDS	32.4	29.6	70.4
All Respondents	22.4	30.2	48.3

Notes: Data are from the 2006 GSS. Sample size = 4,510. Those with no religious preference do not have valid data on these variables, so I exclude them from the table.

because their small numbers make it difficult to study them. Yet there might be significant lessons contained in their financial behavior. I include estimates for Mormons/LDS, Jews, those with no religious preference, and those with some other religious preference (as a single group) in the tables in this chapter and throughout the book. When sample sizes are insufficient, I include these groups with those with other religions. I have not discussed patterns for these groups in detail here because their sample sizes are quite small in the GSS. When possible, I provide additional discussion about small religious groups in other chapters. For example, I address issues related to those affiliated with Mormon/LDS churches because they provide a unique contrast to the religion-wealth relationship. CPs are generally found to have relatively low wealth. Of course, this varies across CP denominations, as we will see, but a strong pattern is present in contemporary data. In contrast, members of Mormon/LDS churches tend to be religiously conservative, but there are reasons to anticipate that they have comparably high net worth. Addressing this unique pattern is important on its own, and it can also provide insights into patterns we find for other groups.

TABLE 1.8. *Religion and Wealth: Median Net Worth*

	% of Sample	Net Worth (NLSY, Child)
White Conservative Protestant (CP)	25.8	$82,400
Black Conservative Protestant (BP)	11.0	$22,800
Mainline/Liberal Protestant (MP)	18.1	$146,000
Catholic		$134,500
White	19.9	$156,000
Hispanic	3.8	$51,500
Jewish	0.5	$423,500
Other Religion	7.4	$65,500
No Religion	12.4	$57,700
All Respondents	100.0	$99,500

Notes: Data are from the 2004 NLSY. Sample size = 4,369. Religion is child-hood religion and net worth is defined in great detail in Chapter 4. Net worth estimates replicate those in Chapter 4. Percentages do not sum to zero because non-white, non-Hispanic Catholics and missing respondents are not included.

Religion and Wealth

Wealth clearly varies with religious affiliation. Table 1.8 provides a first glimpse into how religion and wealth are related. For the entire NLSY sample in 2004, median net worth was slightly higher than $86,000. For comparison, median net worth in the 2004 Survey of Consumer Finances was $93,000. The Federal Reserve Board collects these data every three years on a representative sample of the U.S. population. The Survey of Consumer Finances is widely considered the most reliable data on household wealth ownership in the United States because it includes extremely detailed information, gathered using very reliable methods, and includes an oversample of high-income people (Bucks, Kennickell, and Moore 2006). The oversample of high-income respondents provides additional detail at the critical high end of the wealth distribution, yielding an accurate representation of the distribution and related summary statistics such as average wealth ownership. It is notable that median net worth in the NLSY is very similar to the Survey of Consumer Finances median. The NLSY sample was first drawn in the late 1970s and has not been altered in ways related to this study since. There are two advantages of using the NLSY for this research: (1) it is longitudinal (i.e., includes the same respondents each year) and (2) includes information on respondents' religion. The Survey of Consumer Finances is cross-sectional and does not contain information about religion. The accuracy of the basic wealth information from the NLSY is suggestive of the reliability of estimates I present in the remainder of this book.

Wealth ownership varies both across Protestant groups and between Protestants and other religious groups. MPs and white Catholics have similar wealth, consistent with recent evidence showing a convergence in status for these groups. CPs and BPs have considerably lower wealth than MPs. The median net worth of CPs is approximately $82,000, whereas the median net worth for MPs is about $146,000. The median net worth of BPs is even more extreme, at only $228,000. At the other end of the wealth spectrum, Jews have a median net worth of more than $423,000. Of course, it is important to remember that small sample sizes for Jews make this number a bit difficult to interpret; however, this is consistent with other published sources (Burstein 2007) and with those from other data sets (e.g., the HRS) that I will discuss in more detail later in the book.

My hope is that the remainder of this book will help elucidate the details of the relationship between religion and wealth and provide insight into both the importance of religion and the mechanisms that lead to wealth ownership (or the absence of wealth ownership).

2

Family and Human Capital Processes

Religion, family processes, and education are linked in complex ways to each other and, ultimately, to wealth ownership. Childhood religion and childhood family socioeconomic status (SES) are correlated, and these work together to affect the timing and ordering of educational investments and outcomes, marriage behavior, and fertility and family behaviors. These behaviors and outcomes, in turn, affect job processes and occupation, wages and salaries, and ultimately wealth ownership. In this chapter, I explore how religion, education, marriage, fertility and family, are related. I will refer to Figure 1.1 and elaborate on the portions labeled *background* (family and social, religious, and other), *human capital*, and *adult family and friends*. Throughout this chapter and Chapter 3, I also describe the *intergenerational and demographic mechanisms* identified in Figure 1.1 as one of the three pathways through which the various processes are related. This pathway and the others included in the figure operate across the life course, affecting both transitions from childhood to adulthood and those that occur within adulthood.

In this chapter, I discuss how these processes are linked to each other, and I show patterns in these relationships using data from the NLSY and the HRS. I also discuss how these processes are connected to wealth ownership, in preparation for more detailed discussions and empirical evidence that I provide in subsequent chapters. I explore fertility, marriage, and education processes in a single chapter because they are very closely related to each other. Indeed, it is possible to make the case that these are inseparable processes. At the very least, addressing them separately is cumbersome and suggests that they somehow occur in isolation across the life course. There are work and career issues that are also

TABLE 2.1. *Childhood and Adult Religion: Correlations*

Childhood Religion	Adult Religion
Baptist	0.61
Episcopalian	0.52
Methodist	0.45
Presbyterian	0.37
Other Protestant	0.15
Catholic	0.70
Jewish	0.84
Other	0.20
None	0.16

Source: Data are from the 1979–2004 NLSY. Sample size = 4,369.

intertwined with family and education processes, and I address those in the next chapter in the interest of space. I also reserve discussion of the orientations and values pathway for the next chapter.

Although I attempt to disentangle the components of family and education processes that are responsible for saving and wealth ownership, I approach the questions realizing that these are complex relationships that I will not be able to completely clarify. One complication that will flavor the discussion in this chapter and that will emerge again in other portions of this book is the high correlation between childhood and adult religious affiliation. It has been well-established that if people leave their childhood religious group, they make the change as young adults but frequently find their way back to faith as they start their own families (Sherkat 1991; Sherkat and Ellison 1999). Values, orientations, and priorities change with age, and marriage and childrearing intensify the magnitude of these changes (Johnson 2001; Johnson and Elder 2002), leading many people back to spirituality and affiliation with organized religious groups. Table 2.1 illustrates the relatively high correlation between religion during childhood and adulthood that result. The correlations are particularly high for Catholics and Jews, two groups that are also considered ethnicities. Yet there are also high correlations for large, prominent Protestant groups. A related complication is that even most of the best available data often only allow us to compare parents and their children (and even then with limitations). There are some important exceptions, but those data do not include adequate information on religion and wealth.

TABLE 2.2. *Childhood Religion and Parents' Socioeconomic Status*

	Parents' Income (median)	Father Had a BA (%)	Mother Had a BA (%)	Ever Inherited (%)
White Conservative Protestant (CP)	$15,700	6.5	5.7	49.0
Black Conservative Protestant (BP)	$9,000	2.8	3.9	23.7
Mainline/Liberal Protestant (MP)	$20,000	16.1	11.3	63.6
Catholic	$11,600	12.4	6.9	51.4
White	$17,500	14.2	7.8	57.8
Hispanic	$8,000	3.9	3.1	25.7
Jewish	$35,000	17.2	35.3	83.9
Mormon/LDS	$15,000	8.9	2.9	48.6
Other religion	$18,500	13.4	18.0	70.1
No religion	$14,000	10.7	10.1	49.3
All Respondents	$17,000	10.9	8.0	50.9

Notes: Data are from the 1979–2004 NLSY. Sample size = 4,369 (excluding 19 cases with missing data for childhood religion).

To understand life-course processes, we might ideally use evidence from multiple generations to isolate selection and influence. Eventually, multi-generation studies will be possible, but for now, I will focus on two generations.

The Importance of Background: Linking Origins with Outcomes

The complex story begins with the relationship between childhood religion and adult socioeconomic status (SES). In the very large majority of cases, children assume both the religion and SES of their parents, and these are correlated because the processes that I will discuss throughout this book operated in prior generations as well. Research from early scholarship on religion documented an important connection between religion and SES as early as colonial times (Cantril 1943; Lenski 1961; Pope 1948), and the relationship is equally strong today. Parents' income and education are two essential measures of family background, and Table 2.2 shows that these vary in notable ways with childhood religion. Among today's adults, those raised in Jewish families report the highest family income levels, consistent with research that documents very high levels of achievement among American Jewish families (Burstein 2007; Lehrer 2004a, 2009; Steen 1996). Median household income for NLSY respondents raised in Jewish families was $35,000 (in 1979 dollars) – almost twice the median for the entire sample. Those raised in Mainline

Protestant and white Catholic families also report relatively high childhood household incomes, consistent with research that shows that these groups tend to be relatively high SES (Lehrer 1995, 2009; Smith and Faris 2005; Steen 1996). In contrast, those raised in Conservative Protestant and Mormon/LDS families report much lower childhood household incomes. Black Protestant, black Catholic, and Hispanic Catholic respondents report among the lowest childhood household incomes, although black Catholics report slightly higher values.

Parents' educational attainment follows similar patterns. Table 2.2 illustrates patterns in parents' college graduation rates, an indicator of high educational attainment for parents' of NLSY respondents (who were aged fourteen to twenty-two in 1979). Jewish respondents report extremely high levels of college graduation for both their fathers and mothers. A relatively large percentage of Mainline Protestants' parents, particularly fathers, also completed college. By contrast, parental educational attainment was quite low for those raised in CP, BP, and Hispanic Catholic families. Two noteworthy groups are white Catholics and Mormon/LDS respondents. White Catholics report slightly lower college completion rates for their fathers, and even lower rates for their mothers, consistent with research that suggests Catholic educational attainment rates have begun to increase in recent generations (D'Antonio et al. 2001; D'Antonio, Hoge, and Davidson 2007; Keister 2007). Mormon/LDS respondents report relatively high educational attainment for their fathers and lower levels for their mothers, as other research suggests is common in this group (Lehrer 2004a, 2004b; Steen 1996). Those included in the other religious category have mothers with notably high education levels. Grouping all people raised in religions not otherwise specified here (i.e., other religions) is a bit misleading because there is enormous variation with this group. Because sample sizes within this group are quite small, it is important not to draw causal inferences from these patterns. However, it is worth pointing out that the high levels of mother's education are driven by Unitarians, 34 percent of whom report that their mothers had bachelor's degrees.

Parents' wealth is another important indicator of childhood well-being, and the likelihood of inheriting also varies with family religion. Figure 1.1 does not include a separate box labeled inheritance because inheritance is implied by parents' wealth for most people. Not surprisingly, because parents' incomes and education levels are important determinants of their wealth, patterns in inheritance follow patterns similar to those in family income and parents' education. Table 2.2 uses NLSY data to estimate the percentage of respondents who have ever inherited. The percentages are relatively high, particularly compared to other data sources (Gokhale and Kotlikoff 2000). However, there is a notable lack of reliable data on intergenerational transfers of wealth, and there are unique challenges associated with collecting such data (e.g., substantial and meaningful variations in interpretations of transfers/inheritances). As a result, there is widespread agreement among scholars that overall levels of reported inheritance might not be accurate, but relative levels tend to be reliable given that respondents in a single survey react to the same questions with comparable biases. Thus, when interpreting inheritance patterns from the NLSY data (see Table 2.2), levels of reported inheritance may not be accurate, but relative amounts are likely to reflect real differences.

Table 2.2 shows that people raised in Jewish families are among the most likely to inherit, followed by those raised in other religions and those raised in Mainline Protestant denominations. These patterns are consistent with the knowledge that wealth ownership in prior generations was high for members of these groups. White Catholics are also relatively likely to inherit, consistent with their parents' income and educations, but Hispanic and black Catholics are considerably less likely to receive an inheritance. The comparably low inheritance rates for white Catholics reflect an upward trend in SES and underscore the recency of notable wealth ownership for members of this group. Again, black Catholics have a slight advantage over BPs, following patterns in parents' income and educational attainment. I found no significant differences in the outcomes included in Table 2.2 for more detailed religious groups (e.g., within the large group of CPs).

We also know from decades of research that parents' SES and children's SES when they become adults – including income, education, occupation and work behaviors, and wealth – are highly correlated. This correlation in status across generations is referred to as social reproduction and is well established empirically in the social sciences (Baltzell 1964; Hauser and Warren 1997; Warren and Hauser 1997). The intergenerational correlation in these measures varies across the measure (e.g., there is a higher correlation for some measures of SES than for others), but there is a strong association for each of these indicators of SES. The important point here is that to the extent to which parents' SES and parents' religious affiliation are correlated, there is a relationship between childhood religion and children's adult attainment.

Family and religious background affect nearly all adolescent and adult behaviors and processes through several channels. It is worth identifying and describing the mechanisms that underlie social reproduction because they provide a critical first link between childhood religious/social context and adult SES. One of the most straightforward and consequential effects of childhood SES on adult SES is inheritance: People born into wealthier families are likely to inherit more wealth than people born into less wealthy families. As a result, there is a high likelihood that a person raised in a wealthy family will become a wealthy adult. Although this is an important mechanism, it is one that is sometimes overstated in research, in the popular press, and by casual observers. In reality, the likelihood of inheriting any amount of wealth is very low in the United States, and even those who inherit are likely to inherit a small sum (Gokhale and Kotlikoff 2000; Laitner 2001). There is also evidence that considerable wealth mobility does occur in the United States, and this mobility occurs in all segments of the wealth distribution (Keister 2005). People move up from the lower portions of the distribution, and they also fall from high positions more than we would expect by chance. An important caveat is that a great deal of this movement is to adjacent cells of transition matrices. That is, much of the mobility that does occur does not constitute movement across great spans of the distribution (Keister 2005). More important for my purposes is that factors other than wealth inheritance affect how much wealth people accumulate during their lives.

A second mechanism connecting childhood and adult SES is one that has attracted attention in sociology since the early days of the discipline but that is no less important today: Parents with high levels of education and occupational prestige have children with high levels of education and occupational prestige (Blau and Duncan 1967; Hauser and Warren 1997; Warren and Hauser 1997). This mechanism is a bit subtle, but part of the story is the emphasis parents place on behaviors that lead to educational and occupational attainment. Parents act as role models, and they convey expectations for their children that translate into attainment. There is a sizable literature that demonstrates how parents' occupational experience, in particular, can transmit orientations toward work that affect the intergenerational transmission of status. Kohn and his colleagues have shown that parents who have self-direction in their work have different orientations toward jobs, working, and job-specific tasks than parents whose work forces them to conform to external authorities and rules in their jobs (Kohn 1959, 1969; Kohn et al. 1997). Kohn and his coauthors have shown that under various social, cultural, and economic conditions, this leads to high correlations between parents' and children's valuation of self-direction and likely to an intergenerational transmission of job and other SES.

Third, there is evidence that parenting styles influence the intergenerational transmission of status. Working-class parents use what Annette Lareau refers to as "accomplishment of natural growth," providing necessities but allowing children to discover and engage in leisure activities independently. By contrast, middle-class and upper-class parents are more likely to use "concerted cultivation," deliberately attempting to foster children's abilities and talents by arranging organized leisure activities and experiences. Working-class parents also tend to use directives in addressing children, conveying the importance of following rules, whereas middle-class parents reason with their children, conveying skills necessary to engage in critical thinking and independent decision making (Lareau 2000, 2002, 2003). In reality, these processes are likely to operate together to reproduce social status – including wealth – across generations and, to the extent to which religion and status are correlated in one generation, to reproduce that correlation in subsequent generations.

The final mechanism that some use to explain the intergenerational transmission of social status is processes that occur in the classroom. Those who emphasize this mechanism suggest that the relevant focus is out of the family and in the school building, a place where children spend a good deal of time as they grow. This approach to social reproduction highlights the process by which a society educates its children in formal settings and points to the fact that children tend to be segregated by class in their schools (i.e., working-class children go to school with other working-class children, upper-class children go to school with other upper-class children). This approach also suggests that the intersection between school and the use of a person's labor power is critical to understanding the transmission of SES, including wealth ownership. It is in school that children learn skills and orientations that prepare them for work in class-specific jobs. At its most basic, this approach suggests that working-class children "learn to labor" in classrooms that are rule-based and teach skills that prepare children for occupations in which they will take orders and otherwise engage in manual pursuits (Willis 1981). In contrast, upper-class children tend to spend time in classrooms where critical thinking, leadership, and autonomy are valued. These children are much better prepared for nonmanual positions that will require mental work, decision-making abilities, leadership, and related skills (Willis 1981).

Identifying mechanisms that link childhood religion/SES with adult outcomes suggests that the processes connecting religion and SES are

TABLE 2.3. *Childhood Religion and Childhood Family Structure*

	Number Siblings	Step-parent Family (%)	Single-parent Family (%)
White Conservative Protestant (CP)	3.0	11.6	9.4
Black Conservative Protestant (BP)	4.4	7.3	26.3
Mainline/Liberal Protestant (MP)	2.6	7.8	8.5
Catholic	3.5	6.1	9.4
White	3.5	5.4	5.1
Hispanic	4.5	8.1	15.9
Jewish	1.9	0.0	13.8
Mormon/LDS	4.6	9.3	16.2
Other religion	2.5	9.8	14.6
No religion	3.2	11.9	15.8
All Respondents	3.3	8.2	11.7

Notes: Data are from the 1979–2004 NLSY. Sample size = 4,369 (excluding 19 cases with missing data for childhood religion).

relatively unidirectional. Unfortunately, it is often difficult to disentangle selection from influence processes. That is, it is not simple to distinguish whether people (parents or children) select into religious groups with people of similar status or religious affiliation and beliefs affect social and economic status (i.e., the causal direction). Questions of selection and influence have been common in research on religious influence on various outcomes, and the only certain conclusion they have reached is that this is a complex question. Recent research that engaged this fundamental debate explicitly concluded that selection effects were relevant under some conditions but found that selection did not diminish the independent effect of religion on key outcomes (Regnerus and Smith 2005). For purposes of developing a theoretical explanation for the religion-wealth connection, it is also not necessary to account for every step in the causal process (Cohen 1988). In reality, there is likely to be some degree of causation in both directions: Parents (and prior generations of relatives) select religious groups with people like themselves, and membership in these groups reinforces beliefs, practices, and orientations.

Childhood Family Size and Structure
Childhood religion and childhood family characteristics – particularly family size and family structure – also tend to be correlated. Table 2.3 demonstrates typical patterns. Those raised in Jewish families report having relatively few siblings, followed by those raised in MP families.

Catholics in the generation featured here come from relatively large families. Consistent with prior research, white Catholics report that they came from relatively large families (D'Antonio, Hoge, and Davidson 2007; Keister 2007), although family size for this generation of white Catholics is notably smaller than for their parents' generation. Hispanic Catholics report that they were raised in relatively large families, the largest among Catholics. Again, there is evidence of the black Catholic versus black Protestant difference: Blacks raised in Catholic families came from notably smaller families than those raised in BP families. Those raised in CP and LDS/Mormon families had the largest number of siblings.

There are also important relations between childhood religion and parents' marital status. Very few of those raised in Jewish, MP, or white Catholic families were raised by step-parents or single parents. For those raised as Jewish, step-parent families were particularly rare. The patterns for MPs and white Catholics are nearly identical to each other. Slightly more of those raised in CP families had step-parents or single parents. The most notable pattern in parents' marital status is for blacks. Very high percentages of those raised in BP and those raised in black Catholic families report being raised by single parents. The table does not include details regarding the gender of the parent, but additional exploration of the data indicated that most of the single parents were women. This pattern by race reflects a trend that has been identified clearly in other research on race: Black women in the United States are much more likely to raise their children without a partner than women of other races. There is little reason to believe that religion affects this pattern markedly. However, the pattern is important because it highlights the added disadvantage that blacks face in adult attainment.

Childhood family traits, in turn, are important determinants of adult wealth. *Family size* (i.e., number of siblings) is likely to reduce adult wealth for two reasons. First, larger families have fewer resources, both material and nonmaterial, to devote to children's intellectual development and education. Children are less likely to attend private schools and colleges, and they tend to have fewer educational materials available such as books, newspapers, and computers. Children from large families are also less likely to participate in other educational opportunities such as theater performances and museum trips (Blake 1989; Downey 1995). Similarly, family size reduces the nonmaterial resources that can contribute to educational attainment. In larger families, the time parents have available to assist children with homework, to create educational opportunities at home, to actively encourage their children at whatever activities they do find appealing, and to otherwise nurture and provide positive reinforcement is reduced. Similarly, when more children compete for attention, parents have less time to intervene when any one child is rebellious, delinquent, or otherwise getting into trouble. Likewise, children's opportunities to engage the world – that is, to interact with others and to become involved in meaningful activities that feed into later life outcomes – can be decreased in larger families. Researchers have shown that these nonmaterial resources are critical for children's development and can contribute significantly to adult attainment. In their absence, attainment is likely to be reduced (Blake 1981). I discuss how education affects wealth later in the chapter.

Second, siblings reduce direct transfers of financial resources from parents to children, both *inter-vivos* (during life) transfers and inheritance. Inter-vivos transfers include direct financial transfers of money and other transfers such as payments for college, help paying bills when necessary (i.e., if the child loses a job), purchases of automobiles, particularly early in life, assistance buying a home, and investment capital (i.e., to start a business or investment portfolio). Parental resources can reduce the need for children to accumulate educational debt during college or graduate school. Other life transitions may also be easier for children whose parents have sufficient resources. If their resources are adequate, parents may aid their children in purchasing a first home, establishing a household after marriage, and preparing for and taking care of children. Assistance with homeownership, in particular, can be an important inter-vivos transfer, and homeownership is a core component of a stable wealth portfolio. In addition, because investing in a home is the most typical first investment for Americans, homeowners are more likely to also own stocks, mutual funds, and bonds (Keister 2000b). Because additional siblings reduce the likelihood of parental assistance with a down payment on a home, homeownership will be delayed, and investment in other financial assets, such as stock, may also be delayed. Inheritance is also less likely in large families. A smaller or completely diminished inheritance changes the point at which the child begins to accumulate wealth. Any direct transfer of financial resources from parents to children has the potential to provide a base savings that can grow even if additional savings are never added. A reduced inheritance postpones the age at which wealth accumulation can begin and, because long-term compounding adds significantly to net worth, the long-term rate of accumulation may be significantly decreased when inheritance is lower.

Childhood family structure (i.e., the presence of parents in the household) also affects adult wealth. Family structure varies widely across households in the United States and includes households where no parents are present as well as households where at least one parent is present. Households that include no parents are those where, for instance, the child is in foster care, is being raised by grandparents or other relatives, or is otherwise separated from both biological parents. Households that include at least one biological parent might be single-parent households, households with both biological parents, or step-parent households. Single-parent and step-parent households tend to be relatively common in the United States and tend to negatively affect adult wealth compared to households where both biological parents are present. Growing up in either a single-parent or a step-parent family is likely to affect acquisition of human capital. Single parents have fewer resources, both material and nonmaterial, to invest in children's education. Single-parent households tend to have lower income and wealth than those with two biological parents, and because there is only one parent available, nonmaterial resources such as time and energy also tend to be more limited. As a result, people raised in single-parent households are at a disadvantage in the accumulation of human capital compared to their peers who are raised by two biological parents. Similarly, being raised by step-parents can affect human capital, but the effect is likely to reflect the disruption caused by experiencing a divorce rather than the family structure itself. Being raised in a single-parent or step-parent household is also likely to affect orientations toward such behaviors and processes as marriage and fertility, work and occupational decision making, and saving and investing. I discuss the connection between education and wealth later in this chapter, and I address the role of orientations toward work and money in Chapter 3.

Race and Ethnicity

Race and ethnicity are both strongly comingled with religious affiliation and beliefs, and race/ethnicity are also among the most enduring determinants of wealth ownership. As I explained in Chapter 1, I follow recent research tradition by identifying religious groups based partly on race/ethnicity. Table 2.4 summarizes the racial and ethnic composition of the religious groups on which I focus and confirms that these groups are very racially and ethnically homogeneous. The table shows the percentage of each racial/ethnic group affiliated with particular religious groups. I include this table not because the patterns are particularly surprising

TABLE 2.4. *Childhood Religion and Race (%)*

	White	Black	Hispanic
White Conservative Protestant (CP)	29.6	1.6	6.5
Black Conservative Protestant (BP)	0.2	80.8	0.2
Mainline/Liberal Protestant (MP)	29.1	2.4	2.6
Catholic	32.6	7.5	87.6
Jewish	1.7	0.2	0.4
Mormon/LDS	0.9	0.0	0.6
Other religion	1.7	1.1	0.4
No religion	4.2	6.4	1.7

Notes: Data are from the 1979–2004 NLSY. Sample size = 4,369 (excluding 19 cases with missing data for childhood religion). Cells are the percent of race/ethnic group that is affiliated with religious group (e.g., percent of whites who are CP).

(given my coding strategy) but rather because it is important to underscore the strength of the association between race/ethnicity and religion. Recall from Chapter 1 that these groups are also internally consistent in many of their beliefs and practices, and that my definitions of religious affiliations are consistent with a large body of literature that confirms similarities in the content of the beliefs of these groups. Empirical models that I discuss in later chapters allow me to disentangle race/ethnicity and religious effects to some extent; I discuss the issue in greater detail in relation to those models.

There are very clear, very strong empirical relationships between race/ethnicity and asset ownership, particularly homeownership. It has become apparent that white families are more likely to own homes than black and Hispanic families, that the values of the homes owned by whites appreciate more rapidly than those of blacks and Hispanics, that resale values of homes are greater for whites, and that whites typically receive more favorable terms in home mortgage lending (Conley 1999; Oliver and Shapiro 1995). Because homeownership is an essential part of wealth accumulation for most people in the United States, racial/ethnic differences in the ownership and value of these assets translate into significant differences in overall net worth, which can become extreme over the life course.

There is also evidence that saving from current income and investment strategies (when saving is possible) vary by race/ethnicity in ways that translate into wealth differences. In particular, blacks appear to be less likely than whites to buy high-risk, high-return assets when they do save (Keister 2000a). Although the patterns in ownership are unmistakable, the reasons that these differences persist is far from certain. Some have argued that variations in preferences for saving and consumption are responsible. That is, some have argued that there are racial and ethnic differences in willingness to postpone consumption that are manifested in saving and investment behavior (Brimmer 1988; Lawrence 1991). Others point to differences in opportunities from early in life that create differences in lifetime earnings, employment, education, opportunities to save, and knowledge about how to save and invest as explanations for race and ethnic differences in wealth ownership. Whatever the reason for these differences, it is clear that white Americans enjoy a sizable advantage in wealth ownership over black and Hispanic Americans. Those differences will exacerbate religious differences in wealth ownership where religious affiliation coincides with race.

Human Capital

Human capital, including formal education and related training, is one of the most important reasons that religion and wealth ownership are related. Indeed, human capital is such a critical link that, in other published work, I have depicted human capital as the cornerstone of conceptual models similar to the one in Figure 1.1. I have moved away from that type of illustration because it suggests that other processes are not important and because there is a degree of simultaneous decision making that such a figure does not reflect (see the end of this chapter for more on simultaneous decisions). Yet it is difficult to overestimate the strength of the role human capital plays in creating wealth and in linking religious beliefs with wealth accumulation.

There is an extensive literature documenting the important role that religion plays in educational attainment in the United States (Burstein 2007; Fitzgerald and Glass 2008b; Glass and Jacobs 2008; Lehrer 2004b; Sherkat and Darnell 1999), and education, in turn, is one of the strongest predictors of wealth accumulation. Table 2.5 shows that there are, indeed, notable patterns in educational attainment by religious group. Educational attainment is particularly high among those raised in Jewish families: Both years of education completed and the percentage of respondents with an advanced degree (beyond a bachelor's degree) are exceptionally high for Jews. Mainline Protestants also stand out in their educational attainment. White Catholics are similar to MPs in the number of years of education they attain, but they still lag behind in completing advanced degrees – a pattern that is consistent with knowing that education levels

TABLE 2.5. *Childhood Religion and Educational Attainment*

	Years of Education	Has Advanced Degree (%)
White Conservative Protestant (CP)	13.2	10.7
Black Conservative Protestant (BP)	12.7	4.2
Mainline/Liberal Protestant (MP)	14.3	19.5
Catholic	13.6	11.0
White	14.0	12.3
Hispanic	12.5	6.4
Jewish	16.0	33.4
Mormon/LDS	13.8	8.1
Other religion	14.9	25.2
No religion	12.7	9.5
All Respondents	13.6	12.5

Notes: Data are from the 1979–2004 NLSY. Sample size = 4,369 (excluding 19 cases with missing data for childhood religion).

have only recently begun to increase for white Catholics. The table suggests that CPs have relatively low educational attainment (Darnell and Sherkat 1997; Fitzgerald and Glass 2008b; Glass and Jacobs 2005; Greeley and Hout 2006; Smith and Faris 2005). In contrast, Mormon/LDS respondents have notably higher levels of education – a pattern that sets them apart from other conservative Protestant groups. Black Protestants, black Catholics, and Hispanic Catholics report the lowest levels of educational attainment, particularly completion of advanced degrees. Those in the "other religion" group also have high education levels. As was the case in Table 2.2, this value is largely driven by Unitarians, 50 percent of whom report having advanced degrees.

There are two general categories of reasons given for the strong effect that religion has on education. The first is a rational choice (in sociology) or human capital (in economics) approach. From this perspective, people face opportunities and constraints throughout their lives and make decisions regarding the importance of education within those constraints. Religious beliefs and ideology affect both the opportunities/ constraints and the decisions that people make. Within this general class of approaches, sociologists (rational choice and status attainment researchers) emphasize the importance of constraints such as family background and other structural factors (e.g., school quality during childhood) in shaping educational decisions and outcomes (Ellison and Sherkat 1995; Finke and Stark 2005; Sherkat and Darnell 1999; Sherkat and Wilson 1995). Rational choice sociologists and status attainment researchers are not typically grouped together, but in this case, their approach tends to be similar. Economists tend to emphasize individual preferences (demand for education) and contextual or macrolevel conditions (supply of education) that determine options (Lehrer 1999, 2004a, 2004b, 2010).

Second, particular characteristics of religious groups are often identified to explain patterns in educational attainment and human capital acquisition. Conservative Protestants, for example, tend to be skeptical of the approaches taken in secular schools and universities that propagate secular humanist values and promote scientific investigation rather than acceptance of divine truths (Darnell and Sherkat 1997; Sherkat 2009; Sherkat and Darnell 1999; Sikkink 1999). These unique orientations contribute to low levels of education among CPs (Fitzgerald and Glass 2008b; Glass and Jacobs 2005; Sherkat and Darnell 1999). In contrast, particular traits have also been cited as significant factors in producing high levels of educational attainment among Jews (Burstein 2007) and Mormons/LDS (Shaefer and Zellner 2007). Burstein (2007) points out that cultural emphasis on pursuits in this life are important contributors to educational success for Jews. Shaefer and Zellner (2007) discuss the important major educational efforts of the Latter-Day Saints, including a system of seminaries and institutes that focus on retaining adolescent members. They also emphasize the important position that higher education, particularly Brigham Young University, plays in producing well-educated, committed LDS adults.

Particular group traits have also been used to explain *change* in a group's attainment levels. For instance, recent generations of white Catholics have been cited as an important group for whom educational attainment has changed (Keister 2007). Distance from the immigrant experience may be part of the explanation for Catholic educational achievement (Borjas 1999, 2000). Indeed, white Catholics in the NLSY are relatively similar to MPs in their proximity to immigration. Table 2.6 shows the percent of NLSY respondents whose fathers and mothers were immigrants. For MPs, approximately 2 percent had a father who was an immigrant, and approximately 3 percent had a mother who was an immigrant. White Catholics were significantly more likely than MPs to have immigrant parents. Hispanic Catholics make an interesting and important contrast to white Catholics because they tend to be much closer to the immigrant experience. Indeed, more than 40 percent of Hispanic Catholics report that their father was an immigrant and the same percent report that their mother was an immigrant. In addition, there are

TABLE 2.6. *Childhood Religion and Family Background (%)*

	Father Was Immigrant	Mother Was Immigrant
White Conservative Protestant (CP)	2.5	3.4
Black Conservative Protestant (BP)	1.1	0.8
Mainline/Liberal Protestant (MP)	2.5	3.0
Catholic	12.1	12.2
White	5.8	5.6
Hispanic	41.5	41.6
Jewish	18.4	26.3
Mormon/LDS	15.3	19.9
Other religion	24.2	34.2
No religion	3.2	4.9
All Respondents	6.1	6.9

Notes: Data are from the 1979–2004 NLSY. Sample size = 4,369 (excluding 19 cases with missing data for childhood religion).

important advantages resulting from Catholic school attendance, as I will discuss in more detail in Chapter 6.

That education improves life chances and financial well-being is so certain, it is largely taken for granted in the social sciences. Education interacts with other family processes, including marriage and fertility, usually leading to behaviors that enhance saving and asset accumulation. Indeed, there is evidence that the timing of life course transitions, including marriage and childbirth, can affect educational attainment in ways that may also affect other measures of attainment for some groups. In particular, family formation may be partially responsible for low educational attainment for people raised in both CP and BP families. In multivariate models of educational attainment for women, introducing the timing of family formation (net of other controls) reduced the negative effect of being raised CP to insignificance (Fitzgerald and Glass 2008a). For BP women, the timing of family formation reduced but did not completely eliminate the religion effect. For CP and BP men, control variables explained the negative effect of childhood religion on adult educational attainment (Fitzgerald and Glass 2008a).

Of course, education is also critically important in its own right. Education improves job prospects, occupational prestige, career trajectories, wages and salaries, and benefits. Saying that education improves life chances also suggests that there is a positive relationship between education and wealth. And there is excellent empirical evidence that human capital does increase wealth ownership (Keister 2000b, 2005). Of all of the predictors of adult net worth, educational attainment is among the strongest. College graduates enjoy a very large increase in their total net worth, and those with advanced degrees enjoy even greater wealth. Education also increases the likelihood of homeownership, ownership of financial assets, saving for retirement, and the pace of wealth accumulation over the life cycle.

Net of its many other benefits, educational attainment improves adult wealth for a number of reasons (Keister 2000b; Oliver and Shapiro 1995; Wolff 1998). First, education improves financial literacy and financial decision making. At all income levels, those who have completed more education save more, assume less debt, and make decisions regarding investments that yield larger overall portfolios. In addition, those with more education are likely to begin saving earlier in life, allowing them to accumulate assets more rapidly throughout their careers and into retirement. Investing in high-risk, high-return financial assets such as stocks, for example, as opposed to relatively conservative instruments such as Certificates of Deposit, can have dramatic effects on total wealth accumulated over the life course (Keister 2000a). Likewise, the timing and ordering of financial decisions can shape wealth accumulation in important ways. Beginning to save in early adulthood can have significant advantages over postponing saving until later. Because there is a degree of path dependence built into saving and consumption decisions, people tend to follow paths through their lives that influence in important ways the amount of wealth they accumulate over time. For example, a traditional trajectory might involve first buying a house then investing in financial assets only later in life. In contrast, investing in financial assets early is likely to increase total accumulation across the life course because the returns on these assets tend to be relatively high and compounding can create a sizeable portfolio with time. A positive early saving trajectory also tends to provide somewhat of a buffer against financial emergencies and economic downturns that could otherwise create a crisis and prevent additional accumulation.

Second, education can provide important social contacts that provide information, assistance, and referrals to those who can provide these important things. Social contacts may also provide direct assistance such as capital for starting a business, making an initial financial investment, or making a down payment on a home. Informal education regarding saving can also come from social contacts and might contribute to the positive education-wealth relationship. Knowledge about the importance of saving, avenues available for saving, and saving strategies are at least partly gained through exposure to the saving behavior of parents and others a person encounters over the life course (Chiteji and Stafford 1999). Parents who save and invest teach their children to do the same. Likewise, other social contacts during childhood and adolescence (e.g., other relatives, parents' friends, church members) or young adulthood (e.g., friends, professors, other contacts in college) can have a similar effect.

Third, there is a possible social-psychological process connecting education and wealth. That is, it is possible that some people are more inclined than others to postpone consumption, and those people are more likely to acquire human capital and to save money (Dynan 1993). A person with a relatively high propensity to postpone consumption is likely to begin saving early in life and to benefit from compounding. Such a person is also likely to make education, training, and other types of human capital a priority from early in life and to benefit from the effects of these investments over the life course. Because this is a challenging mechanism to study empirically, it has not attracted a great deal of research attention, making it difficult to conclude how important this mechanism is relative to others explaining how education and wealth are related. However, even if the education-wealth connection is spurious (i.e., both are caused by a third, psychological factor), this does not diminish the centrality of education to understanding how religion and wealth are related.

Adult Processes

Religion shapes marriage, fertility, and related behaviors, and these behaviors are important determinants of adult saving and net worth outcomes. Most religious faiths incorporate ideas about marriage, family, divorce, and related processes as an important part of their teachings. Marriage is considered a sacred relationship in many faiths, the importance of marriage occurring prior to fertility permeates western religious teachings, and admonitions against divorce are also extremely common. Similarly, many spiritual traditions incorporate teachings about family formation, childrearing, and related practices. The effect of religion on family processes stems from both childhood and adult religious affiliation and beliefs. Childhood beliefs provide the foundation for behaviors related to marriage and family formation, and adult religious beliefs have a strong effect as well (Alwin 1986; Alwin and Felson 2010; Bartkowski and Ellison 1995; Wilcox 1998). When a person stays with the same faith over the life course or returns to a childhood religious affiliation as an adult, the effect of religious teachings and beliefs on adult behaviors such as marriage behavior can be intensified. In the next two sections, I describe in more detail how religion, family, and wealth are related.

Marriage Processes and Wealth

There is, indeed, an important effect of religion on marital processes. Religious beliefs affect orientations toward the desirability of marriage, age at which people should first marry, and related decisions about cohabitation (Hammond, Cole, and Beck 1993; Lehrer 2004c, 2010; Mosher, Williams, and Johnson 1992). Decisions about marriage and cohabitation, in turn, are closely linked to orientations and decisions regarding family, education, and work. In relatively conservative faiths, women are encouraged to focus on home and family activities, are encouraged to have large families, and are exposed to others who marry early and focus on home activities. As a result, early marriage may be perceived as both desirable and acceptable in these faiths (Lehrer 2004a). Women in conservative faiths also tend to have low education levels, which limits job prospects and increases the appeal of early marriage (Hammond, Cole, and Beck 1993; Lehrer 2004c, 2010; Mosher, Williams, and Johnson 1992). In more liberal faiths, early marriage and childbearing are not typically discouraged explicitly, and cohabitation is not encouraged. However, because early marriage is uncommon, cohabitation is relatively common, and educational and career attainment are encouraged, early marriage is less appealing.

Table 2.7 relates childhood religion to adult marriage outcomes. The table shows that a very high percentage of those raised in Jewish families are currently married. White Catholics and MPs are close behind and very similar to each other. BPs report very low rates of current marriage, but this is consistent with other research that documents that marriage rates among blacks are quite low, rather than reflecting a religious effect. However, it is noteworthy that marriage rates among black Catholics are high relative to rates for BPs. Those with no religious preference are less likely than the average respondent to be currently married, consistent with the argument that delayed marriage has contributed to growth in claims of no preference (Hout and Fischer 2002). The effect of childhood religion on marriage can be intensified by adult religious beliefs and orientations. Comparing adult religion to marriage behavior produce very similar patterns (not shown to conserve space).

Religion also affects the choice of a spouse – including whether the couple practices the same religion (homogamy) or not (Lehrer 1998;

TABLE 2.7. *Childhood Religion and Marriage (%)*

	Married	Divorced
White Conservative Protestant (CP)	70.0	17.2
Black Conservative Protestant (BP)	38.1	15.7
Mainline/Liberal Protestant (MP)	72.4	12.5
Catholic	69.2	13.1
White	71.8	12.4
Hispanic	61.2	14.7
Jewish	81.3	2.2
Mormon/LDS	61.6	19.0
Other religion	66.4	11.7
No religion	52.5	16.4
All Respondents	65.6	14.2

Notes: Data are from the 1979–2004 NLSY. Sample size = 4,369 (excluding 19 cases with missing data for childhood religion). Married and divorced refer to current status.

Sherkat 2004) – marital stability and satisfaction (Lehrer 1996a; Lehrer and Chiswick 1993), and the likelihood of divorce (Call and Heaton 1997; Filsinger and Wilson 1984; Lehrer 2010). The selection of a marriage partner is strongly motivated by homogamy (e.g., on education, background, and other traits), and religion is a critical dimension on which people select a partner. Religious homogamy, in turn, is an important predictor of marital stability and satisfaction, and religious heterogamy (when a couple has different religious affiliations) can be destabilizing and lead to divorce. Couples who share the same religious beliefs can share spiritual experiences, participate jointly in religious observances and activities both at home and in other settings, and develop overlapping social relations originating from religious groups. Religious homogamy also increases the likelihood that couples are similar on a large number of demographic behaviors and processes, including education, childrearing, time allocated for various life activities, work patterns, decisions about where to live, social relationships, and decisions about finances. In contrast, religious heterogamy and the processes it affects can be destabilizing and divorce can become more likely (Lehrer 1998, 2004a). As Lehrer (Lehrer 1998, 2004a) has documented, there are three conditions under which religious intermarriage can be particularly problematic: when the marriage includes people whose religious beliefs are very different, as in the marriage between a Jew and a Christian; when one or both partners' religious groups seek separation from the broader culture; or when one partner has no religious affiliation. In all three cases, the effect is more

extreme because both religious and other demographic differences can be
radically different in the couple, exacerbating the destabilizing effect of
all traits.

Religious beliefs – separate from the effect of religious homogamy –
can also affect the likelihood of divorce. In faiths where divorce is explicitly prohibited, the social costs associated with marital dissolution are
high and the decision to divorce can generate severe social and spiritual
consequences. Catholicism, for instance, has a well-known prohibition
against divorce. Catholic doctrine regards marriage as a sacrament, and
any valid marriage between two baptized Catholics cannot be dissolved
(D'Antonio, Hoge, and Davidson 2007; Tropman 1995, 2002). Catholics
point to several Biblical passages to support this teaching, including
"Everyone who divorces his wife and marries another commits adultery,
and he who marries a woman divorced from her husband commits adultery" (Luke 16:18, Mark 10:11–12). In the Catholic Church, the only time
a couple can remarry after divorce is when an annulment is granted, most
often indicating that the two parties did not exchange valid matrimonial
consent initially. In the absence of an annulment, a divorced Catholic
is not permitted to participate in other church sacraments, making it
extremely difficult to be an active member of the church. Until relatively
recently, divorce was very rare among Catholics, adding social pressure to
the spiritual pressure to remain married. Although divorce has increased
in recent decades among Catholics, particularly among white Catholics,
the likelihood of divorce is still lower for Catholics than for those from
other spiritual traditions with comparable educations, incomes, and other
demographic traits (D'Antonio, et al. 2001; D'Antonio, Hoge, and Davidson 2007). Table 2.7 shows that divorce is particularly rare among Jews
and low for white and Hispanic Catholics. CPs and black Catholics are
slightly more likely than average to be divorced.

Marriage has a very clear, positive effect on wealth ownership (Keister 2005; Lupton and Smith 2003). There is some evidence that marriage increases earnings (Waite and Lehrer 2003) which would allow
for additional saving. More directly, there is evidence that asset levels
increase after marriage. Part of the increase reflects the tendency for
married couples to combine their assets and to begin treating formerly
separate assets as joint property (Keister 2005). Couples join savings and
checking accounts and combine investments, they purchase homes rather
than rent, and they otherwise consolidate finances into jointly owned
property. Marriage allows couples to pool risks (e.g., if one person is
unemployed, the other can continue working), creates economies of scale

(e.g., in housing costs), and allows people to take advantage of a division of labor (Waite and Lehrer 2003). Marriage also creates common goals (e.g., children and children's educations, home improvements and upgrades, and retirement objectives) that encourage couples to save. Early marriage is likely to reduce attainment of other outcomes such as education, which suggests reduced wealth, but early marriage also has the potential to increase saving and lifetime wealth accumulation by increasing the likelihood of early saving and homeownership.

Religious homogamy can intensify the effect of marriage on wealth accumulation. Marriage between two people of the same faith increases the likelihood that a couple has similar values, priorities, and competences regarding finances. When those values favor saving, religious homogamy can increase saving and wealth. Homogamy also reduces the likelihood of divorce, as noted earlier, and divorce has a relatively straightforward and severe negative effect on wealth. In just the opposite fashion as combining assets, separating assets decreases the net worth of both parties who begin to live independently and to maintain two households. Divorce can also be costly and force a couple to use savings to cover legal fees, the cost of arbitration and other professional services, moving costs, and increased health care costs (often associated with psychological services and increased illness resulting from stress). If the couple had children, the effect of divorce on wealth can be even higher as the expenses associated with maintaining two homes are often quite high.

As this section suggests, the relationship among religion, marriage, and other processes that affect wealth (e.g., education, work behavior) are complex. It is easy to think of human capital acquisition as preceding marital behavior and processes, and the majority of people still finish their education prior to marriage. That is, the likelihood of continuing education after marriage drops dramatically. However, marriage does not preclude continued human capital acquisition. In fact, more people are returning to school later in life today than ever before, and more people are cohabiting prior to marriage. For these reasons, it is difficult to make claims about the precise order in which education and family processes occur that holds true across people. What is important is that educational and marital processes interact with each other, and both affect wealth accumulation.

Fertility and Wealth

Fertility behavior is clearly an important part of the causal processes linking religion, education, and family processes with wealth outcomes. It is well documented that religion influences orientations toward premarital sex and the onset of sexual activity, attitudes regarding birth control and the use of contraception, whether a person or couple has any children, the age at which people have their first child (i.e., age at first birth), family size, and even behaviors such as taking virginity and secondary abstinence pledges (Lehrer 1996a, 2004a; McQuillan 2004; Sherkat and Ellison 1999). More traditional religious groups tend to have more traditional approaches to sexual activity and family formation. There is some evidence that well-established patterns are not as clear when looking at transitions to premarital births, but when marriage is treated as a competing risk, familiar religious patterns reemerge (Pearce 2010).

Recent research also shows that premarital and nonmarital sex are, indeed, less common in faiths such as CP denominations that explicitly discourage them (Regnerus 2007). Regnerus (2007) also shows an interesting pattern of religious youth delaying sexual intercourse or pursuing "technical virginity" (engaging in oral sex, anal sex, and other sexual acts without actually having vaginal intercourse) in an effort to retain future marriage prospects. Virginity and secondary abstinence pledges (returning to abstinence after having lost virginity) have also become more common in recent years, and members of conservative religious groups are more likely to take such pledges (Regnerus 2007). There is also evidence that youth who take such pledges do delay the onset of sexual activity, have fewer sex partners than nonpledgers, and are more likely than nonpledgers to abstain from sex until marriage (Bearman and Brückner 1999). There is also evidence of nuanced interactions between religion, race, and sexual activity (Regnerus 2010). For example, African-American youth, particularly boys, are among the earliest to engage in sexual intercourse and, therefore, are at high risk of early fertility. Even though African-American youth are also likely to be members of relatively conservative religious groups, there is little empirical evidence that religion delays sexual activity for these young men (Regnerus 2010).

In addition, some religious teachings and traditions include social and psychological rewards for having large families. In such pronatalist faiths, early fertility is approved and even encouraged both by formal teachings and rules and through norms, and having many children can provide considerable social status (Lehrer 2004a; McQuillan 2004). Mormon/LDS fertility rates have been notably high in the United States at least in part in response to such incentives (Lehrer 2004a, 2010; Stark and Finke 2000). Catholicism also strongly discourages contraceptive use and abortion, and Catholic family size has also been quite large historically. Fertility

TABLE 2.8. *Childhood Religion and Fertility (%)*

	Have Any Kids (%)	Age at First Birth	Number of Kids
White Conservative Protestant (CP)	81.7	24.4	1.9
Black Conservative Protestant (BP)	80.3	22.1	2.1
Mainline/Liberal Protestant (MP)	76.7	26.8	1.7
Catholic	79.8	26.1	1.9
White	79.3	26.8	1.8
Hispanic	80.9	23.6	2.2
Jewish	77.0	30.6	1.7
Mormon/LDS	79.5	25.4	1.7
Other religion	62.9	26.7	1.4
No religion	74.5	24.1	1.7
All Respondents	78.9	25.3	1.8

Notes: Data are from the 1979–2004 NLSY. Sample size = 4,369 (excluding 19 cases with missing data for childhood religion). Age at first birth only recorded for females (*n* = 3,100, excluding 8 cases with missing data for childhood religion). Sample percentage refers to the total sample (i.e., males and females).

rates among white Catholics have declined since the 1970s, in part as a result of declining adherence to church teachings regarding children, but family size remains large among Hispanic Catholics where adherence remains high (Lehrer 2004a; Mosher, Williams, and Johnson 1992). There is considerable variation in pronatalism across CP and BP sects, but many have strong norms and teachings encouraging large families. By contrast, Mainline Protestant denominations and non-Orthodox Judaism place less emphasis on large families, and fertility rates in these groups has historically been correspondingly low. Table 2.8 summarizes religious patterns in fertility. The table suggests that although the likelihood of having any children does not vary dramatically by religious background, there are notable religious differences in the age at first birth and family size. Black Protestants and CPs tend to have kids slightly younger than the average, whereas Jews tend to have children relatively late. BP and CP families also tend to be larger than average, whereas Jewish families are small (note that very small differences in the number of children born indicate important differences in this context).

Fertility behaviors, in turn, have important effects on saving, wealth accumulation patterns, and overall net worth. There tends to be a curvilinear relationship between family size and wealth: Saving and wealth accumulation tend to increase somewhat in families with one to two children (compared to households with no children) as parents increase saving and buy homes, but it then declines in families with more than two children as expenses rise and saving becomes more difficult (Keister 2005). Having children early in life is particularly difficult because having a family can make it difficult to finish or complete schooling, makes career development more challenging, and can reduce initial saving and investing that can contribute to lifelong asset appreciation (Keister 2005). For this reason, in faiths where early childbearing is encouraged or simply common, wealth accumulation is likely to be slower and overall wealth reduced. Likewise, in faiths where large families are desirable and common, wealth accumulation slows and net worth is likely to be lower than in faiths where smaller families are the norm. In contrast, remaining childless is an extremely strong, positive predictor of wealth ownership. Delayed fertility or childlessness increase wealth because they facilitate educational attainment, career development, occupational advancement, and initial saving and investing. Thus in faiths where childbearing occurs later in life or where people are more inclined to remain childless, wealth accumulation is likely to occur faster and overall wealth is likely to be relatively high.

Like marriage behavior, fertility behavior is complicated because it interacts with education and marriage as well as directly with wealth. In the past, marriage preceded children for the majority of adults. While this is still the case for the majority of people, childbirth outside of marriage is increasingly common. It is also increasingly common for people to return to school after having children or to simply plan to have children while they are completing schooling. Again, this suggests that marriage, fertility, and education interact with each other in ways that can exacerbate the effect of any one process on wealth ownership.

Simultaneous Processes

The relationships among demographic traits can be discussed as isolated processes, but in reality, the behaviors and events that affect these traits occur simultaneously. People usually make decisions regarding education, marriage, fertility, union dissolution, and related behaviors simultaneously rather than separately. For example, decisions regarding marriage often involve simultaneous decisions about fertility, labor force participation, and saving. Research from economic demography is particularly relevant to understanding how religion simultaneously affects various demographic processes. The arrows in Figure 1.1 indicating that human capital, work behavior, adult religion, and other adult family processes affect each other refer to the simultaneous nature of these decisions. The arrows are intended to indicate that each process in column 2 is dependent on the other processes in that column. Lehrer (2004a, 2008) has articulated how religious affiliation relates to various demographic processes and resulting measures of attainment. Lehrer proposes that investments in human capital, fertility behavior, union formation and dissolution, and other demographic processes are interrelated behaviors and that internalized religious teachings affect the perceived costs and benefits associated with these decisions. Lehrer's model is similar to the one I propose in that she acknowledges both direct and indirect effects of religion on attainment (via demographic processes).

The family and education processes that I describe in this chapter are critical to understanding the connection between religion and wealth, but the relationship involves work and income behaviors and outcomes that I deliberately did not discuss in this chapter. I address those processes in the next two chapters before moving on to an explicit discussion of the connection between religion and wealth.

3

Work, Occupation, and Income

The aim of this book is to explore the relationship between religious beliefs and the behaviors and processes that lead to wealth accumulation. In the previous chapter, I showed that religion is related to family processes and human capital acquisition. I proposed that these, in turn, affect wealth ownership through several mechanisms, including through their effect on work, job outcomes, and income. In this chapter, I continue to investigate the relationship between religion and the processes that connect it to wealth indirectly. In particular, I explore in more detail the role that work and money play in linking religion to wealth by discussing the boxes in Figure 1.1 that are labeled *work*, *job traits*, *income*, and *charitable giving*. These behaviors and processes are also partially driven by intergenerational processes and can be considered demographic. As such, this chapter continues my discussion of the pathway labeled *intergenerational and demographic processes* in Figure 1.1.

In my discussions, *work* includes measures such as age at first birth, time spent in the labor force, hours worked, occupation, and related traits. Work behavior is likely to vary with gender as women often interrupt labor force participation for childbirth and when they have young children. *Job traits* (e.g., occupational prestige, job satisfaction) are not chosen but rather result from human capital, work behavior, and other adult behaviors and processes. *Income* refers to the sources and amounts of income earned by individuals and households. *Charitable giving* includes the amount of money donated, the percentage of available resources devoted to philanthropy, and the frequency of giving. Charity also includes gifts of time.

In this chapter, I also address the pathway labeled *orientations and values*. Religious beliefs affect orientations and values toward a large number of behaviors and processes, including work and money. Religious beliefs might, for example, have implications for the number of hours a person works, and they might suggest that working in some occupations or jobs is more desirable than working in others. Similarly, there are religious variations in orientations toward the meaning of money, saving, investing, the relative importance of work/money/family, reasons to work hard, and even the means by which money should be saved (e.g., buying a home versus investing in financial assets). An important starting point for this discussion is the fact that work and money have meaning beyond their economic value, that general orientations toward living affect finances, and that Americans recognize these connections (Wuthnow 1994; Zelizer 1978, 1989).

Throughout this chapter, I briefly address how work processes, occupation, and financial orientations affect asset accumulation and wealth ownership, but I reserve the bulk of the discussion of wealth for Chapters 4 and 5.

Religion, Work, and Occupation

There are important associations between religious affiliation, the amount of time spent working, and the nature of the jobs people hold. Work and occupation affect income, and income, in turn, affects the wealth outcomes that are the focus of this book. Some of these connections are unrelated to the content of religious beliefs, but they are important to understanding the religion-wealth connection all the same. Other connections do have origins in religious beliefs. For example, in faiths that value traditional family relations, the importance of spending time with young children may affect whether both parents work, the number of hours parents spend away from home, and even the type of job parents are willing to take. Similarly, religious conservatives are more likely than others to advocate for women taking primary responsibility for childcare and men taking responsibility for working outside the home. These values can also affect work behaviors, occupational decisions and outcomes, and related behaviors and processes. There are also important generational and peer processes that reinforce patterns of work. As I mentioned in Chapter 2, intergenerational correlations in occupational status and work behaviors are quite high, and peer influences on various adult behaviors can be strong. Both family and other social relations certainly reinforce work

TABLE 3.1. *Adult Religion and Hours Worked*

	Hours Per Week, NLSY (median)	Hours Per Week, HRS (median)	At Least 40 Hours, NLSY (%)	At Least 40 Hours, HRS (%)
White Conservative Protestant (CP)	40.0	37.0	83.4	49.3
Black Conservative Protestant (BP)	40.0	35.0	83.6	42.8
Mainline/Liberal Protestant (MP)	42.0	30.0	82.8	38.5
Catholic	40.0	35.0	83.1	43.5
White	40.0	35.0	81.9	41.3
Hispanic	40.0	40.0	87.3	55.4
Jewish	40.0	30.0	64.1	37.4
Other Religion	40.0	32.0	80.1	45.6
No Religion	42.0	30.0	84.4	41.1
All Respondents	40.0	35.0	83.1	43.4

Notes: Data are from the 1979–2004 NLSY and the 2006 HRS. NLSY sample size = 4,369; HRS sample size = 8,113. Religion was measured in 2000 in the NLSY and in 1992 in the HRS.

and occupational behaviors. In turn, there is a fairly direct connection between work behaviors and income, benefits, and other compensation. Work, occupational attainment, and income combine to affect saving and investing in financial assets; purchases of real assets, such as a home and other real estate; debt; and, ultimately, wealth accumulation.

The NLSY includes considerable detail on work behaviors, occupation, and related activities, which is useful in exploring connections between religion and these important outcomes. Hours worked is one very important behavior that signals a person's approach to work and that affects other work outcomes, including income. Table 3.1 shows how hours worked vary by religious group, as identified by religion in adulthood. Separate analyses (not shown, to conserve space) show that hours worked and income vary with religious group similarly regardless of whether childhood religion or adult religion is used to create religious groups reflecting, at least in part, the high correlation between childhood and adult religious affiliation. I use adult religion throughout this chapter to draw on data from both the NLSY and HRS without providing overwhelming amounts of data. The tables in this chapter also omit the separate black Catholic and LDS/Mormons groups because sample sizes for these groups are small as a result of missing data on work and income outcomes. To create Table 3.1, I draw on detailed NLSY information about work patterns over time to create two measures: a continuous measure of total hours worked per week and a dichotomous indicator that the respondent works full time or forty or more hours per week (both were measured in 2004). I report median hours worked because the variable is skewed by a relatively small number of people who report very long workweeks.

Religious affiliation is associated with hours worked, but Table 3.1 suggests that the relationship reflects other SES measures rather than the content of religious beliefs. The first column in Table 3.1 compares median hours worked in a typical week by religious groups and shows that Americans are extremely uniform in their work behavior. There is remarkably little difference for the working-age (ages thirty-nine to forty-seven) adults in the NLSY sample. Comparing mean number of hours worked (not shown) does not reveal any marked differences either. Rather, mean hours worked is simply higher than the median, reflecting the small number of people who worked very large numbers of hours, but is still roughly uniform across religious groups. Median hours worked is naturally lower for the older HRS sample (aged forty to eighty-nine, with an average age of approximately sixty-eight; see Chapter 1 for details on the data than for the NLSY sample. However, patterns across religious groups in the HRS reveal SES-based differences by religion. In particular, the HRS data show that MPs and Jews – groups with relatively high educational levels – work few hours in retirement compared with religious groups with lower educational levels, such as CPs, BPs, and Hispanic Catholics. Those with other religious affiliations also work relatively few hours, reflecting high educational levels, particularly for the LDS/Mormon respondents included in this group. The next column in Table 3.1 shows the percentage of NLSY respondents who work at least forty hours per week. There is much more variation here than in the median number of hours worked, and the variation is suggestive of SES-based influences on work. For instance, relatively high percentages of Hispanic Catholics (who tend to have low educational levels and high SES) in both the NLSY and HRS report working full time, while relatively low percentages of Jews (who tend to have high educational levels and high SES) in both samples report working full time. As a whole, this table shows that the majority of Americans work full time regardless of religious affiliation; however, the table also provides some initial evidence of important variations by religious group. Although the patterns that are evident here appear to be SES-based, they are likely to be important influences on income and wealth outcomes.

Although overall work patterns do not appear to be a primary suspect in linking religion to wealth outcomes, gender differences in work

TABLE 3.2. *Adult Religion, Gender, and Hours Worked*

	Hours Per Week, Men (median)	Hours Per Week, Women (median)	At Least 40 Hours, Men (%)	At Least 40 Hours, Women (%)
White Conservative Protestant (CP)	45.0	40.0	96.3	70.8
Black Conservative Protestant (BP)	44.0	40.0	92.8	74.0
Mainline/Liberal Protestant (MP)	46.0	40.0	95.2	70.1
Catholic	45.0	40.0	94.8	70.1
White	46.0	40.0	95.5	66.1
Hispanic	40.0	40.0	90.2	84.3
Jewish	50.0	33.0	93.1	38.5
Other Religion	46.0	40.0	87.2	72.8
No Religion	45.0	40.0	91.5	75.0
All Respondents	45.0	40.0	93.9	71.4

Notes: Data are from the 1979–2004 NLSY. Sample size = 4,369. Religion was measured in 2000. There are statistically equivalent numbers of men and women in the sample used here, and missing data do not vary significantly by gender.

behavior that reflect religious conservatism/liberalism may be important. Specifically, median hours worked vary with gender and religion in ways that are consistent with SES differences – particularly educational differences that I explored in Chapter 2 – and with religious traditionalism (see Table 3.2). The median hours worked do not vary notably either for men or women, with the exception of Jewish men and women. I use only the NLSY data here because too many of the HRS respondents are out of the labor force. The NLSY data contain nearly equal numbers of men and women, and missing values do not vary by gender. Jewish men work significantly more hours than the average, and Jewish women work significantly fewer. Additional inspection of the data (not shown, to save space) indicates that the Jewish women who work few hours are those with young children.

Yet, more noteworthy differences exist between men and women and by religious group in patterns of working at least forty hours per week (columns 3 and 4 in Table 3.2). For men, significantly more CPs work full time than average – a pattern that could reflect either SES differences or religious differences, or both. That is, educational differences might account for differences in occupation and, thus, differences in hours worked. Alternatively, traditional religious beliefs might discourage working more than forty hours per week to allow for time with family. For women, significantly more BPs and Hispanic Catholics work full time compared with the overall sample. In contrast, significantly fewer white Catholics and Jews work full time. Again, these patterns could reflect both SES differences and differences in religious beliefs. Patterns of unemployment by religious affiliation – including ever having been unemployed and the number of unemployment spells – follow patterns similar to those for working more than forty hours weekly. That is, groups such as CPs, BPs, and Hispanic Catholics with low educational levels are more likely to experience unemployment.

One might also wonder whether there are differences in work behavior by marital status or religious attendance, where attendance may reflect strength of religious convictions. Additional examination of the data (not shown, to conserve space) reveals that separated and divorced men, regardless of religion, work more hours than other men. Otherwise, there are no notable patterns in work by both religious affiliation and marital status. Similarly, one might wonder whether the intensity of religious convictions, measured by attendance at religious events and services, is related to work behavior. However, additional data analysis (again, not shown, to conserve space) reveals few notable patterns in hours worked by religious attendance.[1]

Occupation also matters. Occupation affects income, which directly increases or decreases wealth. Recall from Chapter 1 that occupational similarities between parents and children is at least part of the reason that childhood and adult SES are connected (Blau and Duncan 1967; Hauser and Warren 1997; Warren and Hauser 1997). Parents' occupational experience, including the amount of self-direction they have in their jobs, can transmit orientations toward work that affect the intergenerational transmission of occupational status (Kohn 1959, 1969; Kohn, et al. 1997). As a result, occupational similarities can also intensify the effect of religion on SES outcomes, including both income and wealth.

There are, indeed, differences in occupation by religious group that contribute to cross-group variations in financial well-being. Labor and service occupations are two of the most common among Americans, and nearly one-half of NLSY respondents who are currently working report that their primary occupation is one that falls into the labor/service category (see Table 3.3). Once again, I use NLSY data for this table because

---

[1] I base religious attendance on HRS data because the data are more consistent with other published research. Because most respondents in the HRS sample have neared or reached retirement, additional research is necessary to draw more certain conclusions regarding the relationship between religious convictions and work behaviors.

TABLE 3.3. *Adult Religion and Occupation (%)*

	Managerial/ Administrative	Professional	Sales	Labor/Service	Other
White Conservative Protestant (CP)	16.1	13.6	10.0	49.0	11.3
Black Conservative Protestant (BP)	10.2	7.1	4.7	63.6	14.5
Mainline/Liberal Protestant (MP)	26.3	15.4	6.8	39.1	12.4
Catholic	22.5	12.2	8.9	46.9	9.5
White	24.4	12.4	9.5	45.1	8.7
Hispanic	13.0	10.4	7.2	55.1	14.2
Jewish	24.0	25.5	9.3	14.1	27.1
Other religion	18.9	15.9	5.0	45.0	15.2
No religion	17.2	14.9	7.2	51.5	9.2
All Respondents	19.1	13.2	8.0	48.2	11.6

Notes: Data are from the 1979–2004 NLSY. Sample size = 4,369. Religion was measured in 2000. The *Professional* includes medical workers; law, engineering and technical trades, and the sciences. *Other* includes counselor, social, and religious workers; teachers; education, training, and library workers; entertainment/sports workers; media and communication personnel; protective services; funeral professions; and military.

the majority of respondents to this survey are still active members of the labor force. CPs are quite typical on this measure, with nearly one-half of them reporting that their primary occupation is labor/service. A significantly larger-than-average percentage of BPs and Hispanic Catholics are in labor/service jobs, and a significantly smaller-than-average percentage of Jews and MPs are in labor/service jobs. In contrast, Jews, MPs, and white Catholics are more likely than average to be in managerial/administrative occupations. Jews are also significantly more likely than average to be in professional occupations. Looking horizontally across rows in Table 3.3, one notices that labor/service occupations are the most common jobs for CPs, BPs, and Hispanic Catholics. MPs and white Catholics are distributed bimodally: Managerial/administrative and labor/service jobs are both common. Jews most typically find themselves in managerial/administrative or professional occupations. As with hours worked, these patterns likely reflect SES differences, and they are certain to contribute to income and, ultimately, wealth accumulation.

Of course, with these descriptive patterns, one cannot be certain that there is a causal relationship or identify the nature or even the direction of causation if it does exist. Religious beliefs may affect work behaviors directly. Religious beliefs may affect education and family processes that affect work behaviors. Alternatively, SES may affect choice of religious group. Regardless, the patterns that emerge here can affect wealth, and it is important to identify the patterns before claiming a relationship with wealth. In later chapters, I present multivariate analyses to delve deeper into the causal component of these patterns.

Orientations toward Work

Underlying work behaviors and wealth accumulation patterns is an important relationship between religion and orientations or values by religious groups. The moral codes articulated in religious doctrine are typically manifest in ideal orientations or values. *Orientations* or *values* are guiding principles or ideals that express the worth associated with particular actions or outcomes (Joas 2000; Maio et al. 2003; Schwartz and Bilsky 1987). Orientations/values are cognitive representations that are enduring, that tend to be grouped (e.g., those regarding work, money, and family), and that transcend specific situations. Orientations/values can be terminal (i.e., directed toward particular outcomes) or instrumental (i.e., directed toward means of achieving those outcomes). Orientations/values are usually directed toward particular behaviors or states and follow from religion (Hitlin 2003; Hitlin and Piliavin 2004; Joas 2000; Kohn et al. 2000). More precisely, religious belief is typically considered an ideology or a general orienting approach; it is a collection of ideas often adopted as a whole and maintained regardless of events. Religious beliefs affect orientations/values, which, in turn, affect attitudes and specific preferences. Attitudes and preferences then affect behaviors.

That religious beliefs affect orientations is relatively straightforward, but the subsequent connection between orientations and behaviors is extremely difficult to demonstrate empirically (Hitlin 2003; Hitlin and Piliavin 2004; Maio et al. 2003). Part of the difficulty lies in measuring each of the constructs in this causal chain, and attempts to measure values both explicitly (i.e., based on individual self-reports) and implicitly (i.e., invoking values from behavior) produce challenges that are not yet completely resolved (Hechter, Kim, and Baer 2005). Fortunately, many standard data sets provide reliable measures that can be used to understand the role of orientations/values in determining behavior. Moreover, it is not necessary to show empirical evidence for each component of a causal chain to provide adequate empirical evidence of a social relationship (Cohen 1988). Partly as a result of measurement challenges, notions of *orientations* and *values* fell out of favor in sociology, including in the sociology of religion, following some controversial uses of the terms decades ago. However, the terms are receiving a more favorable reception in current research that has demonstrated that values are essential to understanding, among other processes, how religion affects behaviors and outcomes (Hechter 1992; Hechter 1993; Hitlin 2003; Hitlin and Piliavin 2004). For instance, research showing that religion is associated with behaviors and outcomes such as family processes, gender roles in the home and in the workplace, human capital acquisition, and work and career decisions often invokes notions of values, albeit not always explicitly (Glass and Jacobs 2005; Lehrer 1995; Peek, Lowe, and Williams 1991; Sherkat 2000).

Most important for this work, religion can affect the particular orientations/values people have toward work and money (as I noted briefly in Chapter 1). Religious beliefs affect orientations toward working for certain organizations and in some occupations; for example, being a minister, working for a social service agency, or becoming a career missionary are considered desirable in some faiths. Religious beliefs also influence notions of the relative importance of work and family commitments and time allocation; the willingness to relocate to improve job prospects and career advancement; the desirability of self-employment; and the relative importance of income, advancement possibilities, and job content (Edgell 2006; Glass and Jacobs 2005; Johnson 2001; Keister 2007). Religious beliefs also affect orientations toward money and financial decisions, including budgeting, active saving, the importance of charitable giving, the selection of worthwhile charities, and the amount of money given to charities (Chaves and Miller 1999; Hoge, et al. 1999; Keister 2008; Regnerus, Smith, and Sikkink 1998). Status attainment researchers have invoked similar thinking when they point out that the allocation of personal resources (e.g., toward certain educational, work, and financial pursuits) reflects learned and acquired orientations that can have origins in religious beliefs (Kerckhoff 1976).

The EVS is a survey that contains detailed information on orientations/values regarding work and money that can be used to assess whether there are differences in orientations by religion. One question asked respondents whether their religion influenced their career choice. Specifically, respondents were asked, "In deciding what kind of work to go into, did your religious values influence your decision?" Possible answers included "yes, definitely," "maybe," and "no, definitely." Only 12 percent of the sample answered affirmatively, including only 3 percent

TABLE 3.4. *Religion, Career Choice, and Biblical Lessons on Work (%)*

	Religion Influenced My Career Choice	I Think a Lot About What the Bible Teaches About Work
White Conservative Protestant (CP)	0.18	0.22
Black Conservative Protestant (BP)	0.14	0.28
Mainline/Liberal Protestant (MP)	0.08	0.09
Catholic		
White	0.10	0.09
Nonwhite	0.08	0.08
Jewish	0.02	0.02
Other Religion	0.16	0.15
No Religion	0.03	0.03
All Respondents	0.12	0.14

Notes: Data are from the EVS. Sample size = 2,013.

of those with no current religious affiliation (see Table 3.4). CPs were significantly more likely than all others to respond "yes, definitely." In contrast, the percentage of MPs, nonwhite Catholics, and Jews who agreed that their religious beliefs affected their work decisions was significantly smaller than the sample mean.[2] The percentages of BPs and white Catholics who agreed that religion affected their decisions about work were indistinguishable from the sample mean. It is notable that BPs are more similar to white Catholics than to nonwhite Catholics on their response to this question, given that black Catholics are included with nonwhite Catholics. Consistent with this pattern, multivariate models (not shown) suggest that the effect of religion is definitely separate from the effect of race for blacks. EVS respondents were also asked whether they think about what the Bible teaches about work. Responses to this question were similar to those given to the question regarding religion and career choice, with one notable exception: BPs were significantly more likely than all other groups to say that they think a lot about what the Bible teaches about work. Again, multivariate models suggest that race and religion operate separately and that the effect of religion remains for BPs once race is controlled. The multivariate models suggest that there is

---

[2] Because the EVS codes race differently from the NLSY and HRS, I am forced to report different religious-race subgroups. Specifically, the EVS only identifies white, black, and other races and does not indicate Hispanics as a separate group. This prevents me from separating Hispanic Catholics from other Catholics.

TABLE 3.5. *Work, Family, and Self-Worth, by Religion (%)*

	Factors that are Essential to My Self-worth			
	Success	Money	Work	Family
White Conservative Protestant (CP)	0.66	0.40	0.81	0.97
Black Conservative Protestant (BP)	0.80	0.63	0.81	0.93
Mainline/Liberal Protestant (MP)	0.67	0.39	0.84	0.98
Catholic				
White	0.73	0.50	0.82	0.96
Nonwhite	0.82	0.69	0.90	0.95
Jewish	0.71	0.40	0.86	0.94
Other Religion	0.72	0.38	0.76	0.95
No Religion	0.75	0.50	0.77	0.85
All Respondents	0.71	0.46	0.82	0.96

Notes: Data are from the EVS. Sample size = 2,013.

a separate effect of race and religious belief on orientations toward work and beliefs about God's role in work decisions.[3]

The relative importance of work, money, and family in creating a person's identity, or self-worth, can be suggestive of approaches to work and finances. The EVS asked respondents to answer a series of questions that began, "How important is each of the following to your basic sense of worth as a person: absolutely essential, very important, somewhat important, not very important?" CPs were significantly less likely than other groups to indicate that success and money were essential to their self-worth (see Table 3.5). By contrast, BPs were significantly more likely than others to respond that money is essential to their self-worth, but they were similar to the rest of the sample on other factors. Another notable group is nonwhite Catholics, who were more likely to say that success, money, and work were essential to their self-worth – a pattern that is driven by black Catholics (not shown in the table) and that underscores findings from the NLSY described earlier and in the previous chapter. In contrast to patterns shown in Table 3.4, BPs and nonwhite Catholics are more similar in their response to the questions highlighted in Table 3.5. Again, Table 3.5 does not control for race, but work I published elsewhere shows that these patterns persist when race and other demographic traits are controlled (Keister 2008).

[3] In tables using EVS data, I separate white and nonwhite Catholics because the survey does not include sufficient detail to create more precise categories. I also exclude Mormons/LDS from these tables because the sample does not include sufficient numbers of them to permit reasonable conclusions.

Evidence from other research suggests that religious beliefs affect the way people make work-family trade-offs – that is, the way orientations toward work and family affect behavior (Ammons and Edgell 2007; Kmec 1999; Mennino and Brayfield 2002). Ammons and Edgell (2007) pay particular attention to religious influences on decisions regarding employment and family trade-offs, and show that there are important differences not only by religion but also by gender within religious subgroups. They find that religiosity (measured by church attendance) encourages both men and women to favor family at the expense of work when making work-family decisions. They also find some evidence of differences between people affiliated with conservative and mainline/liberal Protestant denominations. They do not explore religious groups as detailed as those I show here, and they also face the challenge of having limited ability to make an empirical connection between religious affiliation and behavioral outcomes. However, findings reported in research such as this provide some support for the proposition that religious traditionalism translates into decisions that favor family over employment outside the house.

The factors that motivate people to work hard can also provide important information about approaches to work and money that underlie wealth accumulation and inequality. The EVS asked respondents one question in particular about reasons to work hard that can help clarify the mechanisms that relate religion to financial decision making: "How much does each of the following motivate you to work hard and do your work really well; would you say it motivates you a great deal, a little, or none?" Respondents then responded to this question with regard to an extensive list of potential motivators. Here I focus on three factors to help evaluate the argument that religious beliefs affect orientations to work and money: helping others, money, and being promoted (see Table 3.6). Consistent with the Biblical teaching that good deeds are more important than material possessions and personal success, CPs were significantly more likely than other respondents to be motivated by helping others, but they were average in reporting that money or promotions motivated them. In contrast, BPs were less likely than average to be motivated by helping others but more likely to be motivated by money. Nonwhite Catholics were also more likely than average to report that money and promotion were important motivators, but they were also above average in reporting that helping others motivated them. Jews were significantly less likely than other respondents to report that any of the factors included in Table 3.6 were important motivators of their work behavior.

TABLE 3.6. *Influences on Hard Work, by Religion (%)*

	Factors that Motivate Me to Work Hard		
	Helping Others	Money	Promotion
White Conservative Protestant (CP)	0.71	0.50	0.34
Black Conservative Protestant (BP)	0.58	0.56	0.34
Mainline/Liberal Protestant (MP)	0.75	0.42	0.30
Catholic			
White	0.61	0.47	0.34
Nonwhite	0.70	0.67	0.52
Jewish	0.50	0.40	0.22
Other Religion	0.50	0.36	0.34
No Religion	0.55	0.50	0.33
All Respondents	0.65	0.48	0.33

Notes: Data are from the EVS. Sample size = 2,013.

Religion and Income

Income is essential to understanding patterns of wealth ownership and accumulation, and there is reason to anticipate that religion and income are highly correlated. Although *income* is a fairly common term, it is useful to provide a definition to clarify how income, earnings, and wealth differ. *Income* refers to total resources flowing into a household and is usually measured over time, such as monthly or annually. Income can be measured at the household or individual level because, unlike wealth, it is usually easily attributable to a particular person. Income includes revenues generated from paid work as well as from government transfer payments (e.g., Social Security, Temporary Assistance for Needy Families), alimony, interest and dividends from savings or investments, royalties, rents, proceeds from trusts, prize winnings, and any other source that generates a flow of funds. I use the term *earnings* to refer to income generated from paid work – that is, earnings are the subset of income that individuals receive as wages or salary. Recall that wealth, in contrast, is measured at a single point in time and refers to net worth or savings generated in part from past income.

How does religion affect income? Religion is likely to have an indirect effect on income through education and family processes. As I discussed in Chapter 2, religion, education, and family processes are correlated; there is also evidence that education and family processes are particularly strong predictors of income, particularly of earnings. Likewise, the first part of this chapter showed that religion is related to actual work behaviors and approaches to work. To the extent these factors affect income, religion and income should also be correlated. In addition, employers may use religion as an indicator of desirable traits in workers and, in some cases, may make hiring decisions based on religious affiliation and perhaps on religious beliefs. Because it is both illegal and socially unacceptable to discriminate in hiring based on religion, few employers would admit to using religion as a hiring criterion. As a result, it is extremely difficult to provide empirical evidence for such practices. Nonetheless, discrimination cannot be ruled out as a potential mechanism linking religion and earnings.

Income, in turn, is a very strong predictor of wealth ownership. Income is a measure of the resources available for saving and, to the extent that income is composed of earnings, it is also correlated with job benefits (e.g., pension plans) that directly become wealth. Income makes it possible to save, increases the likelihood of saving, and increases the amount of money saved. Indeed, income and wealth are so strongly related that the two terms are often used interchangeably. This is understandable given that both refer to individual or household financial resources and both are important measures of SES. Although income is a very strong predictor of wealth, however, income and wealth are distinct. In particular, as I noted in Chapter 1, wealth affords its owner important advantages that are not all available to those with high incomes who do not save (e.g., wealth can be transferred across generations whereas income cannot). The close relationship between income and wealth suggests that an exploration of the association between religion and income is in order.

Table 3.7 draws on data from the NLSY and the HRS to show how religious affiliation correlates with earnings. The table shows that median CP income for working-age adults from the NLSY is equal to the sample median. Mean income for CPs is lower than the sample mean, but I report medians reflecting the standard skew in the income distribution. Some important variation appears within the CP category (not shown): conservative Methodists, Pentecostals, and Southern Baptists have incomes that are below the sample mean, whereas Assembly of God members tend to have higher incomes. However, CPs are sufficiently similar in terms of income (as they are in terms of other SES measures) to consider them together. More important, if CPs are shown in subsequent chapters to have low wealth, the finding that their incomes are at the sample median suggests that saving practices, rather than the availability of funds, contribute to low wealth. In contrast, BPs and Hispanic Catholics have markedly lower-than-average incomes. Given the

TABLE 3.7. *Adult Religion and Income*

	Median Household Income, NLSY	Median Household Income, HRS	Below Poverty Line, NLSY (%)	Below Poverty Line, HRS (%)
White Conservative Protestant (CP)	$61,598	$34,592	8.7	6.4
Black Conservative Protestant (BP)	$26,692	$21,438	26.0	19.5
Mainline/Liberal Protestant (MP)	$73,404	$45,120	4.0	3.3
Catholic	$74,717	$37,760	6.4	6.4
White	$79,461	$42,123	4.0	3.2
Hispanic	$46,609	$17,313	18.8	21.5
Jewish	$93,423	$60,278	0.0	0.0
Other religion	$55,077	$39,800	11.2	5.9
No religion	$54,411	$43,019	10.7	5.1
All Respondents	$61,598	$38,473	9.9	6.3

Notes: Data are from the 1979–2004 NLSY and the 2006 HRS. NLSY sample size = 4,369; HRS sample size = 8,113. Median household income is adjusted to 2004 dollars using the Consumer Price Index. *Below poverty line* is based on the U.S. Census Bureau–established poverty threshold for 2005 for the HRS and on the Health and Human Services definition for 2003 for the NLSY. Religion was measured in 2000 in the NLSY and in 1992 in the HRS. Sample size for Jewish respondents in poverty is too low to include a percentage.

well-established connection between black and Hispanic race/ethnicity and income, the low medians for blacks and Hispanics shown in Table 3.7 likely reflect racial/ethnic processes rather than religious processes. MPs and white Catholics have comparable and relatively high incomes, and Jewish respondents have very high median incomes. Similar patterns are evident in income differences for retirement-age adults from the HRS data. Naturally, incomes are lower in the HRS, but the medians suggest that the patterns by religion remain in later life.

To understand saving and wealth accumulation, it can also be helpful to consider whether people have incomes so low that they are considered to be living in poverty. For those living in poverty, concern with meeting basic needs makes saving nearly impossible. To explore whether there are differences across religious groups in the incident of poverty that might contribute to variations in wealth ownership, Table 3.7 also includes the percentage of NLSY and HRS respondents who are have incomes that are below the poverty line. In the NLSY, the poverty line refers to the definition offered by the U.S. Department of Health and Human Services; in the HRS, it refers to the U.S. Census Bureau's poverty threshold for 2005 (the year prior to the survey). Although the definitions are slightly

TABLE 3.8. *Adult Religion and Government Transfers: NLSY (%)*

	TANF/SSI	Food Stamps
White Conservative Protestant (CP)	3.3	3.5
Black Conservative Protestant (BP)	10.1	13.8
Mainline/Liberal Protestant (MP)	1.6	2.0
Catholic	3.3	2.9
White	2.5	1.3
Hispanic	7.3	11.6
Jewish	0.0	0.0
Other Religion	5.0	6.7
No Religion	5.0	6.2
All Respondents	4.1	4.9

Notes: Data are from the 1979–2004 NLSY. Sample size = 4,369. Religion was measured in 2000.

different, the results are comparable, and using the data prepared by the data collection agencies allows me to incorporate information used to create these estimates that is not part of the public data. The patterns of living in poverty by religious group are consistent with patterns of median incomes by religion. CPs tend to have average poverty rates, whereas BPs and Hispanic Catholics have higher-than-average poverty rates. Poverty rates for MPs and white Catholics are comparable to each other and below average, and rates for Jews are notably low.

Relying on government transfer payments for income also makes it difficult to save, and Table 3.8 summarizes relevant patterns by identifying the proportion of NLSY respondents who received transfers in the year prior to the most recent interview. The table includes two broad categories of transfers that target those in financial need: (1) Temporary Assistance for Needy Families (TANF) and Supplemental Security Income (SSI), and (2) food stamps. TANF began in 1997 to provide cash assistance to families with children who need aid. TANF replaced the earlier Aid to Families with Dependent Children (AFDC), which was in effect from 1935 through 1996. Prior to 1997, states administered AFDC and determined eligibility for aid. In contrast, TANF provides block grants directly to states, which both design and administer their own programs. Thus, in survey years prior to 1997, respondents report AFDC receipt; in more recent survey years, respondents report TANF income. Table 3.8 includes only 2003 reports and thus includes only TANF income; however, in subsequent chapters, I will use longitudinal data that will include both forms of income. Changes in the role of states in these programs lead to changes in eligibility and affect the percentage of respondents receiving income of this sort. SSI is a similar income supplement designed to help aged, blind, or disabled people who have little or no income. This program provides cash to low-income people to help meet basic needs (e.g., food, clothing, and shelter). SSI is funded by general tax revenues, rather than social security taxes, and should not be confused with social security income received after retirement. The term *food stamps* is the historical name (and still common shorthand) for the Supplemental Nutrition Assistance Program (SNAP). SNAP is a federal assistance program administered by the U.S. Department of Agriculture that provides cash in the form of a debit card for food purchases. (Historically, the program provided actual paper coupons rather than a debit card.)

Patterns in government transfer receipts by religion provide additional support for the ranking of religious groups by income that is emerging in this chapter. Slightly more than 4 percent of all NLSY respondents receive TANF or SSI payments, and nearly 5 percent of all respondents receive food stamps. Dividing the sample by adult religious affiliation reveals that significantly higher (than the sample average) proportions of BPs and Hispanic Catholics receive these forms of government assistance. The proportion of CPs who receive TANF/SSI or food stamps assistance is below the sample medians, but the difference is not statistically significant in either case, suggesting that CPs are average on these measures. MPs, white Catholics, and Jews are significantly less likely than the average to receive government assistance.

Table 3.9 explores earnings in more detail by breaking total household income into individual earnings by gender. The table also shows the percentage of men and women who have no earnings, by religious affiliation, to further explore the relationship between religion and household financial revenues. Consistent with established facts about gender, the table shows that women are less likely than men to have income; when they do work, women earn less than men. I do not explore the reasons for this pattern here because a large literature provides extremely good evidence regarding the relative importance of factors such as time in the labor force, experience, preferences regarding work and family, and discrimination. The table also shows that consistent with prior evidence in this chapter, CPs have relatively average incomes, whereas BPs and Hispanic Catholics have incomes that are significantly lower than average. MPs and white Catholics have incomes that are similar to each other and that are higher than average. The most striking pattern in this table is the gender difference between Jewish men and Jewish women: Jewish men

TABLE 3.9. *Adult Religion and Individual Earnings, by Gender*

	Earnings, Men	Earnings, Women	No Earnings, Men (%)	No Earnings, Women (%)
White Conservative Protestant (CP)	$41,065	$21,358	8.8	21.5
Black Conservative Protestant (BP)	$26,692	$14,373	17.9	29.2
Mainline/Liberal Protestant (MP)	$49,278	$26,692	7.4	11.2
Catholic	$51,332	$24,126	8.2	21.4
White	$51,332	$24,639	6.9	20.1
Hispanic	$36,959	$15,399	12.3	28.9
Jewish	$92,397	$19,198	0.0	0.0
Other Religion	$39,012	$17,794	9.2	26.6
No Religion	$39,012	$25,206	10.8	16.3
All Respondents	$43,118	$22,073	10.0	20.4

Notes: Data are from the 1979–2004 NLSY. Sample size = 4,369. Religion was measured in 2000. There are statistically equivalent numbers of men and women in the sample used here, and missing data do not vary significantly by gender. Earnings are adjusted to 2004 dollars using the Consumer Price Index. The sample size for Jewish respondents in poverty is too low to include a percentage.

have incomes that are relatively high, whereas Jewish women's incomes are relatively low.

These results are consistent with the few empirical studies that attempt to relate religion and earnings (Lehrer 2010; Steen 1996). Smith and Faris (2005) find similar patterns using GSS data. Their results also include more detailed CP denomination groups and demonstrate that although there are some differences among CPs, the CP groups hold together rather well. Other research shows that the ranking that emerges in my results holds when various individual and family traits are controlled (Lehrer 2010; Steen 1996). Since the early 1980s, other research has provided corroborating evidence for the uniquely high Jewish earnings that are evident in the NLSY and HRS (Burstein 2007; Chiswick 1993; Hollinger 2004; Wilder and Walters 1997). Burstein (2007) summarizes four possible explanations for what he calls Jewish exceptionalism. The first explanation suggests that Jews are successful for the same reasons others are successful: attaining high levels of education, working long hours, and living in high-wage areas. The second explanation is that there is something unique about Jews that leads to their success. For example, there may be religious-based beliefs (similar to those that emerge in the tables above focusing on orientations and values) that lead to success. The third possible explanation starts with the fact that Jews have been marginalized historically. This marginalization may have lead to creativity that feeds into educational and occupational success and ultimately increases earnings. Finally, social capital may be at the heart of Jewish success. As I pointed out in Chapter 2, social relations can be critical to educational, earnings, and wealth attainment. To the extent that Jews have successful social connections, they may be more likely to succeed themselves. Regardless of the mechanism, the Jewish advantage is clear in earnings differences; I address how this affects wealth attainment in more detail in subsequent chapters.

Orientations toward Money

Similar to orientations toward work, orientations toward money (both earning money and using money) differ by religion. Reported attitudes toward money and the role of God in money are essential to assessing how religion affects the orientations that drive people's decisions regarding money and financial decision making. The EVS included many questions that are pertinent for understanding this connection, and differences among religious groups are clear in the responses given to these and similar questions. CP exceptionalism on many of these questions highlights their unique perspectives on finances and illustrates the mechanisms that relate religious beliefs directly to wealth accumulation. According to Randy Alcorn, a prominent CP commentator, "[T]he scripture makes clear that there is a fundamental connection between a person's spiritual life and his attitudes and actions concerning money and possessions" (Alcorn 2005). Indeed, the Bible contains many lessons regarding money and finances: sixteen of the thirty-eight parables and 10 percent of New Testament verses address money or finances. There are approximately 500 total Bible verses on prayer and the importance of faith in the Bible, but there are more than 2,000 verses that deal with money and finances (Kreider 2002). Similarly, Alcorn estimates that "fifteen percent of everything Jesus said related to money and possessions. Our Lord made more references to money and possessions than to either prayer or faith. He spoke about money and possessions more than heaven and hell combined" (Alcorn 2005).

As I noted earlier, it is challenging to link beliefs with behavior, but CP beliefs regarding money and finances provide an important example of how the connection emerges.[4] The central defining trait of CPs is

---

4 Recent growth in prosperity theology suggests that future research may need to further disaggregate the general Protestant label. In particular, there has been growth in churches that share many beliefs and practices with traditional (i.e., not prosperity-oriented) CP

the interpretation of the Bible as the inerrant Word of God. The key assumption that follows and that figures prominently into CP financial values is that money belongs to God, and people are managers of God's money. The Bible includes many references to God's exclusive ownership of worldly goods: "The land must not be sold permanently, because the land is mine and you are but aliens and tenants" (Leviticus 25:23). "To the Lord your God belong the heavens, even the highest heavens, the earth and everything in it" (Deuteronomy 10:14). "The earth is the Lord's, and everything in it, the world, and all who live in it" (Psalms 24:1). "Every animal of the forest is mine, and the cattle on a thousand hills. I know every bird in the mountains, and the creatures of the field are mine. If I were hungry I would not tell you, for the world is mine, and all that is in it" (Psalms 50:10–12). CPs interpret such passages to mean that people are not the true owners of worldly possessions. Rather, they believe that God has entrusted people with the objects they possess, including both real and financial objects. Krieder, another CP commentator (2002: 9) explains, "We must realize that everything we have belongs to God. We are merely stewards (managers) of any material goods we possess. God owns everything we have, but He makes us managers of it." Similarly, according to Alcorn (2003a), "We are God's money managers. He wants us to invest His money in His kingdom."

At least two important orientations/values follow from the assumption that God owns everything. First, it follows that divine guidance in making financial decisions has considerable merit. If God owns all worldly possessions, it would seem prudent to seek his advice when making decisions about how to accumulate and handle those possessions (Alcorn 2003; Kreider 2002). Seeking guidance from clergy and their advice manuals follows as well, because clergy are seen as agents of God (Alcorn 2003; Kreider 2002).

Second, it follows that excess accumulation is undesirable. CPs articulate three reasons to avoid excess accumulation. First, CPs believe that there is a danger of becoming overly focused on material well-being at the expense of spiritual well-being, as articulated in Luke 16:10–13: "No servant can serve two masters. Either he will hate the one and love the other, or he will be devoted to the one and despise the other. You cannot

churches but that encourage accumulation. Many prosperity-oriented CP churches are also megachurches, having more than 2,000 congregants. Despite their growth, both prosperity theology and megachurches are new and relatively rare. As a result, available data on these groups are extremely limited, and I do not consider these groups in greater detail.

TABLE 3.10. *Orientations toward Money, by Religion (%)*

	Purpose of Church/Synagogue is Divine Guidance	I Pray About Financial Decisions	I Thank God for Financial Blessings	Bible Contains Important Lessons About Money
White Conservative Protestant (CP)	0.42	0.45	0.64	0.70
Black Conservative Protestant (BP)	0.42	0.52	0.67	0.63
Mainline/Liberal Protestant (MP)	0.29	0.27	0.49	0.58
Catholic				
White	0.27	0.28	0.54	0.43
Nonwhite	0.42	0.40	0.60	0.54
Jewish	0.06	0.06	0.20	0.14
Other Religion	0.22	0.26	0.41	0.45
No Religion	0.27	0.08	0.10	0.17
All Respondents	0.31	0.32	0.52	0.53

Notes: Data are from the EVS. Sample size = 2,013.

serve both God and Money." The Bible also notes that the "love of money is the root of all kinds of evil" (1 Timothy 6:10), that people "who want to get rich fall into temptation" (1 Timothy 6:9), and that "a man's life does not consist in the abundance of his possessions" (Luke 12:15). That is, savings can be distracting, as suggested by Kreider (2002): "People who place their money in stocks immediately check out the stock market page whenever they receive their daily newspaper. Why? Because that is where their interests lie; they are concerned about where their finances are placed. Where we give both our tithes and our offerings shows what we place value on." Second, CPs argue that excess accumulation is a bad investment: "Christ's primary argument against amassing material wealth isn't that it's morally wrong but simply that it's a poor investment. Material things ... cannot escape the coming fire of God that will consume the material world" (Alcorn 2003). Finally, CPs believe that it is unnecessary to accumulate worldly possessions because God will take care of believers after they die: "When we invest money now in God's kingdom, we will receive great rewards later in heaven.... We provide tangible assets for ourselves in heaven by giving away, for the glory of God and the good of others, tangible assets on earth" (Alcorn 2003).

Consistent with these orientations, CPs are more likely than many other respondents to say that the purpose of religious services is receiving divine guidance and to indicate that they pray specifically about financial decisions (see Table 3.10). CPs are also significantly more likely than average to say that they thank God for financial blessings and to agree that the Bible contains important lessons about money. Although BPs and CPs are different in many ways, their beliefs regarding the role of the divine in finances tend to be similar, and BP responses to questions included in Table 3.10 underscore this similarity. On each question, BPs are also significantly more likely than other respondents (except nonwhite Catholics) to draw a connection between church, God, and the Bible to decisions regarding money.

White Catholics, MPs, and Jews provide a stark contrast to the financial orientations of CPs. Some have argued that white Catholics have an instrumental attitude toward money and are much less likely than CPs to make a connection between the divine and money (e.g., Tropman 1995, 2002). For white Catholics, money is likely to be seen as necessary to meet needs, but it is only a tool rather than something with intrinsic value (DeBerri and Hug 2003; Thibodeau, O'Donnell, and O'Connor 1997). Similarly, MPs and Jews tend to have this-worldly orientations toward money and finances and are unlikely to claim divine ownership of material possessions. The connection between the divine and finances is even more extreme for Jews and for those with no religious affiliation. Only small proportions of either group report that they seek divine advice about their finances, that they thank God for financial blessings, or that the Bible contains important financial lessons. Respondents with no religious affiliation are noteworthy because a surprisingly high proportion of them indicate that the purpose of church/synagogue is divine guidance and that the Bible contains important financial lessons. These responses likely reflect the fact that the questions make no references to the respondent's own decisions. Respondents who report they have no religious affiliation but that they pray about finances and thank God for financial blessings are likely the segment of the U.S. population who are religious but who are not affiliated with an organized religious group (Hout and Fischer 2002).

The connection between the divine and personal finance is also evident in responses to an EVS question regarding how much time respondents spend thinking about the connection between religion and material possessions: "In the past year, how much have you thought about each of the following: a great deal, a fair amount, a little, or hardly any?" Table 3.11 shows the percentage of respondents, by religious group, who think a great deal about what the Bible teaches about money, the connection between religion and personal finances, and the connection between possessions and spiritual growth. CPs and BPs are more likely than other

TABLE 3.11. *Financial Thinking, by Religion*

	I Think a Great Deal About		
	What the Bible Teaches About Money	Connection Between Religion and My Finances	Connection Between Possessions and Spiritual Growth
White Conservative Protestant (CP)	0.21	0.21	0.24
Black Conservative Protestant (BP)	0.23	0.26	0.28
Mainline/Liberal Protestant (MP)	0.09	0.10	0.14
Catholic			
White	0.09	0.10	0.13
Nonwhite	0.06	0.10	0.15
Jewish	0.02	0.02	0.06
Other Religion	0.09	0.07	0.12
No Religion	0.05	0.05	0.09
All Respondents	0.13	0.14	0.17

Notes: Data are from the EVS. Sample size = 2,013.

respondents to say that they think a great deal about all three items. Consistent with the patterns I report earlier, few MPs and white Catholics and very few Jews and unaffiliated respondents report spending a great deal of time thinking about these issues.

There is little reason for survey respondents to exaggerate on a question regarding the amount of time spent thinking about such issues, but it is still difficult to be certain that responses are accurate. Moreover, as with other cognitive processes, it is challenging to demonstrate empirically that there is a connection between reported orientations and behaviors; however, multivariate models (not reported) suggest that thinking about the connection between the divine and finances is positively related to religious giving and negatively related to household financial resources, even with controls for other predictors of these outcomes.

Not only does the relationship between the spiritual and the material reflect cross-group differences, but it is also suggestive of patterns that have changed over time. In particular, the meaning of materialism and material possessions, the ways we separate materialism from the spiritual, and related beliefs regarding the role of the divine in well-being have changed over the decades in ways that might reinforce religious differences in responses to questions about these processes. For instance, during industrialization – indeed, throughout much of the twentieth century – workers were primarily exposed to materialism in the workplace as producers (Wuthnow, 1994). As part of the transition to postindustrialism, materialism is now more likely to be manifest in consumerism, and people are more likely to be exposed to materialism in the media, while shopping, and in other venues that are not as easily separated from the spiritual as the workplace was in prior generations. As a result, some faiths have strengthened their messages regarding the hazards of materialism, and responses to EVS questions regarding materialism may reflect this change. Unfortunately, there are no data comparable to the EVS from prior decades, and the EVS never reinterviewed respondents, making it impossible to look at changes even over short periods. Future research could usefully explore patterns of this sort over time to better understand how time and social conditions affect the relationship between religion and material outcomes.

Decisions regarding charitable giving, including gifts of time and money to religious organizations, are closely related to orientations toward divine guidance in financial decision making. Charitable giving is widespread in the United States. Eighty-nine percent of households gave some amount of money to charity in 2008, and the average gift was slightly higher than $1,600. Although the occurrence of extremely large gifts has increased over time, even in deflated dollars, the percentage of households that make some form of gift has grown (National Philanthropic Trust, 2009). Religious organizations are the most common cause to which Americans give. In 2008, despite an economic recession that was commonly considered the worst financial downturn since the Great Depression, religious groups received $107 billion in contributions. The second most common cause, educational organizations, received only $41 billion in 2008 (Giving USA Foundation 2009). Tithing is a particular kind of religious giving, usually given directly to the church and typically amounting to 10 percent of gross household income.

Although Americans give generously to religious organizations, tithing and other religious giving vary dramatically across individuals and families. Figure 1.1 illustrates that human capital, work, and adult traits and processes combine to affect the amount of time and money people give, the percentage of income given, and giving frequency. Because other researchers and organizations focused on giving have published detailed breakdowns of the relationship between these individual and family traits and charitable giving (National Philanthropic Trust, 2009), I will not address those patterns here. However, there are also important variations in charitable giving by religious affiliation (Hoge et al. 1999), and these variations are likely an important part of the processes I describe throughout this book.

Again, CPs provide a useful starting point for understanding this variation. There is considerable heterogeneity within the large group of churches categorized as CPs, but the importance of tithing is an issue on which there is much agreement across CP denominations. I noted earlier that at least two orientations/values follow from the CP assumption that God owns all material goods. A third orientation/value also follows: If people are managers – not owners – of money, it is necessary to give some money back to God and otherwise to use money to do God's work. The Bible indicates that "from everyone who has been given much, much will be demanded; and from the one who has been entrusted with much, much more will be asked" (Luke 12:48), and " . . . with the measure you use, it will be measured to you" (Matthew 7:2). CPs conclude that God wants to bless His followers materially but that the "real purpose for receiving God's prosperity is to expand the kingdom of God" (Kreider 2002). Sacrificial giving is considered an investment in eternal rewards; Alcorn (2003a) states, "When money and possessions are invested in heavenly treasure rather than earthly, the equation changes radically. The investment takes on eternal value." Most CP churches advocate tithing 10 percent of total family income, and many also suggest using additional funds (offerings) to support other religious organizations such as missions, shelters, and local outreach programs. They believe that tithes should be made on all income, including earned income, transfer payments, business income, and gifts (Alcorn 2003). While the degree to which CPs heed warnings about tithing is likely to vary, some of the literature suggests that interpreting the Bible as the inerrant Word of God leads to relatively generous tithing (Hoge et al. 1999; Regnerus and Smith 1998).

Consistent with these teachings, significantly higher than average proportions of CPs and BPs report that the purpose of church is to give money back to God, that they should give money to their church, and that church is the most important charity (see Table 3.12). Much smaller proportions of MPs respond this way, again reflecting the difference among Protestants in beliefs about God's role in finances. Even smaller proportions of white Catholics, Jews, and those with no religious affiliation respond affirmatively to these questions. Of course, these patterns do not imply that white Catholics, Jews, and unaffiliated respondents are not philanthropic. Indeed, there is evidence, including responses to other EVS questions, that members of these groups are extremely generous.

TABLE 3.12. *Perspectives on Tithing, by Religion*

| | Considering Church/Synagogue | | | |
	Purpose is to Give Money Back to God	I *should* Give	This is Most Important Charity	Amount Given to Religious Causes (2004 $)
White Conservative Protestant (CP)	0.37	0.71	0.47	2,883
Black Conservative Protestant (BP)	0.35	0.75	0.38	1,013
Mainline/Liberal Protestant (MP)	0.25	0.64	0.33	1,189
Catholic				
White	0.19	0.56	0.31	737
Nonwhite	0.37	0.81	0.44	689
Jewish	0.17	0.18	0.08	2,656
Other Religion	0.22	0.50	0.33	1,112
No Religion	0.01	0.13	0.06	765
All Respondents	0.26	0.59	0.34	1,659

Notes: Data are from the EVS. Sample size = 2,013.

In particular, Catholic, MP, and Jewish respondents are more likely than others to give to nonreligious charitable causes mentioned in separate EVS questions. Similarly, as Kadusin and Kotler-Berkowitz (2006) note, "Philanthropy is one of the hallmarks of Jewish life." Consistent with that claim, Jewish respondents to a 1996 Pew Charitable Trusts survey indicated that they give quite generously (Regnerus, Smith, and Sikkink 1998) and evidence from recent data exploration including the charitable giving of Jews shows that American Jews of all denominations give generously (Kadushin and Kotler-Berkowitz 2006).

EVS reports of the actual money tithed underscores patterns that are evident in orientations toward religious-based charitable giving. Table 3.12 includes a column indicating the total amount EVS respondents gave to all religious organizations in the prior year, adjusted to 2004 dollars. The responses suggest that CPs give relatively generously to religious organizations, followed closely by Jews. BPs and MPs report lower levels of giving than CPs and Jews, and Catholics those with no formal religious affiliation report the lowest levels of giving to religious causes. Other published estimates show that giving to religious organizations as a function of income produces similar results; that is, CPs and Jews give large amounts, and other groups give relatively less, as a percentage of total household income (Keister 2008). Similarly, multivariate models show that these patterns hold when other factors such as race, gender, age, marital status, income, education, and family size are controlled (Keister 2008). These responses and the patterns shown in Table 3.11 are consistent with responses given to earlier GSS questions and reported by Hoge and his colleagues in the late 1990s (Hoge et al. 1999). The EVS responses are also consistent with responses to questions about religious giving in the Center on Philanthropy Panel Study, although Catholics reported slightly more giving in this survey (2003). During the 2009 housing-based recession, the commitment of some American Christians to tithe was highlighted by their willingness to continue giving even when they faced personal financial crisis. The Barna Group, a California-based research firm, found that whereas only 5 percent of Americans report that they tithe, 24 percent of CPs tithe (Reuters September 21, 2008, September 24, 2009). The CPs studied by the Barna Group included households that continued to tithe despite having faced foreclosure of their homes. It is not possible to deduce from the Barna data the extent to which families who lost their homes continued to tithe, but anecdotal evidence from financial counselors reported in a Reuters report suggests that this happened regularly. How does tithing affect wealth? This is a challenging question that raises additional questions about data. Current data sets do not contain sufficient information to make a direct link; I discuss this issue in more detail in Chapter 8, a chapter devoted to issues that cannot be addressed sufficiently with available data.

Taken together, the family and education processes described in Chapter 2 and the work, income, and financial processes described in this chapter explain much of the association between religion and wealth. The various behaviors and outcomes that I have discussed interact with each other over the life course to create net worth outcomes that are important indicators of SES and general well-being. In the next chapter, I begin to discuss wealth outcomes in more detail and to document empirical associations between religion and wealth.

4

Wealth I

Net Worth and Real Assets

One of the best-established facts in social and economic research on the United States is that wealth ownership is very unequally distributed. There is little question that a small group of people own the vast majority of net worth. However, the factors that account for this inequality are not well established, and the role of religion in particular has attracted very little attention in prior research. In this chapter, I present and discuss empirical evidence showing how religious affiliation and wealth ownership are associated. I explore a variety of wealth outcomes, including total household net worth and total real assets. Recall that net worth, or wealth, is total household assets less total liabilities. *Real assets*, a subset of total assets, refers to tangible assets such as the primary residence, other homes (e.g., vacation homes), other real estate, business assets, and vehicles. After showing how religious affiliation is related to total net worth and total real assets, I discuss the relationship between religion and extremes in wealth ownership, including both low wealth (asset poverty) and high wealth.

I then explore how portfolio behavior (i.e., the allocation of assets across different financial instruments) and the accumulation of assets over time vary by religious group. In my discussion of portfolio behavior, I briefly examine allocations of assets across both real and financial (nontangible) assets. Finally, I look more closely at the ownership and market value of particular real assets, focusing on ownership of primary and secondary homes.

Looking ahead, I continue my discussion of the relationship between religion and wealth in Chapter 5 with a detailed look at financial asset ownership (e.g., investments in stocks, bonds, mutual funds, and bank accounts) and household debt (e.g., mortgages, consumer debt, and student loans). I also discuss several multivariate models of wealth ownership; these allow me to discuss the relative importance of factors such as religion, race, family background, and educational attainment. Keep in mind that my discussions prior to that are bivariate and are intended to identify initial patterns.[1]

Net Worth and Real Assets

Net worth – one of the most general measures of wealth – is a logical place to begin comparing the wealth of religious groups. I again use both the NLSY and HRS to estimate wealth in order to compare patterns at different points in the life course. Both summary wealth measures (i.e., net worth, total real assets, and total financial assets) and the components of wealth (i.e., the value of the primary residence, other real estate, stocks, bonds, and mutual funds) from the NLSY and the HRS are comparable despite slightly different definitions used in these surveys. The real assets included in net worth are primary and secondary homes, other real estate, business assets, farms, vehicles, and collections worth more than $1,000. The financial assets include savings and checking accounts, retirement plans for respondents and their spouses, certificates of deposit (CDs), stocks, bonds, mutual funds, and other tax-sheltered accounts (e.g., individual retirement accounts [IRAs], Keogh accounts, variable annuities, and 529 plans). Debts include first and second mortgages on the primary residence and other real estate, vehicle loans, student loans, credit card balances, business loans, and loans owed to other people (i.e., informal debt). Researchers studying wealth use various definitions of net worth depending on the data they use and the questions they ask; the definitions I use here are typical of those used in the literature and contain the most commonly studied wealth components.

Although the NLSY and HRS ask respondents to report assets in different ways, the resulting net worth measures in these two surveys are highly similar and are also consistent with other wealth data. Differences between the NLSY and HRS largely reflect generational differences that make using the two surveys appropriate; I will discuss the details of these

---

[1] Some of my descriptive statistics invoke more than two variables. For instance, an examination of wealth ownership among BPs or Hispanic Catholics includes race/ethnicity, religion, and wealth. However, I do not address the relative importance of religion and race/ethnicity until Chapter 5.

differences throughout this chapter and again in Chapter 5. One reporting difference worth noting is that the NLSY and HRS allow respondents to report different numbers of certain types of assets (e.g., all retirement accounts versus the largest three accounts). Even though this is likely to affect wealth outcomes to some degree, the differences are minimal. Wealth measures in the NLSY and HRS are also consistent with estimates from other data sets. As I mentioned in Chapter 1, the Survey of Consumer Finances (SCF) is a panel data set that contains very high-quality, highly regarded wealth data. The SCF is the standard in wealth research because it includes very detailed information on the components of net worth, uses very careful data collection practices that are focused on overcoming the challenges associated with studying wealth (e.g., avoiding missing information on key wealth measures), and oversamples high-income households to more accurately estimate wealth distribution (Kennickell, Starr-McCluer, and Sunden 1997; Wolff 1995). Although the wealth information in the SCF is excellent, the survey includes neither religion data nor longitudinal information (i.e., it is a cross-sectional data set). As a result, the SCF is useful for validating my wealth measures but otherwise is not appropriate for answering the questions I am asking.

There are important differences between the longitudinal wealth data that I use (i.e., from the NLSY and the HRS) and SCF data that result from the nature of the wealth distribution and the age of the samples used. Because wealth ownership is highly concentrated, the SCF strategy of including high-income households more accurately captures high-wealth households and thus the true wealth distribution. Means and medians for wealth and its components in the NLSY and HRS, therefore, tend to be slightly lower than in the SCF and in the general population. However, there are sample differences that counter this pattern. In particular, the SCF uses a cross-sectional sample that reflects current demographics of the U.S. adult population; the NLSY uses a sample that represents young adults aged fourteen to twenty-two in the late 1970s; and the HRS uses a sample that represents adults over the age of fifty in the early 1990s. As a result, means and medians for wealth and its components in the NLSY and HRS tend to be higher than they might otherwise be, because the older samples have had more time to accumulate assets. The net result is that the two surveys tend to be comparable in the aggregate, but differences can become apparent in more detailed comparisons (e.g., by age groups). Most important, there is no reason to expect that religion affects these patterns; and given the rich data on religion in the NLSY and HRS, it is appropriate to use these data here.

TABLE 4.1. *Median Net Worth and Real Assets*

	Net Worth (NLSY, child)	Net Worth (NLSY, adult)	Net Worth (HRS)	Real Assets (NLSY, adult)
White Conservative Protestant (CP)	$82,400	$86,600	$189,088	$134,500
Black Conservative Protestant (BP)	$22,800	$25,500	$50,692	$46,500
Mainline/Liberal Protestant (MP)	$146,000	$150,500	$322,142	$202,672
Catholic	$134,500	$151,500	$287,660	$198,500
White	$156,000	$173,500	$356,999	$210,000
Hispanic	$51,500	$56,500	$58,188	$118,000
Jewish	$423,500	$443,000	$705,564	$347,000
Other Religion	$65,500	$65,500	$269,857	$122,000
No Religion	$57,700	$97,046	$384,172	$139,000
All Respondents	$99,500	$99,500	$249,243	$155,000

Notes: Data are from the 1979–2004 NLSY and the 2006 HRS. NLSY sample size = 4,369; HRS sample size = 8,113. NLSY, child is childhood religion measured in 1979; NLSY, adult is adult religion measured in 2000; HRS religion was measured in 1992. Median wealth figures are in 2004 dollars (adjusted using the consumer price index for HRS data). Net worth is assets (real plus financial) less debts. Real assets included in net worth are primary and secondary homes, other real estate, business assets, farms, vehicles, and collections worth more than $1,000. Financial assets include savings and checking accounts, retirement plans for respondents and their spouses, CDs, stocks, bonds, mutual funds, and other tax-sheltered accounts (e.g., individual retirement accounts [IRAs], Keogh accounts, variable annuities, and 529 plans). Debts include mortgages, vehicle loans, student loans, credit card balances, business loans, and loans owed to other people.

Median household net worth was approximately $87,500 for NLSY respondents in 2004 and $250,000 for HRS respondents in 2006 (see Table 4.1). Median net worth in the SCF was comparable at about $95,000 for respondents aged thirty-five to forty-four in 2004 and about $266,000 for respondents aged sixty-five to seventy-four in 2007. Not reflected in the table but of some relevance is that these medians vary notably by individual and family demographic traits. In particular, net worth increases with individual and household income, educational levels, and the age of working adults in the household. Married couples tend to have more wealth than single people, largely because wealth is considered joint property and couples work to build assets together. Couples without children tend to have particularly high wealth, as do those with dual incomes and high-prestige and, in particular, professional occupations. Whites have considerably more wealth than blacks and Hispanics. Contrary to common assumption, there is very little regional variation in wealth ownership. Although those living in large cities tend to have significantly greater net worth than those living in all urban areas (driven largely by home values), there is less regional variation in net worth than one might expect. Of course, home values drive up net worth in particular areas (e.g., California, New York); but because there are wealthy people in just about every part of the country (e.g., Bill Gates lives in Seattle, WA; Warren Buffett lives in Omaha, NE; Leslie Wexner lives in Columbus, OH), regional variation is not overly pronounced.

Most important to this book, net worth also varies notably by religious affiliation (see Table 4.1). For example, both working-age and retirement-age CPs have net worth that is lower than the average for their age groups. The net worth deficit is statistically significant for working-age CPs; the gap is even larger for retirement-age respondents to the HRS. I include religion measured both in childhood and in adulthood because net worth for some groups, including CPs, is significantly different between these two measures. It is notable that net worth is higher for CPs when religion is measured as adult religion, suggesting that those who became CPs have higher SES than those who were raised as CPs. This pattern is consistent with previous research but suggests that the CP deficit is not as extreme as it was previously. The pattern also suggests that the difference between those raised CP and those who became CPs as adults is less pronounced than in previous studies. In 2000, median net worth for CPs in the NLSY was $26,000 compared with the full sample median of $66,200. The median net worth for all NLSY respondents was nearly $200,000, whereas the median for CPs was only $85,000. Multivariate models confirmed these differences, showing that both those raised as CPs and those who were CPs as adults had significantly fewer adult assets than those raised in Catholic and MP families, even when many other factors are controlled. Previous research also showed that those raised CP were less wealthy than those who became CP, but the difference was more pronounced than we see in the current data.

Consistent with prior research (Keister 2007, 2008) and with other patterns (of family, education, work, and income) that I discussed in previous chapters, net worth for BPs is dramatically lower than the sample median, and wealth for Hispanic Catholics is significantly lower than the sample median but not as low as for BPs. Also consistent with both previous research and prior discussions in this book, MPs and white Catholics have significantly higher-than-average wealth, with white Catholics notably higher than MPs. White Catholics have been upwardly mobile (Keister 2007), and the high wealth levels that appear in these data suggest that their trend upward has continued. Similarly, the Jewish advantage that has been clear both in previous research and in previous chapters in this book is evident in the significantly larger-than-average Jewish net worth value shown in Table 4.1. In Chapter 5, I discuss current multivariate models that control for other influences on wealth and explore how these groups compare once other factors are controlled. In Chapter 6, I explore upward wealth mobility, highlighting and comparing mobility trends for white Catholics and CPs.

Real assets, including the primary home, other real estate, and other tangible assets, are an important component of wealth largely because of their use value. The primary residence is an important example: For those who are able to afford homeownership, monthly mortgage payments and other associated costs contribute both to the maintenance of an asset and to the upkeep of a shelter. In addition, over long periods of history, real estate values have increased, providing a form of saving for those who own. Patterns by religious group in the total value of real assets owned (see Table 4.1) are similar to those for total net worth because the family home is a large component of both groups for most families. Real assets are lower than average for CPs, although the deficit is not as low as it has been in the past. For BPs, real-asset values are dramatically lower than the sample average; and for Hispanic Catholics, real assets are just slightly lower than they are for CPs. White Catholics and MPs have higher-than-average real-asset values, with values for white Catholics exceeding those for MPs. Finally, real-asset values for Jews are much higher than average, consistent with prior research.

In a discussion of wealth that spans the 2004–2010 period, it is important to pause and consider the role that economic conditions play in shaping these patterns. The wealth patterns that I discuss in this book reflect both family decision making and economic conditions. In this period, real gross domestic product (GDP) increased approximately 2.5 percent per year, on average. Yet by the end of 2007 and into 2008, economic activity slowed noticeably, unemployment increased, and inflation increased as a result of escalating food and energy prices (Bucks 2009). Most notably for this research, healthy financial and housing markets experienced significant crises that affected home values, mortgage rates, and thus family net worth. Despite these economic changes, there are still clear patterns by religious groups; moreover, the patterns that persist through the historically extreme economic conditions are quite similar to those that were clear in previous research. Yet, it is important to be aware that some of the differences that emerge in the most recent data (e.g., the upward mobility of CPs) may be a result of economic conditions rather than of something about these families. I explore these ideas in more detail throughout this chapter and in subsequent chapters.

Asset Poverty

In Chapter 3, I discussed patterns in income poverty, the form of hardship that most people think of when they hear the term *poverty*. However, asset poverty (or wealth poverty) is also a fundamental indicator of economic security, and the term has gained increasing attention from scholars in recent years. Asset poverty refers to having insufficient savings to fall back on during a time of economic difficulty. Researchers have used several strategies to measure asset poverty, most of which are designed to identify whether a household can meet its basic needs (e.g., for food, shelter, and clothing) in the absence of income for a limited period of time. One common measure of asset poverty that is also straightforward to identify and easily interpretable is having zero or negative net worth. That is, a household is asset-poor if its total assets less total debts are zero or negative, where negative net worth indicates more liabilities than assets. This measure is less household-specific than other measures that attempt to identify unique household traits that affect needs (e.g., family size, housing payments, and other expenses). However, nearly all families with zero or negative net worth are at risk of financial hardship, and measuring asset poverty as zero or negative net worth facilitates comparisons across data sets that are difficult with other measures. Although there is no official measure of asset poverty that would be comparable to official income poverty rates, some evidence suggests that asset poverty may be even more pervasive than income poverty and that those who suffer asset poverty may be even more vulnerable than those in income poverty (Caner 2004). Predictors of asset poverty are similar to predictors of overall wealth, including race/ethnicity, family size and structure, education, age, and income.

There are also important patterns of asset poverty by religion. For instance, although net worth for CPs is somewhat lower than average, both working-age and retirement-age CPs have average rates of asset poverty. According to NLSY and HRS data (see Table 4.2), CPs are approximately average in their likelihood of having zero or negative net worth. For working-age CPs, rates are slightly lower than average, although this rate is only marginally statistically significant; retirement-age CPs are nearly exactly at the sample mean. Consistent with other patterns for these groups, BPs and Hispanic Catholics in both age groups

TABLE 4.2. *Asset Poverty and High Wealth (%)*

	Low Net Worth		High Net Worth	
	NLSY	HRS	NLSY	HRS
White Conservative Protestant (CP)	11.2	4.1	6.8	21.0
Black Conservative Protestant (BP)	32.5	13.9	0.8	5.7
Mainline/Liberal Protestant (MP)	5.8	2.6	14.2	33.1
Catholic	8.0	4.7	13.7	28.7
White	5.5	2.3	15.9	33.7
Hispanic	18.6	14.9	4.8	6.7
Jewish	2.1	1.3	46.8	60.3
Other Religion	17.8	7.0	12.6	31.0
No Religion	16.4	5.6	10.6	37.3
All Respondents	13.3	4.6	10.6	27.5

Notes: Data are from the 1979–2004 NLSY and the 2006 HRS. NLSY sample size = 4,369; HRS sample size = 8,113. NLSY religion was measured in 2000; HRS religion was measured in 1992. Net worth is defined as in Table 4.1. Low net worth is 0 or less; high net worth is more than $600,000 (i.e., approximately the top 10 percent of the NLSY net worth distribution).

are considerably more likely than average to be in asset poverty. Again, white Catholics and MPs are quite similar to each other in their rates of asset poverty, and both of these groups are relatively financially stable. Finally, Jews are the least likely in either survey to have zero or negative net worth, consistent with overall trends in Jewish attainment.

Grouping all families with zero or negative net worth is appealing because it highlights a form of financial insecurity that underlies most discussions of economic well-being. Yet, one might wonder how varied the financial situations of families in this category are. Indeed, among both NLSY and HRS respondents (and respondents to other data sets), there is a remarkably high level of similarity in the wealth profiles of the asset-poor that is characterized by an absence of owner-occupied housing, limited saving, and high debt (data not shown, to conserve space). These families tend to be persistently asset-poor, rarely having positive net worth; and in all years for which data are available, these families are at risk of significant financial difficulty should they lose their income. There are certainly exceptions to this pattern, including households who have, for example, recently started a business and are carrying relatively high levels of debt that are temporary.[2]

---

[2] It is possible to use longitudinal data sets to isolate families who are asset-poor at early time periods and to explore what ultimately happens to their net worth. In both the NLSY

High Net Worth

At the other end of the wealth spectrum are the people and families that often come to mind in connection with wealth: the wealthy, or high-net-worth households. Having significant wealth, of course, has many advantages for both current and future generations, and members of some religious groups are more likely than members of others to enjoy these advantages. There are many ways to define high wealth; I chose to define it as having net worth in the top 10 percent of households in the survey. Of course, this does not capture the absolute top of the wealth distribution, those with wealth in the top 1 percent or top 0.5 percent of the distribution. Capturing the absolute wealthiest households is extremely challenging because this is a particularly small group that seldom wants to be identified as such for data collection purposes. The challenges of studying the wealth are evidenced by the extra measures used by the Federal Reserve Board to collect the SCF oversamples of wealthy households and also by the unique strategies used by researchers studying elites to collect data on these individuals. The data sets I use are among the only sources of reliable information on both religious affiliation and wealth ownership, but they do not make special efforts to target households in the absolute top of the wealth distribution. More importantly, however, it is not necessary to identify the extremely rich to understand which groups are overrepresented at the top. Focusing on the top 10 percent provides a very good portrait of the wealthy.

Table 4.2 shows that among both working-age and retirement-age adults, MPs, white Catholics, and Jews are significantly more likely than others to have wealth in the top 10 percent of the distribution. The overrepresentation of MPs among the wealthiest households is consistent with decades of evidence that certain MP denominations – particularly Episcopalians, Presbyterians, and Congregationalist/United Church of Christ – have been socially, economically, and politically advantaged since America's colonial period (Pyle 2003). Indeed a well-developed literature on elites provides evidence that a relatively small group of people who occupy positions of power has historically been dominated by (mainline) Protestant men with close social connections, shared backgrounds and experiences, and overlapping institutional positions (Dahl 1961; Domhoff

and HRS, there are families who have recently started a business and who ultimately and often quickly return to having positive net worth. These families are rarer than persistently asset-poor families.

2006; Mills 1959; Zweigenhaft and Domhoff 2006). Research on the so-called Protestant Establishment tends to have a somewhat different focus than I have in this book, but the findings are related to the comparatively strong patterns in wealth ownership by religious affiliation shown in Table 4.2. In the literature on the Protestant Establishment, this group has been variously characterized as cultural leaders, a controlling in-group, or simply as an American elite group.

Regardless of their motivations and role in the formation and development of social, economic, and political institutions, it is clear that MPs have been overrepresented in the Protestant Establishment (Baltzell 1964; Davidson 1994; Davidson, Pyle, and Reyes 1995). Relatively recent evidence suggests that MPs are still more highly represented among America's elite despite major social changes, such as increased religious pluralism (Zweigenhaft and Domhoff 2006). The continued presence of MPs in the elite notwithstanding, recent research evidence also shows that members of historically underrepresented groups have been gaining membership in elite circles. In particular, recent evidence shows increasing numbers of African Americans, Jews, Hispanics, and women in both the national elite and local elite circles (Davidson 1994; Davidson, Pyle, and Reyes 1995; Zweigenhaft and Domhoff 1982; Zweigenhaft and Domhoff 2006). The increasing presence of Jews among the elite is consistent with research on Jewish attainment that shows high – and improving – levels of SES among both Americans who were raised in Jewish households and those who claim Judaism as their adult religion (Burstein 2007). Research on the Protestant Establishment also shows that white Catholics have been gaining ground, but change has been coming more slowly for white Catholics than for Jews (Davidson 1994; Davidson, Pyle, and Reyes 1995). This is consistent with research on the upward mobility of white Catholics, which is the topic of Chapter 6 (D'Antonio, Hoge, and Davidson 2007; Keister 2007). Despite evidence that numbers of African Americans and Hispanics in the elite have increased (Zweigenhaft and Domhoff 2006), Table 4.2 shows that only small numbers of both BPs and Hispanic Catholics in the data I use are among the samples' wealthiest households. Finally, very recent evidence discusses the growing representation of CPs in the power elite (Lindsay 2008). The evidence included in Table 4.2 does not suggest that CPs are particularly well represented among the wealthy in the samples I use; however, I explore patterns of upward mobility among CPs in greater detail in Chapter 6.

Portfolio Behavior

The allocation of assets across various financial instruments at different stages of the life cycle is an important determinant of the overall level of wealth accumulated. There are active and passive approaches to saving and asset allocation that can have very different effects on wealth accumulation. An active strategy involves some degree of conscious and deliberate decision making about saving, consumption, purchasing assets, and/or investing in financial instruments. Decisions to open a checking or savings account, buy a house, save 10 percent of monthly income, use a budget to generate awareness of spending or to control it, invest in a particular stock, and similar choices are active decisions to accumulate some level of wealth or to own particular assets. Some wealth owners are even more deliberate and active in their portfolio behavior. For instance, an active financial strategy might involve allocating financial assets so that 80 percent of a household's financial assets are in stocks and 20 percent are in bonds (a common strategy for those who have moderate risk tolerance and are not approaching retirement). True to its name, a passive strategy is just the opposite. Those who are more passive in their saving behavior might have very little by way of a financial plan and may simply accumulate assets largely as a by-product of other decisions (e.g., opening a checking account to deposit income and pay bills). Most people fall somewhere between these two extremes, making some conscious decisions to save, consume (more or less), purchase assets, and invest, but these decisions are often not designed to reach a particular allocation of assets across types.

Regardless of the motives underlying saving and asset purchases, the realized distribution of financial resources across assets can have a very real and very significant effect on overall wealth, particularly as assets grow at different rates over time. The notion of a turning point in life course research (see Chapter 1) is also important here. Recall that recognizing turning points is important to understanding trajectories, including financial trajectories. Asset allocation during the working years can be an important determinant of a household's financial trajectory and postretirement well-being. It is during the working years that people tend to have relatively high incomes and to save more than at other life stages. For those who are able to save during these years, some assets also play particularly important roles in building wealth. The primary home, other real estate, bank accounts, retirement funds, and other financial assets

TABLE 4.3. *Asset Allocation during the Working Years: NLSY Portfolio Behavior (% of total assets)*

	Housing	Other Real Estate	Bank Accounts	Retirement Funds	Stocks, Bonds, Other Financial
White Conservative Protestant (CP)	51.4	1.7	6.1	12.4	4.0
Black Conservative Protestant (BP)	39.4	0.8	12.8	12.6	2.2
Mainline/Liberal Protestant (MP)	53.9	2.4	6.4	15.6	4.8
Catholic	53.4	1.5	6.5	15.5	4.5
White	54.2	1.6	6.6	16.1	4.9
Hispanic	48.4	0.8	4.9	7.5	1.8
Jewish	57.0	0.5	7.1	17.2	9.0
Other Religion	51.1	1.6	7.7	12.2	4.3
No Religion	47.7	0.9	7.6	13.2	3.7
All Respondents	50.7	1.6	7.2	14.1	4.1

Notes: Data are from the 1979–2004 NLSY. Sample size = 4,369. Religion was measured in 2000. Housing includes both primary and second homes. Asset categories are not exhaustive.

(e.g., stocks, bonds, and mutual funds) are commonly owned and play important roles in building wealth. Tables 4.3 and 4.4 show the average percentage of total assets held in these categories for NLSY and HRS respondents, respectively. As I have mentioned, there are important advantages associated with homeownership, including the combined use-value and investment that is unique to this asset. Allocation of total assets to housing tends to be consistent across households in the United States, and the NLSY data for rates of homeownership among working-age adults confirm this (see Table 4.3). The overall average is about 50 percent, with BPs quite a bit lower at 39 percent. Housing in both Tables 4.3 and 4.4 refers to ownership of the primary residence and second homes. I discuss these categories separately later in this chapter.

However, there is some variation by religion in the allocation of resources to other assets. Owning real estate other than the primary residence and second homes (e.g., investment real estate) is rare, and NLSY respondents report that they allocate about 1.6 percent of their total assets to other real estate. For those who do own other real estate, the wealth advantages can be significant, particularly given that real estate values tend to move upward in the long run. MPs are one group that might benefit from owning this type of asset (see Table 4.3); in contrast, it is notable that Jews allocate significantly less of their total assets to

TABLE 4.4. *Asset Allocation in Retirement: HRS Portfolio Behavior*
(% of total assets)

	Housing	Bank Accounts	Retirement Funds	Stocks, Bonds, Other Investments
White Conservative Protestant (CP)	58.3	13.6	11.1	4.4
Black Conservative Protestant (BP)	69.7	18.8	3.4	1.5
Mainline/Liberal Protestant (MP)	53.7	11.9	12.9	8.6
Catholic	55.9	14.5	11.9	6.8
White	53.8	13.1	13.6	7.8
Hispanic	68.3	10.4	3.2	1.1
Jewish	48.6	14.6	16.3	11.4
Other Religion	62.0	13.0	7.2	6.0
No Religion	56.1	13.2	10.0	6.3
All Respondents	56.8	13.7	11.3	6.4

Notes: Data are from the 2006 HRS. Sample size = 8,113. Religion was measured in 1992. Housing includes both primary and second homes. Asset categories are not exhaustive.

other real estate. Allocation of funds to relatively low-risk bank accounts varies somewhat, with CPs and MPs allocating relatively little to this category and being more similar to each other on this measure than they have been on any other measure discussed so far in this book. Perhaps most importantly, there are notable differences across religious groups in the percentage of assets allocated to retirement funds and to stocks, bonds, and other financial assets. CPs tend to have fewer assets in retirement funds than the sample average, although their ownership of stocks, bonds, and other financial assets is at about the sample mean. (I discuss the details of financial asset ownership in the next chapter.) BPs and Hispanic Catholics have relatively few resources in retirement funds or stocks, bonds, or other financial assets. In contrast, MPs and Jews tend to allocate significantly more resources in these categories than other groups. White Catholics have slightly more resources allocated to these assets than other groups, but they are not as invested in these as MPs or Jews. I discuss the importance of investing in relatively high-risk, high-reward financial instruments in more detail in Chapter 5, but this first glimpse at patterns of asset allocation provides some insight into the differences in net worth that were evident in Table 4.1.

If asset allocation during the working years is indicative of a household's financial trajectory, allocation during retirement years is a good measure of financial health and well-being when income tends to decline and saving becomes more important. Table 4.4 shows the allocation of assets for HRS respondents. It is important to use caution when comparing the HRS and NLSY data because their samples, data collection strategies, and variables are different. However, it is worth observing significant differences to understand variations across the life course. Consistent with general trends across the life course, the relative weight of housing in the average HRS respondent's portfolio is greater than it was in the average NLSY respondent's portfolio. Another important difference is that housing becomes a much more significant component of the portfolios of BPs and Hispanic Catholics, consistent with research that shows that blacks and Hispanics tend to buy homes later in life than whites (Keister 2005). In contrast, housing becomes a less significant component of the overall portfolio of Jews, but for a different reason: Housing values increase with market values, but continued emphasis on building financial assets makes these a more significant wealth component relative to housing. To attempt to control some of the survey differences, I also experimented with comparing the well-being of similar respondents in the two data sets based on age, education, family structure, family size, income, and religion. I found results that look nearly identical to the results presented in Table 4.4 (results not shown, to conserve space). Multivariate models that I discuss in the next chapter speak to this issue as well.

There are also differences in the role of financial assets after retirement, which highlight variations across religious groups. One general financial pattern that most households follow is to own more low-risk assets during retirement; owning assets that are less vulnerable to the cycles in financial markets provide more security when people are more likely to rely on these assets to cover living expenses. Accordingly, the cash held by HRS respondents in bank accounts is greater than for NLSY respondents. BPs still demonstrate a somewhat disproportionate emphasis on low-risk bank accounts, but Hispanic Catholics are below the mean in their bank account holdings in the retirement years. Holdings of retirement accounts and stocks, bonds, and other financial instruments decline for most groups, to a large extent as a result of older members of the sample spending down their savings or transferring assets to children, grandchildren, and other heirs. Notable differences by religion include relatively low holdings of retirement funds and other financial assets by BPs and Hispanic Catholics; in contrast, holdings of these assets by MPs and Jews are notably high. An additional interesting pattern involves white Catholics; their holdings of retirement accounts is relatively high, even compared with MPs, but their holdings of stocks, bonds, and other financial assets are only slightly (and not significantly) higher than the sample average. This is consistent with research suggesting that white Catholics have been upwardly mobile but that they tend to emphasize lower-risk assets, perhaps reflecting an instrument approach to money that differs from that of MPs and Jews (Keister 2007; Tropman 2002).

Talking about risk preferences and tolerances in association with religious affiliation and religiosity is controversial in research on religion (Miller 2000; Miller and Stark 2002). Most discussions that correlate risk preferences and religion, however, concern the extent to which degrees of religiosity constitute risky behavior (Miller and Hoffmann 1995). Being irreligious has been compared to deviant or criminal behavior because, in the West, dominant religious traditions make clear that those who are not affiliated and/or those who do not participate in religious activities will be punished in the afterlife (Miller 2000; Miller and Stark 2002). To varying degrees, Protestant denominations (particularly conservative denominations), Roman Catholicism, Islam, and Orthodox Judaism include doctrine that indicates that nonaffiliation and nonparticipation will be met with divine punishment. This approach to risk preferences is also consistent with rational-choice approaches to religion in which religious beliefs and behaviors are conceived of as resulting from rational responses to perceived costs and benefits (Stark and Bainbridge 1987; Stark and Finke 2000). There has been very little exploration of how particular religious affiliations (i.e., as opposed to religiosity) and religious beliefs might be correlated with, or might cause, risk tolerance in financial decision making. My own prior work and the results I present in this book suggest that there are indeed important relationships between religious beliefs and risk tolerance that manifest in financial strategies and, ultimately, in wealth outcomes (Keister 2003a, 2007, 2008). However, future research could usefully explore the social psychological processes that underlie these patterns.

Financial Trajectories

Underlying much of my discussion of financial well-being over the life course and variations in risk tolerance across groups and over time is the notion of a financial (or wealth accumulation) trajectory – that is, the path on which households accumulate and spend assets over time. Again, the notion of turning points is relevant to understanding accumulation patterns and financial trajectories. To try to capture the nature of these

paths and how the paths differ across families, I used sequence analysis, a statistical method that relies on optimal matching used to identify
common patterns and transitions across people or households.[3] Optimal
matching is a technique designed to identify how similar two sequences
are by determining how difficult it is to transform one into the other
(Abbott and Hrycak 1990). Optimal matching has been used to identify
and understand trajectories such as individual career patterns, but the
method is equally suited for cataloging sequences in saving behavior. To
this end, I used optimal matching to identify common patterns in the
assets respondents owned over time. I included five assets with varying
degrees of risk associated with them: savings accounts, checking accounts,
a home, bonds, and stocks. I then identified a series of possible sequences
that capture ownership patterns over time, represented as os and 1s. For
example, if a person owned no assets in the first time period, the portfolio
would be represented as 00000. If, in the second time period, the person
opened a savings account but purchased no other assets, the new portfolio would be represented as 10000. If, in the third period, the person kept
the savings account, opened a checking account, and bought a house, the
new portfolio would be represented as 11100.

Taking the first two time periods as an example, it would take one
substitution – substituting a 1 for a 0 in the first column – to make the
sequences identical. If each change (insertion, deletion, or substitution)
"costs" the same, a simple count of the number of changes would indicate
the complexity of the transformation; however, some transformations are
inherently more difficult than others. Underlying this strategy is the notion
that ownership of relatively high-risk assets early in life can propel net
worth forward in ways that more conservative investment strategies, or
no investment at all, cannot. If religion shapes investment patterns, it
is possible that this accounts for the relationship between religion and
wealth ownership.

Using this strategy, I identified three dominant patterns in asset ownership over the life course. Many respondents remained permanently
asset-poor – that is, they never owned an asset and always had a portfolio labeled 00000. A traditional sequence – one that has emerged as
quite common – involves an early transition to cash accounts and then
homeownership. Those who followed this sequence typically acquired a
checking or savings account (or both) during late adolescence, eventually

---

[3] In Chapter 5, I also use a type of multivariate model that allows me to capture accumulation rates, providing further information about patterns over time.

TABLE 4.5. *Proportion of People Following Three Typical Trajectories, by Childhood Religious Affiliation*

	Trajectory		
	Permanently Asset-Poor	Early Transition to Cash/Home	Early Transition to Financial Assets
White Conservative Protestant (CP)	.13	.07	.02
Black Conservative Protestant (BP)	.15	.05	.01
Mainline/Liberal Protestant (MP)	.05	.22	.08
Catholic			
White	.07	.23	.05
Hispanic	.14	.06	.01
Jewish	.01	.35	.33
All Respondents	.06	.17	.04

Notes: Data are from the 1979–2006 NLSY. Sample size = 4,369.

bought a home as their first major investment, and may have eventually invested in stocks and bonds. The third common sequence that emerged was an early transition to financial wealth. Those who followed this type of pattern bought financial assets (stocks and bonds) early in life. Most of these people also had checking and savings accounts, and some eventually owned homes as well, but the dominant feature of this group was early entry into ownership of relatively high-risk assets.[4]

The results presented in Table 4.5 indicate that only 6 percent of the NLSY sample remained permanently asset-poor throughout their lives.[5] Significantly more of those raised as CPs (13 percent), BPs (15 percent), and Hispanic Catholics (14 percent) remained asset-poor throughout their adult lives. In contrast, only 1 percent of those who were raised as Jews remained asset-poor. Early transition to cash and homeownership is perhaps the most traditional of these financial trajectories, and 17 percent of the full sample followed a path that could be classified

---

[4] Each trajectory that I have grouped under these names includes multiple paths that were identified by optimal matching as relatively similar. These are not the only trajectories that emerged, but they are the most common paths followed by those in the sample.

[5] Reporting these results as a function of adult religious affiliation produces similar patterns. The results I report here are slightly different from results I presented in earlier research using a similar technique and an earlier version of the NLSY data (Keister, 2003a). because respondents' asset portfolios changed as new waves were added to the data.

TABLE 4.6. *Homeownership (%)*

	Own Primary Home		Own a Second Home	
	NLSY	HRS	NLSY	HRS
White Conservative Protestant (CP)	70.8	86.5	10.7	13.7
Black Conservative Protestant (BP)	48.4	70.5	7.1	8.2
Mainline/Liberal Protestant (MP)	84.5	88.3	13.0	19.7
Catholic	78.5	81.4	12.7	16.7
White	82.3	85.4	14.1	18.8
Hispanic	60.7	64.9	5.8	7.5
Jewish	89.8	82.2	22.5	19.5
Other Religion	71.0	84.3	13.7	15.0
No Religion	67.9	83.5	10.1	15.8
All Respondents	73.7	84.2	12.1	16.0

Notes: Data are from the 1979–2004 NLSY and the 2006 HRS. NLSY sample size = 4,369; HRS sample size = 8,113. NLSY religion was measured in 2000; HRS religion was measured in 1992.

under this heading. Of those raised as MPs, 22 percent followed this path. Similarly, 23 percent of white Catholics followed this trajectory. Perhaps most instructive are the differences across households in following the trajectory of early transition to financial assets, which is the most high-risk, high-return trajectory. In the full sample, only 4 percent of respondents followed this path. Among those raised as Jews, however, a full 33 percent took a financial path that could be classified in this high-risk category. These results imply that the repertoire of skills and decision-making abilities learned in childhood may very well set a course of action that ultimately translates into high wealth.

Homeownership

Given that homeownership plays an important role in the portfolios of the majority of American households, group differences in owning a home can be very informative about more general patterns of financial well-being. A majority of households own their primary residence (see Table 4.6). More specifically, more than 73 percent of working-age respondents to the NLSY and more than 84 percent of retirement-age respondents to the HRS own their primary residence. These percentages are comparable to estimates from other data sources, including from the SCF. According to my estimates from the SCF, 68.3 percent of respondents aged thirty-five to forty-four and 81.3 percent of those aged sixty-six to seventy-four owned their homes in 2004, and 85.5 percent of SCF respondents aged sixty-six to seventy-four owned their homes in 2007.

Homeownership patterns by religion underscore patterns in total net worth that emerged earlier in this chapter. Working-age CPs are slightly less likely than the overall sample to own the primary residence, whereas retirement-age CPs are slightly more likely than average to be homeowners. Neither difference is significant, suggesting that CPs in both samples are rather typical in terms of their homeownership rates. This is also consistent with previous research that suggests that CPs are family-oriented and thus may be inclined to invest in homes rather than other assets. Rates of homeownership for both working-age and retirement-age BPs and Hispanic Catholics are significantly lower than the sample averages, consistent with previous research on race/ethnicity and homeownership (Keister 2000; Oliver and Shapiro 1995) and with findings reported here on the net worth patterns of these groups (see Table 4.1). MPs and Jews are both significantly more likely than the average respondent to own their homes, regardless of age. White Catholics are also more likely than average to be homeowners, but the difference is much higher for younger (working-age NLSY respondents) than it is for older (retirement-age HRS respondents). This is consistent with evidence that white Catholics have been upwardly mobile in recent generations and that younger Catholics have emphasized home purchases as part of their investment strategies (Keister 2007).

Owning a second home is much rarer, but a purchase of this sort can have important long-term implications for wealth and financial well-being. Given that home values have tended to appreciate over long periods of U.S. history, adding a second home (e.g., a vacation home, a rental house) can add notably to a household's wealth portfolio. Ownership of a second home is uncommon because this type of investment can require significant capital for a down payment and other resources for qualifying for a mortgage and paying a mortgage, maintenance costs, taxes, and other costs. Yet, purchases of this sort have increased over time, particularly during the relative prosperity of the years directly preceding the 2004 and 2007 surveys I am using here. Table 4.6 shows that slightly more than 12 percent of working-age households and 16 percent of retirement-age households report owning something that qualifies as a second home. These rates are consistent with SCF estimates that suggest ownership rates of about 13 percent and 17 percent for subsamples of appropriate ages for comparing with the NLSY and HRS. Consistent with other ownership patterns I have discussed, CPs, BPs, and Hispanic

Catholics are less likely than the sample average to own a second home. In contrast, MPs, white Catholics, and Jews are more likely to own a second home.

Other factors that influence homeownership rates might explain the differences by religious group, but I found little evidence in other analyses and extensive data exploration (not reported) to suggest significant influences of other processes. For example, there is some evidence that homeownership rates vary regionally, consistent with well-established patterns of value and the accessibility of homeownership in certain regions. For instance, because housing prices are extremely high in some parts of the Northeast (e.g., New York City, Boston) and on the West Coast (e.g., Los Angeles, San Francisco), rates of ownership tend to be lower in these places (Bucks et al. 2009). There are some differences by religious group that reflect these patterns, but these differences are minimal. Indeed, there are no statistically significant differences in homeownership by both geographic region and religion that would explain the net worth differences across religious groups that were evident in Table 4.1. Similarly, despite common perceptions, there are only minor differences between urban and rural residents in homeownership rates. Recent SCF evidence indicates that approximately 68 percent of urban households and approximately 71 percent of rural households are homeowners (Bucks et al. 2009). Similar patterns are evident in both the NLSY and HRS data, and there is virtually no effect of urbanicity on patterns by religious group. Of course there are also notable patterns in homeownership by income, education, family structure, race/ethnicity, work status, and other traits. As I proposed earlier, these variables are likely to intercede between religion and homeownership. I revisit the role of these other factors in the next chapter.

Home Values

We have seen that large percentages of Americans are homeowners and that Americans invest significant portions of their savings in the family home. Yet, it is possible to be a homeowner and to gain little net worth advantage if the house is of low value. The median NLSY household reported that the market value of their primary residence was $165,000 and that the value of their second home was $90,000 (in 2004 dollars; see Table 4.7).[6] Similarly, the median SCF respondent of the same

---

[6] All values are medians for those households who reported owning the primary residence or a second home.

TABLE 4.7. *Median Home Values*

	Primary Home		Second Home	
	NLSY	HRS	NLSY	HRS
White Conservative Protestant (CP)	$140,000	$131,181	$80,000	$46,850
Black Conservative Protestant (BP)	$85,000	$86,204	–	$42,165
Mainline/Liberal Protestant (MP)	$180,000	$182,154	$100,000	$112,440
Catholic	$200,000	$210,826	$100,000	$93,700
White	$200,000	$223,944	$100,000	$117,125
Hispanic	$145,000	$163,976	–	$46,850
Jewish	$350,000	$421,652	–	–
Other Religion	$160,000	$234,251	$80,000	$112,440
No Religion	$170,000	$239,873	$76,000	$140,551
All Respondents	$165,000	$168,661	$90,000	$84,330

Notes: Data are from the 1979–2004 NLSY and the 2006 HRS. NLSY sample size = 4,369; HRS sample size = 8,113. NLSY religion was measured in 2000; HRS religion was measured in 1992. Median home values are in 2004 dollars (adjusted using the consumer price index for HRS data). Dashed lines indicate that a cell has too few cases for a reliable estimate (*n* < 30).

age reported a primary home value of $143,000 and a second home value of $80,000 in 2004 (Bucks, Kennickell, and Moore 2006). Hispanic Catholics and CPs reported significantly lower values for both the primary residence and the second home. BPs reported even lower values for the primary residence. Not enough (fewer than thirty) CPs or Hispanic Catholics in the NLSY owned a second home to create a reliable estimate of median value, but in the HRS, both groups reported low values for second homes. By contrast, MPs reported significantly higher than average values for both primary and second homes. White Catholics also reported high values, notably larger than those reported by MPs for the primary home but not for the second home. Jews reported home values that were among the highest in the sample for the first home, but too few Jewish respondents in either survey reported owning a second home to create a reliable estimate of home values for this group. Although some Jewish respondents live in large cities, it is important to note that the high values reported for the primary residence do not reflect an overrepresentation of Jewish families residing in New York City or other cities with high property values. Jewish respondents are located throughout the country, and sample weights adjust for overrepresentation of those from particular areas.

Primary and second home values reported by HRS respondents underscore the patterns evident in the NLSY (see Table 4.7). The median HRS respondent in 2007 reported a home value of $168,661 for a primary residence and $84,330 for a second home. Again, CPs, BPs, and Hispanic Catholics had relatively low home values; MPs, white Catholics, and Jews had relatively high home values. Comparing NLSY and HRS values should be done with caution because of sample differences, as I have noted before. However, given that the median for both samples is quite similar ($165,000 for the NLSY and $168,661 for the HRS), considering how group medians differ from the sample median can be instructive. In particular, it is notable that for most groups, home values are larger in the HRS, relative to the sample median, than in the NLSY. This difference reflects at least two factors that I noted earlier. First, HRS respondents are older than NLSY respondents and demonstrate postretirement patterns in asset ownership. Second, the HRS data reflect 2007 survey responses, whereas the NLSY data reflect 2004 survey responses.

The time lapse between the NLSY survey and the HRS survey is particularly important in a discussion of housing values, because the gap between 2004 and 2007 spans the recent housing crisis that started roughly in 2006. Housing values peaked nationally in the United States in early 2005 and began to decline in 2006 in what is now recognized as a housing bubble and subsequent housing market collapse (Mantell 2009). On December 30, 2008, the Case-Shiller home price index indicated that U.S. housing values had experienced their largest decline in history (Mantell 2009). For many individual homeowners, this dramatic drop in value meant that they owed more on their home mortgages than the home was worth – that is, if they sold the house, they could not pay off the debt used to purchase it. This led many owners to simply walk away from the home and stop making payments on the debt. Other homeowners found that they simply had far less home equity – and thus net worth – than they had just months earlier. Indeed, the NLSY-HRS differences in housing values should be larger than they are, given that three years have elapsed, and the relatively small difference reflects the dramatic market decline that affected homeowners across the country.

One group that stands out in comparing NLSY and HRS median home values is CPs: The median value of both the primary and second home for CPs is lower in the HRS than in the NLSY. This might reflect aging (i.e., downsizing as family size drops), upward mobility of CPs (i.e., wealthier, younger people becoming CPs), or declining housing values. Additional analyses suggest that each of the processes is at work; I explore the relative importance of each influence in greater detail in Chapter 5.

TABLE 4.8. *Median Home Equity*

	Primary Home		Second Home	
	NLSY	HRS	NLSY	HRS
White Conservative Protestant (CP)	$60,000	$111,691	$43,000	$46,850
Black Conservative Protestant (BP)	$36,500	$61,842	–	$34,669
Mainline/Liberal Protestant (MP)	$84,900	$141,000	$70,000	$89,015
Catholic	$98,793	$178,031	$70,000	$93,700
White	$100,000	$187,401	$68,000	$104,944
Hispanic	$75,000	$107,755	–	$46,850
Jewish	$280,000	$374,802	–	–
Other Religion	$60,000	$187,401	$70,000	$71,212
No Religion	$82,000	$178,968	$50,000	$74,960
All Respondents	$74,000	$140,551	$60,000	$74,960

Notes: Data are from the 1979–2004 NLSY and the 2006 HRS. NLSY sample size = 4,369; HRS sample size = 8,113. NLSY religion was measured in 2000; HRS religion was measured in 1992. Median home equity is in 2004 dollars (adjusted using the consumer price index for HRS data). Dashed lines indicate that a cell has too few cases for a reliable estimate ($n < 30$).

Home Equity

Home equity or real property value is the difference between a house's market value and the remaining debt (mortgages) on the property. That is, home equity is a homeowner's unencumbered interest in the property; it is the portion of a home's value that is included in net worth. Home equity increases as the value of the house increases and/or as the homeowner pays off the mortgage. Home equity, like the value of other real assets, has a zero rate of return and is not liquid (i.e., cannot easily or quickly be turned into cash). However, home equity can be used as collateral for a home equity loan or a home equity line of credit (HELOC), two forms of debt that can be used for expenses such as home improvements, medical bills, college education, and other major expenses. Home equity loans and HELOCs, usually considered second mortgages, became increasingly common starting in the 1990s. I will return to a discussion of mortgages and loans on home equity when I discuss debt in the next chapter, but having a basic understanding of these liabilities is necessary for understanding home equity.

Median home equity for working-age NLSY respondents was $74,000 and for retirement-age HRS respondents was nearly double at $140,551 (see Table 4.8).[7] Consistent with their home values, both working-age

---

[7] All equity values are medians for those households who report owning the primary residence or a second home.

and retirement-age CPs and particularly BPs have low home equity. Notably, working-age Hispanic Catholics have home equity that is above the median, despite having relatively low home values. Retirement-age Hispanic Catholics have relatively low home equity, suggesting a degree of upward mobility for this group. White Catholics and Jews report home equity values that are higher than average in both surveys, and MPs in the NLSY also report high home equity. However, home equity for retirement-age MPs is not significantly different from the sample median.

Change in home equity between the working and postretirement years – again, comparing group medians to sample medians to avoid inappropriately comparing across samples – suggests that most groups have more equity later in life, consistent with paying off debt over time. CPs are an exception in that retired members of these churches have dramatically more home equity following retirement than during the working years. This large difference is particularly noteworthy given that the value of the homes owned by CPs declined between the working and retirement years. Patterns of equity in second homes are consistent with the ownership and market value of second homes. In both surveys, CPs have relatively low equity when they own a second home, whereas MPs and white Catholics have relatively high equity in these homes. There are not enough data to estimate equity for working-age BPs and Hispanic Catholics, but retirement-age members of these groups have relatively low equity. There are not enough data to estimate equity of second homes for Jews in either sample.

Summary and Concluding Thoughts

This chapter provided a first look at differential wealth outcomes by religious group that result from the family, educational, and work processes described earlier in this book. I showed that there are important patterns by religious affiliation in total net worth, asset poverty, and high wealth status. I also showed that portfolio behavior and financial trajectories vary by religious affiliation. I then provided some additional detail about the role of the ownership and the value of real assets in creating differential net worth patterns. My findings are consistent with past work on religion and wealth ownership showing that Jews, MPs, and white Catholics tend to have higher total wealth than other groups. My findings also showed that these groups have wealth portfolios and accumulation trajectories that account for at least part of their wealth advantage. In addition, I found that BPs, Hispanic Catholics, and CPs tend to have relatively low wealth, consistent with research on religion, race/ethnicity, and wealth.

I continue my discussion of wealth patterns in Chapter 5 by exploring differences by religious affiliation in the ownership and value of other components of net worth, particularly financial assets and liabilities. In Chapter 5, I also explore the relative importance of religion and race/ethnicity and other more complex relationships by introducing multivariate models. Together, Chapters 4 and 5 provide a comprehensive snapshot of wealth ownership by religion. One important new pattern that I identified in this chapter was some evidence of upward mobility among CPs. I return to this question when I address mobility issues in Chapter 6.

One aspect of religion that I have not discussed is religiosity, or the strength of religious convictions. If religious beliefs are related to wealth outcomes, it might follow that those who are more religious (i.e., those who internalize or otherwise place greater emphasis on their religious beliefs) should have stronger associations with wealth. Empirically, however, there is little evidence from the data sets I use that this is the case. Indeed, there is little evidence from these data that religiosity, measured as frequency of attendance at religious services and frequency of participation in religious activities, is associated with wealth outcomes. The absence of a relationship between religiosity and wealth is consistent with findings that I have published elsewhere (Keister 2003a, 2003b, 2007, 2008). It is also consistent with reports that there is no apparent empirical relationship between church attendance and income (Stark 2008). The absence of a relationship may reflect the tremendous consistency within religious groups in beliefs about a range of values and outcomes (Greeley and Hout 2006; Stark 2008). I find a similarly high degree of within-religious-group similarity in the data I use, including the GSS data on which I reported in Chapter 1. Alternatively, the absence of a relationship may reflect poor measurement of religiosity. That is, religious attendance might be a poor measure of religiosity, and preferable measures would be either self-reported religious conviction or (perhaps even more ideally) measures of the manifestation of religious conviction in other behaviors. Unfortunately, current data sets do not contain sufficient information to explore this question in more detail. Future research could usefully fill this gap.

5

Wealth II

Financial Assets, Liabilities, and Multivariate Models

We saw in Chapter 4 that household wealth ownership is unequally distributed in the United States, and that real assets in particular are owned disproportionately by some groups. Although inequality in the ownership of real assets is definitely high, inequality in the ownership of financial assets is even more extreme. Recall from Chapter 1 that financial assets are nontangible assets, monetary assets such as checking and savings accounts, stocks, and bonds. In this chapter, I continue my discussion of religion and wealth by showing how religious affiliation is associated with these components of total net worth. In particular, I examine the association between religious affiliation and ownership of cash (checking and savings) accounts, Certificates of Deposit (CDs), Individual Retirement Accounts (IRAs) and Keogh Accounts, life insurance with a cash value, pension plans, stocks, bonds, Treasury Bills (T-bills), and educational savings plans. I look at religious variation in the ownership of total financial assets, having very high or very low financial assets, the allocation of resources across types of financial assets, and the value of particular financial assets. In addition, I explore the role of liabilities in variations in net worth. Specifically, I explore how religious affiliation relates to total household debt, having extreme amounts (low and high) of debt, and the allocation of debt across categories. I end this chapter with a discussion of multivariate statistical models that synthesize the information I have provided thus far in this book. The multivariate models allow me to address how religion interacts with other influences on wealth ownership – such as family, educational, and work processes – to produce wealth outcomes.

Financial Assets

Financial assets are essential to a well-rounded wealth portfolio, even for those who own relatively little total net worth. Financial assets are liquid – that is, they can be converted relatively easily to cash. Of course, the ease of conversion and the resulting penalties vary widely across financial instruments, but most can be sold or otherwise converted into cash for current consumption or investment. Because they can be easily converted to cash, financial assets provide a buffer against crises such as a loss in income, a medical or other emergency, or unforeseen expenses associated with natural or other disasters. Financial assets have historically increased in value over long periods, and owners of financial assets such as stocks tend to build wealth faster than those who do not own these assets. As stock values increase, those who own stocks tend to see very large increases in the value of their overall portfolios. As a result, those who do not own stocks fall farther behind.

Financial assets vary widely in the amount of risk associated with owning them and, therefore, in the returns an owner can expect to receive. High-risk assets are those that are not guaranteed and that may lose considerable value; of course, they may – and often do – gain considerable value. Stocks or equities, ownership of some portion of a business, can be high-risk. Bonds can also be risky. Bonds are certificates of debt issued by a government (federal, municipal) or corporation that are assets to the households that own them. Stocks and bonds are often packaged and sold as mutual funds to individual and household investors. Relatively low-risk assets include those that are either guaranteed, as by a government, or simply unlikely to lose or gain much value. Bank accounts, for example, are relatively low-risk because they tend to be insured by the federal government.

Median household holdings of all financial assets were $40,000 in the 2004 NLSY and more than $57,000 in the 2006 HRS (see Table 5.1). A small amount of this variation results from sampling differences across the surveys. However, because I took considerable care to create total financial assets measures that are comparable in the two surveys, much of the difference in central tendency reflects age differences in the samples: The HRS sample respondents simply have had more time to accumulate assets. These estimates are also very similar to financial asset values for age-appropriate groups in the 2004 and 2007 SCF samples. Most notable here are patterns by religious group that are consistent with – albeit more extreme than – differences in the ownership of real

TABLE 5.1. *Religion and Financial Assets*

| | Median Value of Financial Assets | |
	NLSY	HRS
White Conservative Protestant (CP)	$33,000	$39,354
Black Conservative Protestant (BP)	$7,500	$2,811
Mainline/Liberal Protestant (MP)	$60,000	$89,015
Catholic	$58,000	$70,275
White	$59,000	$93,168
Hispanic	$19,000	$3,500
Jewish	$239,000	$252,991
Other religion	$19,400	$50,130
No religion	$30,000	$84,330
All Respondents	$40,000	$57,626

Notes: Data are from the 1979–2004 NLSY and the 2006 HRS. NLSY sample size = 4,369; HRS sample size = 8,113. Religion was measured in 2000 in the NLSY and in 1992 in the HRS. Median financial asset values are in 2004 dollars (adjusted using the consumer price index for HRS data). All financial asset figures include bank accounts, IRAs, Keogh accounts, CDs, bonds, treasury bills, stocks, and mutual funds. NLSY totals also include cash-value life insurance, 529 plans, and variable annuities, as well as totals from employer-sponsored retirement plans (if different from IRAs and Keogh accounts). HRS totals include investment trusts.

assets I reported in Chapter 4. In both the NLSY and HRS samples, BPs have the lowest holdings of total financial assets, followed by Hispanic Catholics and CPs. At the other end of the spectrum are Jews, whose holdings of financial assets are more than five times the sample average for the NLSY and more than four times the sample average for the HRS. MPs and white Catholics are relatively comparable to each other in both surveys and located in the middle of the distribution. Notably, white Catholics have slightly more financial assets than MPs in both surveys – another indicator of their recent upward mobility. The patterns that emerge in Table 5.1 are nearly identical if I use childhood religion rather than adult religion to make comparisons.

Low and High Financial Assets

To understand group differences in wealth ownership, it is also instructive to consider patterns in having particularly low or high financial assets. Table 5.2 divides NLSY and HRS respondents into those with low ($600 or less) and high ($315,000 or more) total financial assets. Specifying the cutoff points for these extremes is a somewhat subjective task, but it is standard in the wealth literature to talk about those in the top

TABLE 5.2. *Adult Religion and Low/High Financial Assets (%)*

	Low Financial Assets		High Financial Assets	
	NLSY	HRS	NLSY	HRS
White Conservative Protestant (CP)	12.1	11.9	8.5	13.6
Black Conservative Protestant (BP)	20.8	28.8	3.4	1.8
Mainline/Liberal Protestant (MP)	6.0	5.3	13.1	24.1
Catholic	6.7	9.1	12.4	20.7
White	5.3	6.1	13.4	23.6
Hispanic	11.9	28.0	7.0	2.5
Jewish	0.0	7.5	40.2	41.8
Other religion	11.8	11.7	11.1	19.9
No religion	11.4	9.2	9.5	23.3
All Respondents	10.2	9.8	10.5	19.4

Notes: Data are from the 1979–2004 NLSY and the 2006 HRS. NLSY sample size = 4,369; HRS sample size = 8,113. Religion was measured in 2000 in the NLSY and in 1992 in the HRS. Low financial assets are $600 or less; high financial assets are greater than $315,000 (i.e., approximately the bottom and top 10% of the NLSY financial assets distribution).

and bottom 10 percent of any distribution. Using the top and bottom 10 percent tends to isolate those who are notably secure or insecure financially compared to others in the distribution. I chose to identify the top and bottom of the NLSY survey and use the monetary amounts ($600 or $315,000) to identify low and high wealth respondents in both surveys to ease interpretation, but simply identifying the bottom and top 10 percent in each survey produced identical substantive results, because the distributions are quite similar in the two surveys. Notice, for example, that when we consider all respondents in the NLSY, 10.2 percent have low financial assets and 10.5 percent have high financial assets (by definition, this is nearly 10 percent). Similarly, 9.8 percent of HRS respondents have low financial assets, a value that is not statistically different from 10 percent. However, there are significantly more HRS respondents who are categorized as high asset (19.4 percent) using this method, reflecting the age of the HRS sample relative to the NLSY sample.

Conservative Protestants are slightly more likely than the average respondent to have low financial wealth in both the NLSY and the HRS. Likewise, CPs are slightly less likely than average to have high financial assets in both surveys. In both cases, the differences between CPs and the overall sample are modest and only slightly statistically significant. More importantly, the differences between CP wealth and overall sample wealth reflected in Table 5.2 are lower than shown in previous research, suggesting either a change in CP saving habits or a change in the composition of CP denominations (Keister 2008). I explore these changes in more detail in Chapter 6. Table 5.2 also suggests that CPs may accumulate assets over their lives slower than others. Specifically, the table shows that the gap between CPs and the overall sample in propensity to have high financial assets is much greater in the HRS than in the NLSY. This difference might reflect survey differences, or it might reflect comparatively slow rates of accumulation for CPs. If the pattern is truly a slow rate of accumulation, this is consistent with the argument of a unique orientation towards money, including considering money to belong to God. I use multivariate models of asset growth in the next chapter to explore this pattern in greater detail.

In contrast, the difference between BPs and the overall samples on both low and high financial asset status are extreme in both the NLSY and the HRS. The percentage of BPs who have low financial assets is more than twice as large as the percentage of all NLSY respondents (20.8 percent compared to 10.2 percent) and almost three times as large as the percentage of all HRS respondents (28.8 percent compared to 9.8 percent). Similarly, very few BPs have high financial assets. Recall that more than 10 percent of all working-age NLSY respondents have high financial assets by definition, whereas only 3.4 percent of BPs fall into this high-wealth category. The difference is even more extreme among postretirement HRS respondents. Nearly 20 percent of HRS respondents have more than $315,000 in financial assets, but only 1.8 percent of BPs are that wealthy. Hispanic Catholics are notably different across the two samples. In the NLSY, Hispanic Catholics are nearly identical to CPs in their propensity to be low-wealth: 11.9 percent of Hispanic Catholics and 12.1 percent of CPs are in this group. These groups are also similar in their propensity to be high-wealth: 7 percent of Hispanic Catholics and 8.5 percent of CPs are in the high-financial-assets group. For the older HRS sample, Hispanic Catholics are much more similar to BPs than to CPs, suggesting that there may have been a generational change for Hispanic Catholics. In particular, 28 percent of Hispanic Catholics and 28.8 percent of BPs in the HRS are in the low-financial-asset category; 2.5 percent of Hispanic Catholics and 1.8 percent of BPs are in the high-financial-asset category.

Consistent with other findings that I report in this book, MPs and white Catholics are similar to each other in their propensity to be either low- or high-wealth. MPs and white Catholics are less likely than average to be low-wealth and more likely than average to be high-wealth. Also consistent with patterns than have begun to emerge in this book, Jews are very unlikely to have low financial assets and very likely to have high financial assets. Indeed, no NLSY respondents who claimed Judaism as their adult religion reported assets low enough to place them in the bottom 10 percent of the distribution for that sample, and significantly fewer than average Jewish HRS respondents (although the difference is only marginally significant) are in the bottom of the financial asset distribution for that survey. Again, the patterns that emerge in Table 5.2 are nearly identical if I use childhood religion rather than adult religion to make comparisons.

The Allocation of Financial Assets, Part I: The Working Years

The allocation of financial assets across investment alternatives can be one of the more pronounced determinants of wealth accumulation patterns. A portfolio that is biased toward low- risk, low-return assets is likely to grow slowly (albeit safely) and to yield relatively low overall wealth in the later stages of the life course. Alternatively, a portfolio that is biased toward high-risk, high-return assets can lead to significant wealth accumulation even in the absence of substantial additional saving from current income. Very few people are truly willing to assume very high levels of risk because most people who save have some long-term objective in mind for which they intend to use their savings. The most common reasons people save are retirement and liquidity: 33.9 percent of respondents to the 2007 SCF cited retirement as the most important reason for saving, and 32 percent cited liquidity as their primary motivator (Bucks et al. 2009). Purchases (10 percent), education (8.4 percent), for the family (5.5 percent), and purchasing a home (4.2 percent) were the other top reasons people gave for saving. There have been some modest changes in the importance attributed to these reasons over time, but the rank-order of the categories has stayed roughly the same since the 1990s (Bucks et al. 2009).

Watching surplus saving that was earmarked for purposes as important as retirement, education, and home purchases disappear can be difficult and discouraging. As a result, an all-stock portfolio – or other extremely high-risk portfolio – is rare. A balanced portfolio that grows consistently but not extremely quickly is more common. A typical medium- to high-risk portfolio would include 70 percent or more in stocks; a medium-risk portfolio would include between 20 percent and 70 percent in stocks; and a low-risk portfolio would include less than 20 percent in stocks. In each

TABLE 5.3. *The Allocation of Financial Assets: NLSY (%)*

	Bank Accounts	Retirement Accounts	Bonds, CDs, T-bills	Stocks, Stock Mutual Funds
White Conservative Protestant (CP)	38.6	40.2	2.5	10.5
Black Conservative Protestant (BP)	43.2	37.0	2.0	3.6
Mainline/Liberal Protestant (MP)	31.1	46.2	2.6	11.5
Catholic	32.2	45.9	2.8	9.4
White	31.5	46.1	2.9	10.2
Hispanic	37.5	42.3	2.2	4.6
Jewish	29.9	41.5	3.2	21.1
Other religion	40.3	39.7	1.8	9.4
No religion	38.4	40.9	2.2	9.8
All Respondents	35.9	42.7	2.5	9.7

Notes: Data are from the 1979–2004 NLSY. Sample size = 4,369. Religion was measured in 2000. Retirement accounts refer to plans offered by employers as well as other IRAs and Keogh accounts. Asset categories are not exhaustive.

scenario, the remainder of the portfolio would include bonds, Certificates of Deposit, bank accounts, and other financial assets. Of course, the cutoffs I cite are subjective, and individuals and their financial planners have various approaches and definitions of risk categories. However, the portfolios I describe are consistent with expectations of risk, and thus growth, associated with each approach to asset allocation. For the purpose of understanding religious variations in wealth ownership, it is useful to consider the implications of portfolio behavior, as decisions about asset allocation can have important consequences for individual and group differences in wealth accumulation over the life course.

Indeed, there are important differences by religious group in asset allocation that may affect patterns in wealth ownership. Table 5.3 identifies variations by adult religion in the allocation of financial resources to four broad categories. The cells refer to the percentage of total financial assets, for NLSY respondents who own any financial assets, held in each category. For example, for the entire sample (all respondents), 35.9 percent of total financial assets are kept in bank accounts, 42.7 percent are kept in retirement accounts, 2.5 percent are kept in bonds/CDs/T-bills, and 9.7 percent are kept in stocks and mutual funds. I include a separate category for retirement accounts because the survey uses this as a unique category, even though retirement accounts can include a range of investments. This makes it somewhat difficult to ascertain the risk associated with a portfolio, but most people would not be able to describe the details of their retirement plan accurately. Moreover, in most cases, retirement accounts would be higher risk than bank accounts and lower risk than stocks, providing some evidence of the risk – and thus potential growth – associated with asset allocation. I also include bonds, CDs, and T-bills in a single category despite important differences in these investments. I do this to compare asset allocation between NLSY and HRS respondents, as the HRS combines these assets into a single category. Moreover, although bonds, CDs, and T-bills are different, they tend to involve somewhat similar risk and growth potential, providing useful information about risk and potential portfolio growth. The NLSY estimates in Table 5.3 are consistent with age-restricted estimates from the 2004 SCF (Bucks et al. 2009), suggesting that the NLSY sample continues to represent the population in this generation well despite sample aging and attrition.

Differences across religious groups in asset allocation are least evident in holdings of low-risk assets and most evident in holdings of the highest-risk assets. There is some variation, for example, in the percentage of assets households hold as bank accounts, and these differences are consistent with patterns we have seen in overall wealth. The higher the percentage of assets held in bank accounts (i.e., cash accounts), the lower the growth associated with the portfolio. Table 5.3 shows that working-age BPs hold a relatively high percentage of their assets in bank accounts. Similarly, working-age CPs and Hispanic Catholics tend to hold higher-than-average percentages of their financial assets in bank accounts. Although on this dimension, Hispanic Catholics are more similar to CPs than to BPs. MPs and white Catholics hold nearly identical – and slightly lower than average – percentages of their assets in bank accounts. Jews hold the lowest percentage of their assets in bank accounts. At the other end of the financial risk spectrum are holdings of stocks (i.e., stocks and stock mutual funds). The average NLSY respondent holds just less than 10 percent of total financial assets in stocks. If BPs have any financial assets, they hold only 3.6 percent of those in stocks, and if Hispanic Catholics have any financial assets, they hold only 4.6 percent in stocks. By contrast, MPs who have financial assets have 11.5 percent in stocks, and white Catholics have 10.2 percent in stocks. The average Jewish respondent to the NLSY holds more than 20 percent of financial assets in stocks.

An important social process reflected in asset allocation patterns that can affect overall wealth is distrust of banks and other financial organizations. That is, there are households that do not own even a checking account (considered the most basic of financial instruments), and there is evidence of group variation in being completely disconnected from financial markets. Between 15 percent and 20 percent of respondents to the NLSY and SCF between the mid-1980s and 2007 report not owning a checking account (Bucks et al. 2009; Bucks, Kennickell, and Moore 2006; Keister 2005). The exact percentage varies, of course, but it tends to be just under 20 percent of the population. The SCF probes respondents about their reasons for not owning a checking account, and the responses are also relatively consistent over time. Between 18 percent (in 1998) and 25 percent (in 2007) of respondents who do not own a checking account say that the reason is they "do not like dealing with banks" (Bucks et al. 2009). The second most common reason given is "do not write enough checks to make it worthwhile;" between 18.7 percent (in 2007) and 28.4 percent (in 1998) of respondents give this as the primary reason they do not have a checking account. Other reasons that are less common include high service charges, high required minimum balances, not having enough money, and credit problems. Most important here are racial/ethnic differences in banking behavior that might underlie religious differences in portfolio behavior. Specifically, blacks and Hispanics are significantly overrepresented among those who do not own checking accounts and significantly more likely than other respondents to distrust banks. Consistent with this, other research shows that blacks and Hispanics are more likely to use check-cashing outlets (e.g., Pay Day loans) and pawn shops for banking than those from other racial and ethnic groups (Caskey 1994). These nonmainstream organizations tend to charge very high interest rates and fees for basic services such as check cashing and are considered by many to be predatory. Respondents to surveys about using these outlets indicate convenience and distrust of banks as motivating them (Caskey 1994). These patterns are also consistent with evidence from the Economic Values Survey that BPs, Hispanic Catholics, and CPs participate at lower rates in mainstream banking. The multivariate models that I discuss later in this chapter adjudicate the relative importance of race and religion in determining overall wealth and to wealth components, including checking accounts.

The Allocation of Financial Assets, Part II: Retirement

Not surprisingly, the allocation of assets changes for most households over the life course. Priorities and goals change, income changes, families grow and then shrink, and assets change value even when their owners do not consciously add to them or withdraw from them. These processes interact in complex ways to alter the allocation of financial assets that households own, and the changes in portfolio composition can be particularly noticeable between the working and postretirement phases of the life course. Retirement itself also necessitates changes in both saving and asset allocation. Reduced income lowers active saving, and households that have accumulated assets may begin to deplete those assets to cover current expenses. This pattern of saving and depletion is referred to as life cycle saving, and although it is intuitive, there is no abundantly clear empirical evidence that households systematically deplete their assets following retirement. A desire to bequeath assets to children and uncertainty about the timing of death are the two most significant reasons households may, in fact, continue to accumulate wealth after retirement. Even if they continue to accumulate assets, however, most households do change the allocation of those assets across financial instruments. For instance, it is common to reduce the risk associated with a portfolio following retirement by selling high-risk assets and purchasing low-risk assets that are more reliable for generating current income. There are also generational differences in saving that might be reflected in comparisons of working age and postretirement households. There is evidence, for example, that Baby Boomers and their parents save in different ways, reflecting generational differences in experience with financial markets (Keister and Deeb-Sossa 2001). For all of these reasons, it is useful to look separately at postretirement asset allocation to understand group – including religious group – differences in wealth ownership.

Postretirement HRS respondents are typical of older Americans in their allocation of assets. Table 5.4 shows the percentage of total financial assets held in four types of financial instruments for HRS respondents who owned any financial assets. The asset categories in this table are as similar as possible to the categories I used in Table 5.3. However, as is always the case when making comparisons across surveys, it is important to remember that sample differences and variations in data collection methods may affect estimates such as these. Despite the differences across surveys, there is a remarkable amount of similarity in the asset allocation patterns of members of religious groups during the working years (shown in Table 5.3) and following retirement (shown in Table 5.4). Similar to working-age BPs, postretirement BPs keep the majority (77 percent) of their financial assets in bank accounts and very little in bonds, CDs and T-bills (6.6 percent) or stocks and stock mutual funds (5.2 percent). Once again, BPs and Hispanic Catholics are quite similar in their asset allocation. Hispanic Catholics also keep the majority

TABLE 5.4. *The Allocation of Financial Assets: HRS (%)*

	Bank Accounts	Retirement Accounts	Bonds, CDs, T-Bills	Stocks, Stock Mutual Funds
White Conservative Protestant (CP)	51.1	27.9	10.0	11.1
Black Conservative Protestant (BP)	77.0	11.1	6.6	5.2
Mainline/Liberal Protestant (MP)	39.3	30.3	11.1	19.3
Catholic	45.6	29.3	10.4	14.7
White	40.4	32.1	11.1	16.4
Hispanic	77.9	13.1	5.8	3.1
Jewish	31.3	36.8	7.7	24.1
Other religion	52.0	23.5	8.5	15.9
No religion	46.4	26.0	11.6	16.0
All Respondents	46.9	28.0	10.2	14.9

Notes: Data are from the 2006 HRS. Sample size = 8,113. Religion was measured in 1992. Investment trusts are also included in the stocks and mutual funds category.

(77.9 percent) of their assets in bank accounts and relatively small percentages in bonds, CDs, and T-bills (5.8 percent) and stocks and stock mutual funds (3.1 percent). Both BPs and Hispanic Catholics do have some assets in retirement accounts, but both groups have moved assets from these accounts to cash accounts, likely to fund retirement spending. The asset allocation that BPs and Hispanic Catholics share is a relatively low-risk allocation; although it is common to reallocate resources to reduce risk during retirement, the BP and Hispanic portfolios shown in Table 5.4 are somewhat extreme even among retirees. CPs are more typical of retirees: They have slightly more than one-half of their financial assets in cash and have moved some savings out of retirement accounts, but they continue to have significant holdings of bonds, CDs, and T-bills (10 percent) and stocks and stock mutual funds (11.1 percent). There are also generational differences that affect the comparability of portfolios of HRS and NLSY respondents. In particular, options for retirement saving have changed in recent decades, altering individual incentives and saving behavior. Defined-benefit savings plans (i.e., plans that guarantee a fixed payout after a defined length of service to an organization) were once the norm. However, defined-contribution plans (i.e., plans that allow participants to contribute a defined amount to a plan – an amount often matched by the employer – and to invest these contributions in stocks, bonds, or other financial instruments) have become more common. The higher incidence of defined-benefit plans among older generations accounts for some of the movement of assets out of retirement accounts.

In contrast, MPs and white Catholics – who are again similar to each other – have as sizable holdings of stocks and stock mutual funds in retirement as they did during the working years. MPs held 19 percent of their total financial assets in stocks and stock mutual funds, and white Catholics held 16.4 percent of their financial assets in these relatively high-risk assets. Both MPs and white Catholics had also transferred noticeable portions of their financial assets from retirement accounts to bank accounts, but they still allocated smaller percentages (about 40 percent) of their assets to bank accounts than BPs, CPs, and Hispanic Catholics. Jews report asset allocation strategies that are even more heavily weighted toward high-risk assets (i.e., stocks and stock mutual funds) than other groups. Indeed, postretirement Jews report having 24.1 percent of their total financial assets invested in stocks and stock mutual funds; 7.7 percent in bonds, CDs and T-bills; 36.8 percent in retirement accounts; and only 31.3 percent in bank accounts. Allocating resources to high-risk assets following retirement suggests that the portfolios of MPs, white Catholics, and Jews are likely to continue to grow, or to decline slower, than those of others with lower-risk asset allocation strategies. Again, some of this change in assets results from differences in types of accounts that are grouped together as retirement accounts, but differences by religious groups in asset allocation are still clear and consistent with patterns in total net worth (Chapter 4) and total financial assets (this chapter).

Financial Asset Values

The allocation of assets affects total financial wealth, and thus net worth, by affecting the accumulation of resources within each asset category. That is, to understand variations in net worth, we need to consider the value of the components of net worth. Table 5.5 shows how median holdings of the four financial asset categories highlighted in the previous two tables vary by religious group for working-age NLSY respondents. The typical respondent held $5,000 in bank accounts, $37,000 in retirement accounts, $3,500 in bonds, CDs, and T-bills, and $20,000 in stocks and stock mutual funds. BPs and Hispanic Catholics held significantly less in each category, with BPs having lower values on average than Hispanic Catholics in three of the four categories. In the fourth category – stocks

TABLE 5.5. *Adult Religion and Financial Asset Values: NLSY*

	Bank Accounts	Retirement Accounts	Bonds, CDs, T-Bills	Stocks, Stock Mutual Funds
White Conservative Protestant (CP)	$4,000	$33,000	$5,000	$20,000
Black Conservative Protestant (BP)	$1,700	$14,000	$1,000	$3,000
Mainline/Liberal Protestant (MP)	$7,000	$50,000	$4,000	$21,000
Catholic	$7,000	$47,000	$3,000	$20,000
White	$8,310	$50,500	$3,000	$20,000
Hispanic	$3,200	$25,000	$6,000	–
Jewish	$15,000	$130,000	–	$100,000
Other religion	$4,500	$30,000	$2,500	$15,000
No religion	$5,000	$38,000	$3,000	$17,000
All Respondents	$5,000	$37,000	$3,500	$20,000

Notes: Data are from the 1979–2004 NLSY. Sample size = 4,369. Religion was measured in 2000. Median financial asset values are in 2004 dollars (adjusted using the consumer price index for HRS data). Dashed lines indicate that a cell has too few cases for a reliable estimate (n < 30).

and stock mutual funds – there were too few Hispanic Catholics who owned any amount of these assets to produce a reliable estimate.

Working-age MPs and white Catholics are once again quite similar to each other and different from BPs and Hispanic Catholics in their holdings of the financial assets highlighted in Table 5.5. An important pattern that stands out in this table is that CPs are much more similar to MPs and white Catholics than they are to BPs and Hispanic Catholics. MPs and white Catholics own nearly identical amounts of each type of financial asset included in Table 5.5. Their bank accounts include about $7,000 to $8,000 in cash, their retirement accounts are worth about $50,000, they own between $3,000 and $4,000 in bonds/CD/T-bills, and they own approximately $20,000 in stocks and stock mutual funds. In contrast, BPs have less than $2,000 in their bank accounts, their retirement accounts are worth $14,000, they have only about $1,000 in bonds/CDs/T-bills, and their stocks and stock mutual funds are worth about $3,000. The financial holdings of Hispanic Catholics are also relatively low in value: Their bank accounts average slightly more than $3,000, their retirement accounts are worth about $25,000, and they own about $6,000 in bonds/CDs/T-bills. Once again, there are too few Hispanic Catholics who own any stocks or stock mutual funds to generate reliable medians. Working-age CPs

TABLE 5.6. *Adult Religion and Financial Asset Values: HRS*

	Bank Accounts	Retirement Accounts	Bonds, CDs, T-Bills	Stocks, Stock Mutual Funds
White Conservative Protestant (CP)	$7,496	$67,464	$23,425	$56,220
Black Conservative Protestant (BP)	$1,874	$46,850	$9,370	$15,929
Mainline/Liberal Protestant (MP)	$9,370	$84,330	$28,110	$93,700
Catholic	$9,370	$74,960	$32,795	$74,960
White	$9,370	$81,519	$32,795	$74,960
Hispanic	$1,874	$39,354	$28,110	$23,425
Jewish	$28,110	$126,469	$56,220	$126,496
Other religion	$9,370	$74,023	$37,480	$93,700
No religion	$13,587	$98,385	$46,850	$93,700
All Respondents	$9,370	$79,834	$28,110	$74,960

Notes: Data are from the 2006 HRS. Sample size = 8,113. Religion was measured in 1992. Median financial asset values are in 2004 dollars (adjusted using the consumer price index for HRS data). Median financial asset values are adjusted using the Consumer Price Index.

have notably high financial assets. Their bank accounts contain about $4,000, and their retirement accounts are worth about $33,000. They also own more in bonds/CDs/T-bills than either MPs or white Catholics, and their holdings of stocks and stock mutual funds are nearly identical to the holdings of MPs and white Catholics. Jews are again at the top of the continuum, with $15,000 in bank accounts, $130,000 in retirement accounts, and $100,000 in stocks and stock mutual funds. There are too few Jews in the sample to create reliable medians.

Financial asset values for postretirement HRS respondents are predictably higher than for NLSY respondents, and there are some slight differences in patterns by religion that are worth noting (see Table 5.6). MPs and white Catholics are again quite similar to each other in their holdings of financial assets, particularly bank accounts and retirement accounts. MPs own more stocks than white Catholics, with $93,700 in stocks and stock mutual funds compared to $74,900 for white Catholics. White Catholics own slightly more bonds/CDs/T-bills than MPs, but the difference (nearly $33,000 for white Catholics compared to slightly more than $28,000 for MPs) is minimal. MPs and white Catholics are also typical of the average HRS respondent: Their holdings of each of the highlighted financial assets are nearly identical to the overall sample median. In contrast, postretirement Jews have financial assets that are larger than the sample median by a substantial margin. At the other end of the spectrum, BPs have very low values of each asset, and Hispanic Catholics own more than BPs but still notably less than the average HRS respondent. Compared to working-age NLSY respondents, both BPs and Hispanic Catholics still have very low bank account values, but their other financial assets are somewhat more valuable, reflecting both appreciation and continued saving. Postretirement CPs have financial assets that are greater than those owned by working-age CPs, but the financial wealth of CP respondents to the HRS is lower than average.

These tables do not show how financial asset values have changed over time, to save space, but it is worth noting that these values have increased slightly for all groups, consistent with general economic trends. Since the mid-1980s, the financial holdings of both NLSY and HRS respondents have increased, with a slight downturn for the median respondent in the early 1990s when the U.S. economy experienced a recession. During that recession, holdings and stocks and stock mutual funds declined, consistent with declining stock values that were common during the recession. Otherwise, the general trend in both surveys has been for asset values across categories to increase. There are some differences in rates of accumulation across religious groups that might underlie overall wealth levels. In particular, there is some evidence that CPs and BPs accumulate assets more slowly than other groups. Slow accumulation rates can reflect differences in saving from current income and/or decisions about how to save. I explore religious differences in accumulation rates in the next chapter.

Liabilities

There is, of course, more to net worth than assets. Liabilities, or debts, make up the other half of the net worth equation, and Americans are an indebted group. For households, liabilities are any sums of money owed to other individuals or organizations for amounts previously borrowed; liabilities include both the principle borrowed and any interest associated with that principle. The Federal Reserve reports a measure called the debt service ratio (DSR) that attempts to estimate the degree to which households are indebted and able to meet their debt obligations. The DSR is the ratio of all debt payments owed to disposable (or after-tax) income. In 2009, the DSR was approximately 13 percent; that is, households spent 13 percent of their disposable income to make payments on mortgages, credit card debt, car loans, education loans, and other liabilities (Federal Reserve Board 2009). The Federal Reserve also publishes a broader measure of financial constraints faced by households, called the financial obligations ratio (FOR). This measure captures more of the mandatory payments made by households by adding to the DSR other financial commitments including car lease payments, rental properties, property taxes, and homeowners insurance. At the end of 2009, the FOR was about 17 percent for homeowners and 25 percent for renters (Federal Reserve Board 2009:273). Most survey data sets that include information on debt are unable to collect enough information to assess this broader measure at the household level, but it is important to be aware that standard debt measures are underestimates of total household liabilities.

Liabilities secured by residential property are the most common type of household debt. These include mortgages, second mortgages, and any other debts secured by both the primary residence or other residential properties, such as vacation homes, owned by the household. Since 2000, American households have held about 75 percent of their total debt in loans secured by the primary residence, up from approximately 71 percent in the late 1990s. Loans secured by other residential properties have increased from 7.5 percent of total household debt in the late 1990s to slightly more than 10 percent in 2007 (Bucks et al. 2009). Installment loans (e.g., education loans, vehicle loans), credit card balances, and lines of credit not secured by residential property are the next three largest types of loans (Bucks et al. 2009). The median value of debt secured by the primary residence for all Americans, from the 2004 SCF, is slightly more than $136,000 (all values are in 2004 dollars for households holding the debt); median debt secured by other residential property is $183,000 (Bucks et al. 2009). Medians in the NLSY and HRS for age-restricted samples are comparable. Other forms of debt tend to be much lower: Median holdings of installment loans are approximately $21,000; median credit card balance is $5,600; and median lines of credit not secured by residential property are $40,000. Again, NLSY and HRS medians are comparable.

The role of debt in net worth is complicated by the fact that liabilities can be positive or negative, and the benefits vary depending on other characteristics of the debt, the household, and even the economic context in which the household takes on the debt. Some liabilities tend to be beneficial to building net worth (e.g., education loans, home loans), whereas other debt tends to detract from net worth accumulation (e.g., home equity loans to pay for consumer goods). The difference between positive and negative liabilities is their investment potential. Education loans are likely to generate future income, home loans tend to build home equity, and business loans can create wealth by enabling the formation of successful organizations. Loans can also be used directly as financial investments. Indeed, borrowing to finance financial ventures is common and can generate more wealth when the investment generates returns that exceed the interest associated with the loan. In contrast, taking a home equity loan (i.e., a loan against the equity built up in residential property) to buy consumer goods reduces net worth with no potential to add to it in the future. Of course, problems arise when credit encourages spending that exceeds the resources needed to pay for the spending, and the financial characteristics and other traits of the household can affect whether debt is beneficial. A household with modest income may be less able to meet debt obligations than one with greater income; likewise, a household that is already highly leveraged may find it difficult to make payments on additional debt regardless of the use of the acquired funds. Even more complex are the nuances associated with debt that might otherwise be beneficial but that is borrowed under conditions that change the effect of the liability on net worth. The recession of 2007–2009 underscored this by demonstrating that housing debt is not always good. During that recession, households that might have been able to make payments on their mortgages faced foreclosure because interest rates dropped and other challenges, such as job loss, affected household income and other aspects of household's financial well-being.

To understand how liabilities affect variations in net worth by religious group, it is useful to compare households based on whether they have very low or very high total debt.[1] Having no debt (zero debt), for example, can be particularly instructive. Using other definitions of low debt did not change the results. Approximately 18 percent of NLSY respondents and almost one-half of HRS respondents are debt free (see Table 5.7). Nearly one-half of BPs in the NLSY – more than twice the sample average – have no debt. Although it is tempting to interpret this as positive, the high number of debt-free BPs reflects a large number of households that do not own a home and who, therefore, are not building home equity. Blacks are also more likely than Hispanics and whites in the United States not to have a credit card (Keister 2000a); this contributes to the high levels of debt-free BP households as well but is a less important factor than home debt. Twenty percent of Hispanic Catholics have no debt; this is

[1] Group variations in median debt values can be instructive; however, because medians for many groups are zero, particularly for those who are postretirement, variations that affect wealth can be obscured. In contrast, having particularly high or low debt highlights patterns that underlie net worth trends.

TABLE 5.7. *Extreme Liabilities: Zero Debt and High Debt*

	Zero Debt		High Debt	
	NLSY	HRS	NLSY	HRS
White Conservative Protestant (CP)	15.4	51.5	9.5	2.3
Black Conservative Protestant (BP)	42.9	41.5	1.4	3.0
Mainline/Liberal Protestant (MP)	12.2	48.8	13.2	2.8
Catholic	13.8	50.8	12.8	3.3
White	11.9	50.9	12.9	3.2
Hispanic	20.7	51.9	13.3	3.5
Jewish	14.4	46.2	32.9	10.0
Other religion	15.8	40.9	9.3	4.8
No religion	18.9	47.5	8.1	5.3
All Respondents	18.3	49.2	10.0	3.2

Notes: Data are from the 1979–2004 NLSY and the 2006 HRS. NLSY sample size = 4,369; HRS sample size = 8,113. NLSY religion is measured in 2000; HRS religion is measured in 1992. Debt is defined as in Table 4.1. High debt is greater than $230,000 (i.e., approximately the top 10% of the total debt distribution for the NLSY).

not significantly different from the sample median, but it is significantly higher than the percentage of debt-free households from other religious groups. Again, this somewhat high median reflects a slightly higher-than-average propensity to rent rather than own the primary residence. MPs, white Catholics, CPs, and Jews are all quite similar to each other and somewhat less likely than the typical NLSY respondent to be debt-free. The typical respondent in each of these groups is likely to be a homeowner and to at least be paying a mortgage. The likelihood that a household is debt-free increases dramatically following retirement as many households pay off their mortgages and reduce other types of spending. There is notably little variation across religious groups in having zero debt in retirement with the exception of BPs who are now less likely than the sample average to have zero debt because the spending and borrowing of BPs changes little following retirement compared to other respondents.

It is difficult to live debt-free today given the pervasiveness and even convenience of many types of borrowing. The vast majority of households will eventually purchase a home with a mortgage, use credit cards, and assume other forms of liabilities that are now taken for granted. Although it is unusual to live debt-free, there is a group of households who live at the other end of the spectrum: having very high levels of debt. Table 5.7 also shows the percentage of respondents who have particularly high levels of total outstanding liabilities. In this table, I define high debt

TABLE 5.8. *Debt Allocation (% of total debts)*

	Home	Vehicles	Credit Card	Education
White Conservative Protestant (CP)	61.0	16.2	10.5	2.9
Black Conservative Protestant (BP)	44.5	19.6	13.3	5.3
Mainline/Liberal Protestant (MP)	69.8	13.1	8.4	1.5
Catholic	68.6	13.9	8.6	1.9
White	71.6	13.1	7.6	1.7
Hispanic	51.8	19.6	14.9	2.5
Jewish	81.6	7.9	6.4	3.3
Other religion	58.2	11.5	11.7	4.2
No religion	56.6	15.3	14.3	3.5
All Respondents	62.5	14.7	10.2	2.8

Notes: Data are from the 1979–2004 NLSY. Sample size = 4,369. Religion was measured in 2000. Debt categories are not exhaustive.

as having more than $230,000 in total outstanding liabilities, or being in the top 10 percent of the debt distribution in the NLSY. There are many ways I might have defined high debt, but preliminary investigations suggested that the patterns by religious group did not vary based on the definition. BPs are again extreme in this regard, having very low debt, particularly mortgage debt. Jews are also extreme, but in contrast to BPs, a large percentage of Jews have high debt both before and after retirement. This pattern reflects two patterns. First, Jews are more likely than other households to own expensive homes (primary residence) when they are homeowners (see Chapter 4 for details). Second, Jews are more likely than other respondents to be business owners and to have sizable business debt. Both home debt and business debt can translate into higher net worth, and both contribute to relatively high net worth among Jews.

How do religious groups differ in their allocations of debt across types? Table 5.8 breaks total debt into four categories, using NLSY data. Allocations are nearly identical for HRS respondents; I do not include those, to conserve space. This table provides further evidence that BPs and Hispanic Catholics have low levels of debt on their homes and disproportionately high percentages of their total debt as credit card debt and vehicle loans. This is despite low levels of credit card ownership among blacks. BPs and Hispanic Catholics differ in the amount of debt committed to education loans: BPs have a relatively high percentage of their debt as education loans, whereas Hispanic Catholics are not different from the sample mean. CPs are at the sample mean on all measures – a pattern that is again suggestive of upward mobility among CPs. MPs, white Catholics, and Jews are very similar on three of the four debts. All three groups have relatively high percentages of their debt in home mortgages and relatively low percentages in vehicle loans and credit card debt. On the relative importance of education loans, MPs and white Catholics are slightly lower than the sample average, and Jews are slightly higher. However, neither difference is statistically significant, suggesting that the three groups are indeed similar on this dimension as well.

Bringing It All Together: Predictors of Family Background

Up to this point, I have discussed relatively simple bivariate relationships between religious affiliation and SES outcomes, including wealth and the factors that contribute to wealth. What emerges is a relatively complex set of interactions among family, education, work, occupation, and other behaviors and processes that ultimately lead to net worth. Pulling each of the elements together and ascertaining the relative weight of each requires more complex, multivariate models. In the remainder of this chapter, I discuss a series of such models that allow me to bring together each of the elements I have discussed so far and to create a more complete picture of how religion and other processes interact to produce financial well-being.

To create the multivariate models, I used the NLSY and large number of the variables I have discussed up to this point in the book. Using the HRS produces substantively similar results but provides less information because of the more restricted ages of the HRS respondents. I used the entire 1979–2004 NLSY as person-year data; that is, I modeled the data using each person in each year as a separate observation. This strategy allows me to take full advantage of the extraordinarily rich information contained in all twenty-five years of the data. I include tables for models of family background (father's education, mother's education, and inheritance) and total adult net worth. First, I model family background to identify religious differences in SES in childhood – that is, in order to identify the starting point people faced from early in life under the assumption that this starting point is a critical determinant of the trajectory and destination people experience. I used two indicators of family background: parents' education and inheritance.[2] Father's and mother's educations are

---

[2] I experimented with modeling family income, parents' occupational prestige, residential traits, and other indicators of well-being. The results were substantively the same as the results I present.

dichotomous indicators that the respondent's biological father or biological mother had ever earned a bachelor's degree or more education.[3] Inheritance is a dichotomous variable indicating that the respondent had ever received an inheritance of more than $1,000. I modeled parents' education as a function of other relevant family characteristics, including religious affiliation, in the same year; I modeled inheritance as a function of both family background and adult traits. Second, I model wealth using measures of total adult net worth in 2004. I also discuss models of the ownership and value of the primary residence, the ownership and value of checking and savings accounts (i.e., cash accounts), and the ownership and value of stocks. I do not include separate tables for these models because they do not provide dramatically different substantive information compared to the models of net worth.

My measures of religious affiliation are identical to the measures I have used throughout the book. The omitted category for religion is Mainline Protestants and white Catholics. I use these two groups for comparison because, as we have seen, they are remarkably similar to each other on many measures I have explored and because they tend to be at the population average on most dimensions. In the models of family background, I include results in the tables for religious affiliation, race, family income, and family size (number of siblings). I also control for childhood family structure, parents' work status, (full time, part time, unemployed), parents' immigration status, respondent's immigration status, a dichotomous indicator that the respondent did not report childhood family income, gender, age, and region of residence. In the models of adult wealth, I include results in the tables for religious affiliation, race, parents' education, family size, respondent's education, respondent's marital status, and respondent's income. I add to this controls for parents' education and respondent's age at first birth, number of children, age at first marriage, and family work status (i.e., one earner versus two earners).

Table 5.9 shows the association between childhood religion and parents' education (having a bachelor's degree or not). I use childhood religion in these models to show how religious background and childhood SES are related. The table shows that CPs, BPs, and Hispanic Catholics

---

[3] Using other indicators such as years of education produced substantively similar results. I opted to model attainment of bachelor's and advanced degrees because, for the generation that included parents of the NLSY sample, these are important indicators of high socioeconomic status. Modeling the completion of a bachelor's degree and advanced degrees separately produced comparable results, although very few mothers and relatively few fathers had advanced degrees.

TABLE 5.9. *Logistic Regression Models of Parents' Education*

	Father Had a BA		Mother Had a BA	
	Estimate	Standard Error	Estimate	Standard Error
White Conservative Protestant (CP)	−.81***	.04	−1.01***	.08
Black Conservative Protestant (BP)	−1.51***	.14	−1.3***	.20
Catholic, Hispanic	−.37	.23	−.64**	.25
Jewish	1.50***	.57	1.00***	.13
Other religion	1.0***	.07	1.12***	.10
No religion	.15*	.06	.45***	.10
Black	−.04	.09	−.22**	.13
Hispanic	−.57	.21	.26	.22
Family income (log)	.31***	.06	−.01	.01
Siblings (number)	.15***	.01	−.20***	.01

Notes: Data are from the 1979–2004 NLSY. Sample size = 4,369. Religion was measured in 1979. The omitted category for religion is Mainline Protestants and white Catholics (see text for an explanation). Also controlled but not displayed are age, gender, family structure, parents' work status (full time, part time, unemployed), region of residence, parents' immigration status, respondent's immigration status, and a dichotomous indicator that the respondent did not report childhood family income.
*p < .05 **p < .01 ***p < .001

had parents with relatively low education levels, all else held constant. That suggests that people raised in each of these groups had a relatively disadvantaged starting point, compared to MPs and white Catholics. Recall, however, that the substance of the findings does not change when I use different omitted categories. BPs were the most disadvantaged, followed by CPs and then Hispanic Catholics. Respondents raised in Jewish families and in families with some other religion or no religion had more advantaged upbringings. These models highlight two important patterns. First, because the models control for race as well as religion, we can see that the negative effects of being raised BP or Hispanic Catholic persist with controls for being black (i.e., black, non-BP) or Hispanic (i.e., Hispanic, non-Catholic). Indeed, the independent effects of being black or Hispanic are not significant in the model of father's education, and only the effect of being black is significant (and negative) in the model of mother's education. Second, these models again suggest that CPs might have been upwardly mobile in recent years. CPs had less educated parents than Hispanic Catholics, yet we have seen that adult CPs outperform adult Hispanic Catholics on some SES measures. I return to this discussion in Chapter 6.

TABLE 5.10. *Logistic Regression Models of Inheritance*

	Ever Inherited	
	Estimate	Standard Error
White Conservative Protestant (CP)	$-.24^{***}$	.02
Black Conservative Protestant (BP)	–	–
Catholic, Hispanic	–	–
Jewish	1.01^{***}	.02
Other religion	$.24^{**}$	.08
No religion	$-.15^{**}$	.05
Black	–	–
Hispanic	–	–
Father's education	$.83^{***}$	.04
Mother's education		
Siblings (number)	$-.03^{***}$	.01
Education		
High school	$.47^{***}$	.03
Some college	$.79^{***}$	.04
College graduate	1.15^{***}	.04
Advanced degree	1.5^{***}	.05
Married	.004	.02
Family income (log)	$.02^*$	.01

Notes: Data are from the 1979–2004 NLSY. Sample size = 4,369. Religion was measured in 1979. The omitted category for religion is Mainline Protestants and white Catholics (see text for an explanation). Too few blacks and Hispanics in the sample inherited to estimate a race effect. Parents' education refers to having an advanced degree. Also controlled but not displayed are other childhood family income, childhood family structure, parents' other education levels, parents' work status (full time, part time, unemployed), parents' immigration status, respondent's immigration status, a dichotomous indicator that the respondent did not report childhood family income, gender, age, and region of residence.
$^*p < .05$ $^{**}p < .01$ $^{***}p < .001$

Inheriting is another indicator of family background and is another important signal of a person's starting point in life. Multivariate models of inheritance show patterns that are similar to models of parents' education, although these models are more limited because inheriting is somewhat rare. Again the reference category is MPs and white Catholics; those raised as CPs are significantly less likely than the reference group to ever inherit, and those raised as Jews are significantly more likely than the reference group to ever inherit. Using adult religion produces similar results. Again, these findings suggest that CPs started with a relative wealth disadvantage on average, whereas Jews started with a relative advantage. Other factors that are usually related to inheritance are also significant and in the

TABLE 5.11. *GLS Regression Models of Net Worth*

	Total Household Net Worth	
	Estimate	Standard Error
White Conservative Protestant (CP)	−15.3***	5.5
Black Conservative Protestant (BP)	−32.4***	6.7
Catholic, Hispanic	−49.3*	32.9
Jewish	124.6*	55.4
Other religion	−17.0	26.8
No religion	3.6	16.1
Black	−36.3***	7.4
Hispanic	19.0	32.2
Father's education	29.6	16.8
Mother's education	18.1	19.9
Siblings (number)	−2.4*	1.1
Education		
High school	15.7***	4.1
Some college	24.8***	5.9
College graduate	45.4***	8.2
Advanced degree	49.4***	11.9
Married	16.4***	4.3
Family income (log)	11.2***	2.0

Notes: Data are from the 1979–2004 NLSY. Sample size = 4,369. Religion was measured in 1979. The omitted category for religion is Mainline Protestants and white Catholics (see text for an explanation). Also controlled but not displayed are other childhood family income, childhood family structure, parents' other education levels, parents' work status, (full time, part time, unemployed), parents' immigration status, respondent's immigration status, a dichotomous indicator that the respondent did not report childhood family income, gender, age, region of residence, age at first birth, number of children, age at first marriage, and having a two-earner household.
*p < .05 **p < .01 ***p < .001

expected direction. Education, for example, is positively associated with receiving an inheritance, but the causal relationship usually flows from inheritance (i.e., family wealth) to education. Similarly, family income and inheritance tend to be positively related, as they are in this model.

Bringing It All Together: Predictors of Adult Wealth

I proposed in Chapters 2 and 3 that family processes (including family background and adult family processes), race/ethnicity, education, work, and income mediate the relationship between religion and adult wealth ownership. Table 5.11 brings all these processes together in a single model of adult net worth to explore the relative importance of these behaviors and processes. Consistent with my expectations, race/ethnicity is related to adult wealth: Black respondents have significantly less wealth than white respondents. Once other factors are controlled, there is no remaining significant effect of being Hispanic. In preliminary models, parents' education is a significantly positive determinant of adult wealth, but as the results in the table show, parents' education is not significant once other factors are controlled. The effect of siblings is significant and negative, even when other controls are included in the model, consistent with arguments that people from larger families ultimately accumulate less wealth. Respondents' educations and incomes are strong, positive predictors of adult wealth; similarly, married respondents have significantly more wealth than never married, divorced/separated, and widowed respondents. Other control variables are not included in the table but are significant in the expected directions.

Even with all of these factors controlled, religion is a very strong, significant predictor of adult wealth. CPs, BPs, and Hispanic have significantly less wealth than MPs and white Catholics. Jewish respondents have significantly greater wealth than MPs and white Catholics. Preliminary models indicated that the effect of all the religion variables is much stronger prior to the addition of control variables to the model, but that adding controls such as family background, race/ethnicity, education, income, adult family size, and marital status slightly reduces the strength of the religion effect, suggesting that the effect of religion on wealth is mediated by these other processes.

These models highlight an issue that has been a recurrent theme throughout this book: Is religion or race/ethnicity responsible for the patterns we are observing? Naturally, the answer is nuanced and depends on which group we are talking about. For example, blacks tend to own dramatically less wealth than whites in the United States regardless of family background and at all levels of adult income and education. Even controlling for various adult family structure traits, the black-white difference in wealth ownership is extreme (Keister 2005, 2008; Oliver and Shapiro 1995). This suggests that the strong effect of BP on SES outcomes – including wealth – that have become clear throughout this book might reflect race effects rather than religion effects. Table 5.11 can clarify this issue to some degree. The model shown in this table includes separate indicators for BPs and CPs as well as for black race (i.e., non-BP blacks). The BP and CP effects are strong, negative, and significantly different from zero; however, the BP effect is much larger than the CP effect.

More importantly, even with black race controlled, the BP effect is still very strong, negative, and significant. There is no significant difference between the independent BP and black effects. Together, these findings suggest that religion is a very important correlate of wealth, independent of race. Preliminary analyses using separate equations for blacks and whites indicated that the processes that relate religion to wealth are nearly identical for blacks and whites and that separate models did not provide additional information.

Results for Hispanics and Hispanic Catholics are less helpful in clarifying the independent effects of religion and ethnicity. The model shows that there is a very strong, negative, and statistically significant effect of being Hispanic Catholic, but there is no independent effect of being Hispanic, non-Catholic. This is important information, but there are few Hispanic non-Catholics in the sample. As a result, the finding does reflect sample issues more for Hispanic Catholics than for BPs.

A third group for whom ethnicity and religion are comingled is Jews. For many American Jews, Judaism is also an ethnicity (Sklare 1971; Waxman 1983, 2001). Waxman (2001) is particularly interested in the degree to which Jewish identity has waned since the Second World War. He finds evidence that, among Jewish Baby Boomers, there has been a rather significant decline in identification as Jewish. He explores patterns of residential segregation and mobility, socioeconomic behavior, language, and mate selection, and argues that there has been a dramatic waning of a sense of Jewishness in this cohort in recent decades. Yet even if there has been a decline in Jewish ethnic identity, there is still little doubt that Jewishness is an ethnicity, particularly when compared to other dominant religious groupings in the United States such as Protestantism and Catholicism. Unlike other religious groups in the United States, Jews are more likely to live with other Jews, to attend Jewish schools, to have other friends who are also Jewish, and to marry other Jews. For these reasons, it would be useful to be able to distinguish more specifically categories within the Jewish group, because there is evidence that financial behavior varies by Jewish denominations. Waxman (2001) found a difference of about $10,000 a year in income between Reform and Conservative Jews, and a similar difference between Conservative and Orthodox Jews. That means that Reform Jewish families have, on average, $20,000 a year higher income than the Orthodox Jewish families. Waxman also proposes that many of the factors that I discuss with respect to the conservative Protestant similarly account for the lower incomes among the Orthodox Jews. Unfortunately, relatively small sample size makes it very difficult to make more precise denominational distinctions among those who report that they are Jewish.

A related issue to which multivariate models can speak is the relationship between religion and socioeconomic class. If cultural orientation – including religion – is part of social class, the religion effect indicates that class is related to material well-being. In fact, these findings are important because they demonstrate how an important component of social class correlates with material well-being. Yet, my results provide evidence that religion is not a strict proxy for economic class: Religion is significant despite controls for class background (parents' education, income, work) and adult class (welfare receipt, occupation, rural residence). I experimented with other class controls (e.g., childhood welfare receipt, parent's occupation, childhood residence, income quintile), but none of these improved model fit or reduced the religion effect. I have also experimented with including restrictive inheritance measures, and the religion effect is still strong. Because class is an amorphous concept, it is difficult to conclude with certainty that religion is independent of class. However, these results suggest that religion is an important and unique correlate of wealth ownership.

Multivariate models of the components of net worth provide additional evidence of the patterns that Table 5.11 summarizes. Models of homeownership (both the primary residence and other residential property), home value, business ownership, the value of business assets, owning cash accounts, the value of cash accounts, owning stocks and stock mutual funds, the value of stocks and stock mutual funds, owning other financial assets, and the value of other financial assets suggest a ranking of religious groups consistent with the ranking that is clear in the models of total net work. Because the information is largely consistent with the results in Table 5.11, I do not include separate tables. Once all other control variables (i.e., those controlled in net worth models described earlier) are held constant, CPs and BPs are significantly less likely than MPs and mainline Catholics to own residential property, businesses, cash accounts, stocks and stock mutual funds, and other financial assets. Moreover, when they do own these assets, the value is significantly less than for MPs and white Catholics. With no control variables, Hispanic Catholics are also less likely than MPs and white Catholics to own these assets and, for owners, to have lower value assets. However, the effect of being Hispanic Catholic is no longer statistically significant once other factors, particularly education level, are controlled. At the other end of the spectrum, Jews are more likely than MPs and white Catholics to own each of these assets and have higher-value assets with all other factors controlled. One exception is that the effect of being Jewish on owning the primary residence is negative but is only marginally significant – that is, Jews are somewhat less likely than MPs and white Catholics to own their primary home. However, when they are homeowners, Jews own homes that are significantly greater in value than the homes owned by other respondents. This effect is constant across geographic regions and does not reflect an overrepresentation of Jewish families living in New York City. However, Jews do have a higher empirical propensity to reside in urban areas, and the control for urban residence does absorb some of this effect. I explore unique Jewish patterns of achievement in more detail in Chapter 7.

6

Upward Mobility

Social change can provide valuable insight into the processes that generate well-being. When a person or, perhaps more importantly, an entire group changes social position, the events and conditions that created that change may provide clues into basic but otherwise difficult-to-study social processes. Imagine a simple example of a group that experiences an increase in average education levels; this change is likely to lead to a subsequent change in income for both individuals and households and, ultimately, to an increase in wealth. If other factors are held constant, this change may underscore the conditions under which educational attainment affects income and wealth attainment or mobility. *Social mobility* is the general term used to describe movement in a person or a group's social standing over time and usually refers to changes in education, income, occupation, wealth, and other SES measures. *Wealth mobility* – a change in position in the wealth distribution – is a specific type of social mobility, one that has been relatively rare throughout most of history. *Upward wealth mobility*, as the term suggests, implies an improvement in conditions over time, whereas *downward wealth mobility* is a decline in well-being. *Intergenerational wealth mobility* refers to changes in wealth status between parents and children; *intragenerational wealth mobility* is changes in wealth within a single generation. Both intergenerational and intragenerational mobility are still unusual today, because social reproduction is a powerful generator of stability. As I pointed out in Chapter 2, inheritance, cross-generational reproduction of educational and occupational status, parenting styles, and educational processes lead to social reproduction and limit wealth mobility.

Although social mobility of any sort is uncommon, there are note-worthy instances in which groups have changed positions in the wealth distribution. These unique cases are important because they highlight the processes that lead to change and also provide evidence for more general patterns that underlie social processes. In this chapter, I take advantage of the unique opportunities created by changes in the wealth ownership of members of three religious groups to study the relationship between religion and wealth. First, I discuss a group for whom mobility appears to be complete. That is, I look closely at non-Hispanic white Catholics (i.e., white Catholics), a group that was upwardly mobile in the wealth distribution in recent decades. Less than a generation ago, white Catholics were relatively disadvantaged on many measures of well-being, particularly relative to Mainline Protestants (Glenn and Hyland 1967; Lenski 1961; Sherkat and Ellison 1999). In recent years, however, white Catholics experienced dramatic changes in important demographic behaviors that affect wealth ownership, including fertility, education, and income. Previous research (D'Antonio, Hoge, and Davidson 2007; Keister 2007) and much of the evidence I have presented in previous chapters of this book suggest that white Catholics are no longer asset-poor and may even be among the wealthiest groups of adults in the United States today (Sherkat and Ellison 1999; Keister 2003b, 2005). In this chapter, I update previous research and look closely at the degree to which wealth ownership has changed for this group. I also explore the factors that explain their mobility.

Second, I study two groups for whom wealth mobility may be in process: CPs and Hispanic Catholics. There is no previous research evidence to suggest that these groups have been upwardly mobile; indeed, most previous work shows both groups rank relatively low on standard measures of well-being and attainment. However, the empirical findings that I have presented so far in this book suggest that there are at least the beginnings of mobility for both groups. I spend time in this chapter presenting additional evidence to ascertain the extent and potential causes of this mobility, and I offer some ideas for the future potential for additional changes. CPs and Hispanic Catholics are likely to be different in the degree to which they have been upwardly mobile, given patterns that I have found in previous chapters. It is likely that CPs have experienced more mobility than Hispanic Catholics but less than white Catholics. In this chapter, I also investigate whether this is true and why. I conclude the chapter with a brief discussion of some more general underlying processes that are operative when the wealth ownership of a group changes.

That is, I talk about whether the changes we see reflect rising tides or groups trading places: It is possible that changing wealth reflects general improvements in economic conditions that benefit all groups; alternatively, one group might move up while another moves down. The three examples that occupy the bulk of my discussion are examples of upward mobility, or an increase in relative position in the wealth distribution. Of course, an upward change for one group implies that at least someone experienced downward mobility. I briefly address which groups have been downwardly mobile and which have stayed in a relatively constant position. A final note: I use the NLSY in this chapter because it is in that data that the changes I study are evident.

Mobility Accomplished: White Catholics since the 1980s

Demographic changes appear to be an important reason that white Catholics have been upwardly mobile. For example, family behaviors and processes have changed in important ways in recent decades for this group, and as I showed in Chapters 1 and 2, family outcomes are important predictors of wealth accumulation. In prior generations, white Catholics tended to have larger families than MPs (Alwin 1986; Lenski 1961; Sherkat and Ellison 1999), but as I showed in Chapter 2, they are now similar to MPs in their propensity to remain childless and the age at which they first have children (Lehrer 1996; Pearce 2010; Sherkat and Ellison 1999). Total fertility for white Catholics is also now comparable to that of MPs (Mosher, Williams, and Johnson 1992; Sander 1995; Sherkat and Ellison 1999). The reasons for these changes are not perfectly clear, but there is some consensus that assimilation is an important part of the story. Most white Catholic adults are now two to three generations from immigration (Alba 1981), and distance from the immigrant experience can create fertility changes (Borjas 1999, 2000). Many white Catholics have retained their religious identity as Catholic while adopting an American ethnic identity, which has contributed to assimilation. This separation of religious and ethnic identity is unique in the particulars but is somewhat similar in process to the assimilation of other religious-ethnic groups such as Italian Protestants (Form 2000). Whatever their origin, fertility changes can facilitate wealth accumulation and lead to upward wealth mobility. Similarly, marriage behaviors matter for wealth ownership and are an important part of the mobility trends experienced by white Catholics. White Catholics have somewhat high marriage rates, high rates of marital stability, low divorce rates, and high rates of homogamy (Lehrer 1998; Sherkat 2004; Sherkat and Ellison 1999).

Education and educational changes also likely contribute to wealth mobility for white Catholics. Both men and women raised in white Catholic families have achieved high levels of education in recent years, even though white Catholics tended to have parents who achieved relatively modest levels of education (Lehrer 1999; Sherkat and Ellison 1999). This has translated into increases in wage and salaries that are likely to affect wealth ownership (Ewing 2000). Again, distance from the immigrant experience may be part of the explanation for Catholic educational achievement (Borjas 1999, 2000). There are also important advantages of Catholic school attendance. Attending Catholic school is associated with higher test scores (Bryk, Lee, and Hollan 1993; Hoffer, Greeley, and Coleman 1985; Sander 1995), higher probabilities of completing high school and attending college (Evans and Schwab 1995; Neal 1997), increased rates of college graduation (Neal 1997), and higher adult salaries and wages (Neal 1997). The success of Catholic school students may be a result of stricter discipline, increased social capital produced by dense parental networks, and governance structures that allow for more parental choice and consensus than is possible in public schools (Coleman, Hoffer, and Kilgore 1982a, 1982b). More recent work suggests that relatively high levels of religiosity (which tends to be positively correlated with general well-being, see Chapter 8) may underlie the Catholic school effect (Altonji, Elder, and Taber 2005; Cohen-Zada and Sander 2008). As a result, some researchers have raised objections to this finding, but the empirical relationship between attending Catholic school and educational achievement is highly robust. Although not all people raised in Catholic families attended Catholic schools, the majority of those who were Catholic and elementary school age in the 1970s did. Indeed 60 percent of American Catholics surveyed in 1999 had attended Catholic school as a child for at least a short period of time, and 36 percent had attended seven or more years (D'Antonio et al. 2001; Greeley 2004).

The importance of education for Catholics is highlighted by the reality that many Catholic religious orders promote education in both their teachings and the activities they support (Coleman 1993; Greeley 2004). The Franciscans and Jesuits are particularly well known for their involvement in education, but devotion to running schools and colleges with secular as well as social and religious missions is central to nearly every Catholic religious order. The Catholic commitment to education originally developed as way to deal with existential questions about human existence as early as the 1200s, and the tradition has remained an integral part of the faith since (Bryk, Lee, and Hollan 1993). There is a history of Catholic immigrants to America encouraging their children to pursue educational opportunities, and from the late 1800s on, both male and female Catholics began to enter colleges and universities at increasing rates (Oats 1989). There are no apparent gender differences in the encouragement of lay educational pursuits, either, and if there are gender differences in educational success among Catholics, they favor girls (Bryk, Lee, and Hollan 1993). There are certainly gender differences among Catholics, most apparent in the restriction on women becoming priests. Yet female religious leaders such as nuns do pursue education themselves, and they do contribute to Catholic education goals by becoming teachers, school administrators, and pursuing other education-related careers (Hamington 1995).

Finally, there may be a connection between unique white Catholic orientations toward work and money and upward wealth mobility. Some have argued that compared to other religious groups, white Catholics tend to have an instrumental attitude toward both work and money. That is, there is evidence that Catholics approach work as an activity that produces a result rather than something that is pleasurable in itself (Tropman 1995, 2002). Work is a way to earn money to buy necessary things. Catholics also tend to have a strong orientation toward family, and their motivation to work is extrinsic, usually oriented toward the family (Tropman 2002). Again, some of this family orientation may derive from the recent immigrant experience and the strong ethnic ties that immigration involved (Borjas 1999, 2000). While white non-Hispanic Catholics have largely assimilated, there is some evidence that the strong family focus has persisted (Tropman 2002). Although an instrumental attitude toward work might reduce the incentive to work, the added effect of a strong family orientation has lead Catholics to work relatively hard (D'Antonio et al. 2001; Greeley 1979). They may satisfice at work (Tropman 1995) – that is, Catholics may work only as long or as hard as necessary to provide for their families – but they work hard nonetheless (D'Antonio et al. 2001). Egalitarian gender roles suggest that there are also likely to be two earners in Catholic households with two adults (Oats 1989), and wealth research shows that having two earners is an important predictor of asset accumulation (Keister 2005). Together, hard work and having two earners suggests that Catholics will have sufficient income to save and accumulate assets.

Similarly, Catholics have an instrumental attitude toward money. As with work, there is evidence that Catholics tend to see money as a means to acquire necessities (Tropman 1995, 2002). Money is necessary to meet needs, but it is only a tool rather than something with intrinsic value (DeBerri and Hug 2003; Thibodeau, O'Donnell, and O'Connor 1997). Again, the strong family orientation is important in speculating about how this value will shape wealth ownership. Catholics tend to save in order to care for their families (Tropman 2002). That is, although an instrumental view of money might reduce saving, having a strong extrinsic motivation will, in contrast, lead Catholics to save and invest in ways that will ensure their families are secure. This suggests that there should be a direct effect of religious affiliation on wealth for Catholics.

In addition, their instrumental attitude toward money suggests that Catholics tend to save in ways that are relatively low-risk. For example, Catholics are likely to prefer homeownership and stable financial investments (e.g., investments with guaranteed rates of return from banks) to volatile financial investments (e.g., stocks) because they can meet their needs without unnecessarily risking their capital. In addition, the Catholic church does not have a strong tradition of tithing that would dilute the amount of income available to save in Catholic families (Chaves and Miller 1999; D'Antonio et al. 2001). There is some evidence that Catholics are community-oriented (Greeley 1989; Tropman 2002) and may be relatively more likely to volunteer and otherwise be generous (Nelson and Greene 2003; Regnerus, Smith, and Sikkink 1998). Yet there is little evidence that tithing reduces their disposable income in a way that would slow wealth accumulation (Steen 1996).

Data that I have presented in previous chapters of this book suggests that white Catholics are indeed well positioned on important measures of SES. White Catholics have relatively high education levels and are comparably likely to have advanced degrees (Table 2.5). They have relatively high-prestige occupations (Table 3.3), high household incomes (Table 3.7), are relatively unlikely to receive government transfer payments (Table 3.8), and have high individual earnings for both men and women (Table 3.9). White Catholics also have fairly high wealth. They have high net worth (Table 4.1), low levels of asset poverty (Table 4.2), high rates of homeownership (Table 4–6), high home values (Table 4–7), and high home equity (Table 4.8). Finally, it was clear in Chapter 5 that white Catholics also have relatively high levels of financial assets. Their total financial assets are high (Tables 5.1 and 5.2) and their debt levels are low (Table 5.7). One exception is their ownership of high-risk assets

TABLE 6.1. *Logistic Regressions of Family Background Traits, NLSY 1979–2004*

	Father's Education		Mother's Education		Ever Inherited	
	Estimate	Standard Error	Estimate	Standard Error	Estimate	Standard Error
Catholic, white	−.43***	.04	−.69***	.07	−.10***	.03
White Conservative Protestant (CP)	−.99***	.05	−1.28***	.10	−.29***	.06
Jewish	1.22***	.08	.48***	.14	.97***	.13
Other religion	.92***	.08	.92***	.11	0.19*	.11
No religion	−.17***	.09	.35***	.10	−.20***	.05

Notes: Data are from the 1979–2004 NLSY. Sample is 4,745 white, nonimmigrant respondents who reported religion as Roman Catholic in 1979. The omitted category for religion is Mainline Protestants (see text for an explanation). Also controlled but not displayed are age, gender, family structure, parents' work status (full time, part time, unemployed), region of residence, parents' immigration status, respondent's immigration status, and a dichotomous indicator that the respondent did not report childhood family income.
*p < .05 **p < .01 ***p < .001.

such as bonds, stocks, and stock mutual funds. White Catholics are comparable to the overall NLSY sample in their ownership of these assets (Table 5.5), consistent with a group that has been upwardly mobile and with the argument that white Catholics may have an instrumental orientation toward money and investing.

Any advantage white Catholics have today is a change from prior generations. Table 6.1 provides an example of the sort of evidence that can be used to demonstrate relative disadvantage in prior generations. The table shows how childhood religion is related to parents' education; the dependent variables for the two models are whether the respondent's biological father and biological mother had advanced degrees. The analyses are a revised version of the analyses presented in Table 5.9 but use a different omitted category for religion to highlight the childhood SES of white Catholics. In Table 5.9, recall that white Catholics and MPs were the omitted category. In Table 6.1, MPs are omitted. All variables that I discussed in Chapter 5 and that I controlled for in the results presented in Table 5.9 are controlled in the models presented in Table 6.1. Similarly, Table 6.1 includes a revised model of the model presented in Table 5.10 in which the dependent variable is ever inheriting. Again, the model in Table 6.1 is identical to the model in Table 5.10, including all control variables, except the omitted category for religion in Table 6.1 is MPs only. The results in Table 6.1 provide strong evidence that compared to MPs, white Catholics were likely to have parents who did not have high

TABLE 6.2. *Wealth Mobility: White Catholics versus All Respondents (%)*

	All Respondents	White Catholics
Quintile 1 to Quintile 4 or 5	24	31***
Quintile 2 to Quintile 4 or 5	26	33**
Quintile 3 to Quintile 4 or 5	37	44**

Notes: Data are from the 1979–2004 NLSY. Sample size = 4,369. Cells indicate the percent of respondents who were in the first quintile in the distribution of net worth in 1985 and in the either of the second quintiles in 2004.
**p < .01 ***p < .001.

education levels; white Catholics were also less likely than MPs to ever inherit. Moreover, using other measures of childhood status (e.g., family income, parents' occupational prestige) produced similar results. Taken together, these results provide important evidence that Catholics were raised in relatively disadvantaged families.

Perhaps more interestingly, white Catholics have experienced relatively high levels of intragenerational wealth mobility. That is, non-Hispanic whites raised in Catholic families have moved up in the wealth distribution more rapidly than average. Table 6.2 compares the percentage of Catholics who were upwardly mobile between 1985 and 2004 to the percentage of the entire NLSY cross-sectional sample who were upwardly mobile. I used 1985 as a starting point because all respondents were at least twenty years old in that year and could be considered adults, and I used 2004 as the end year because it is the most recent year for which data are available. These points capture the sample at early adulthood and when most were in their prime working years and had at least begun to establish their net worth portfolios. I first show the percentage of respondents who moved from the bottom quintile of the distribution of wealth (i.e., net worth, or total assets less total debts) to either of the top two quintiles of the distribution. Of those in the full sample, 24 percent were in the bottom quintile of wealth owners in 1985 and in one of the top two quintiles in 2004. For white Catholics, the number of upwardly mobile respondents was 31 percent. Similarly, a significantly larger percentage of Catholics moved from the second quintile (33 percent) and third quintile (44 percent) to either the fourth or fifth quintiles. The results are comparable if I compare movement in the distribution at comparable ages (e.g., between the ages of twenty-five and thirty-five or between the ages

TABLE 6.3. *White Catholics: GLS Regressions of Adult Net Worth, NLSY*
1985–2004

	Base Model		Add Education, Family	
	Estimate	Standard Error	Estimate	Standard Error
Catholic, white	23.14***	5.41	16.08*	7.12
Mainline/Liberal Protestant (MP)	15.72**	6.18	7.97	7.39
Jewish	100.98*	41.89	107.3*	56.37
Other religion	5.36	23.30	−9.55	34.43
No religion	10.35	16.76	20.70	18.61
Fertility				
Age at first birth	–	–	−0.23***	.03
Number of children	–	–	17.61***	5.47
Number of children (square)	–	–	−2.00*	1.07
Marriage				
Ever married	–	–	17.04*	8.34
Number of marital changes	–	–	−13.40**	5.75
Both Catholic	–	–	13.17*	7.42
Education				
College degree	–	–	59.04***	9.00
Advanced degree	–	–	60.23***	13.16
Financial resources				
Family income (log)	–	–	14.23***	2.70
Two–earner household	–	–	.41***	.13

Notes: Data are from the 1979–2004 NLSY. Sample size is 4,745 white, nonimmigrant respondents who reported religion as Roman Catholic in 1979. The omitted category for religion is CPs, BPs, and Hispanic Catholics (see text for an explanation). Also controlled but not displayed are other childhood family income, childhood family structure, parents' education, parents' work status, (full time, part time, unemployed), parents' immigration status, a dichotomous indicator that the respondent did not report childhood family income, gender, age, other marital statuses and education levels, and region of residence.
*p < .05 **p < .01 ***p < .001.

of thirty-five and forty-five for those with valid data for each year). As the NLSY sample continues to age, their wealth will increase and these differences are likely to become even more pronounced.

How do white Catholics compare to other groups in terms of wealth accumulation? Table 6.3 provides some evidence; the tables includes results of two multivariate models that both use total household net worth as the dependent. The models are comparable to the models presented in Table 5.11, but the omitted category for religion was MPs and white Catholics in Table 5.11 and is CPs in Table 6.3. I change the omitted category to focus on the wealth accumulation of white Catholics. The models presented in Table 6.3 is also a more restricted sample; that is, I estimated the models on only white, nonimmigrant respondents to the NLSY to isolate the wealth accumulation processes unique to white Catholics. I include two models to assess the relative importance of religion and other demographic behaviors and processes, including fertility behavior, marriage behavior, education, and financial processes.

The first model shown in Table 6.3 shows that white Catholics have an important wealth advantage controlling only for basic individual attributes (e.g., childhood family income, childhood family structure, parents' education, parents' work status, parents' immigration status, a dichotomous indicator that the respondent did not report childhood family income, gender, age) and religion. The coefficient estimate for white Catholic is positive and significant, and it is larger than the coefficient for Mainline Protestant. Table 6.1 showed that white Catholics grew up in lower-status families than MPs, but Table 6.3 provides evidence that white Catholics have equal or greater adult wealth than MPs. Even though the descriptive statistics shown throughout Chapters 4 and 5 suggested that average wealth for Catholics and Mainline Protestants is comparable, the multivariate results in Table 6.3 suggest that whites raised in Catholic families have significantly more wealth than we would expect *given their other background traits.*

The second model in Table 6.3 introduces measures of respondents' fertility, marriage behavior, education, and adult financial resources. The measure for the age at first birth is positive and significant. Similarly, the coefficient estimate for the number of children ever born is positive, while its square is negative and significant. Each of these patterns is consistent with other research that shows that having children reduces wealth but that the effect of the number of children is curvilinear (i.e., increases initially but then tapers off) (Keister 2005). More importantly, the effect of a Catholic upbringing on adult wealth is weaker in Model 2 of Table 6.3 than in the basic model (Model 1). This indicates that at least part of the effect of being white Catholic on adult wealth (shown in Table 6.3, Model 1) is a result of the effect of fertility processes on wealth. This finding is consistent with other research on the advantages Catholics have in earnings and provides support for my proposal that fertility patterns contributed to wealth mobility for Catholics.

Marriage behaviors and processes also intercede between religion and wealth for white Catholics. Table 6.3, Model 2 also introduces three indicators of marriage behavior to the basic model to assess the importance of marriage. Consistent with prior research and with my arguments, the indicator that the respondent was ever married is positive and significant, and the indicator of the number of marital transitions prior to the current year is negative and significant. Likewise, the indicator of marital homogamy (respondent and spouse are both Catholic) is positive and significant. Controlling for all three variables in the same equation allows me to appropriately model homogamy and transitions for those who have never been married without assigning missing values to those respondents. I do not control for respondents who were ever divorced because the effect is captured by the measure of transitions. However, in separate models (not shown), the measure of ever divorced produces results that are consistent with my other findings. Again, the introduction of these variables reduces the strength of the effect of the variable, indicating that the respondent was raised in a Catholic family. Statistical tests (Cox tests) confirm that this difference is statistically significant. The addition of the marriage variables also contributes (with the introduction of the fertility variables) to reducing the strength of the religion indicator, suggesting that marriage accounts for a portion of the religion effect. Notably, however, the religion effect remains strong.

Education, income, and work behavior also affect the relationship between religion and wealth for white Catholics. Table 6.3, Model 2 also introduces measures of educational attainment, household income, and a dichotomous indicator that both members of a couple work (where the respondent is married; controlling for marital status accounts for other family types such as never married and divorced respondents). The results included in Table 6.3 show that, compared to those with less than a high school education, those with a college degree or more education have significantly more wealth. The models also control for having a high school degree and for having some college. I do not display all the results, to save space, but consistent with other research, the effect of each of these indicators is positive and strongly statistically significant. Similarly, the measures for total household income and having two earners are both positive and significantly different from zero. These findings are consistent with other research on the advantages white Catholics have in earnings (Lehrer 1996) and provide support for my proposal that educational mobility and work behaviors contributed to wealth mobility for this generation of white Catholics. Upward educational mobility improves occupational outcomes, including occupational prestige and income. Highly educated people also tend to experience greater career stability and enjoy greater benefits such as opportunities to save before taxes in instruments such as 403(b) accounts. It is also possible that being Catholic signals desirable traits that employers seek. As Ewing (2000) argues, employers may see Catholics as disciplined, honest, trustworthy, and motivated. Ultimately these patterns lead to wealth accumulation and upward wealth mobility for white Catholics. The education, income, and work measures also contribute to the reduction in the strength of the effect of being white Catholic. In separate models (not shown), I introduced fertility, marriage, and education variables separately. Each set of variables reduced the religion effect. I do not display each set of findings, to conserve space.

In additional models that I do not show here, I find that white Catholics own somewhat unique combinations of assets – a pattern that contributes to their total net worth. I suggested that an instrumental orientation toward money would lead Catholics to save in ways that are relatively low-risk, and my results provide strong support for this argument. Logistic models of three dichotomous dependent variables (the home, saving and checking accounts, and stock/mutual fund ownership) and general linear models of three linear dependent variables provide evidence for this argument. Each model includes the religion measures and all control variables including family background, education, and adult variables. The results show that Catholics are more likely than CPs to own a home and cash accounts (e.g., checking and savings accounts). Both of these assets are considered low-risk, whereas stocks and related financial instruments are higher-risk assets. The value of the housing and cash assets that white Catholics own are also significantly higher than those owned by CPs, suggesting that these assets play a central role in the portfolios of Catholics. On the contrary, white Catholics are more likely to own stocks and mutual funds, but the value of their holdings are not significantly larger than for other groups. Together, these findings suggest that white Catholics do have portfolios that emphasize relatively low-risk stocks, likely reflecting their instrumental attitude toward money.

Because it is rare for an entire group to make such a dramatic move in the wealth distribution, the changes white Catholics experienced in recent years provide important information about the factors that lead to mobility. White Catholics are largely descendents of Irish, Italian, German, and Polish immigrants who arrived in the United States starting in the 1840s and 1850s and initially settled in ethnic communities in medium-sized and large cities in the Northeast (Alba 1981). I mentioned earlier that distance from the immigrant experience may have facilitated the fertility changes and education patterns. Yet Catholics are still close enough to their relatives who immigrated to retain some values that derive from recent immigration. Both male and female Catholic immigrants worked primarily in manufacturing jobs and quickly established themselves as hard-working and reliable (Oats 1989). It is also notable that immigrant Catholic women participated in the labor force and in labor movements in relatively high numbers, primarily in textile and garment mills and as domestic servants. The early participation of women in the workforce set the stage for rather rapid assimilation by increasing household earnings and contributing to occupational opportunities (Oats 1989). There is some evidence that Catholic immigrants also developed a pro-assimilation, pro-education ethic that they actively and consciously passed along to younger Catholics (Kennelly 1989; Oats 1989). Although it is difficult to determine with certainty whether a pro-assimilation ethic contributed to this transformation, it is clear that the change has been rather pronounced. The change in wealth ownership is consistent with this history.

An important question about white Catholics is: What happens next? Will this group continue to move up in the wealth distribution, or is there likely to be a threshold? There are certain to continue to be important changes for white Catholics if only those originating from simultaneous increases in wealth and decreases in fertility. For example, given that more white Catholics are remaining childless and accumulating sizable fortunes, there are likely to be more inheritances not left to offspring. Perhaps nieces and nephews will benefit, but white Catholics have fewer nieces and nephews as well, suggesting that some of these fortunes will benefit organizations such as universities and churches. There is some evidence that white Catholics are generous with their time but less inclined than members of other faiths to contribute sizable amounts to their churches (Chaves and Miller 1999; Tropman 1995), but growing net worth and declining fertility may change the nature of donations for white Catholics. Currently, the data needed to answer these questions are not available, but future research may be able to explore how white Catholics and their churches change going forward.

Will white Catholics continue to move up in the wealth distribution? If they have an instrumental attitude toward work and money, there is a possibility that they will not continue to increase their wealth but will be satisfied with being rich enough. Other priorities – such as family – may continue to be more important, and they might simply accumulate enough wealth to have a secure financial cushion. Moreover, if their propensity to invest in relatively low-risk assets is an enduring preference rather than a characteristic of an upwardly mobile group, the upward wealth trajectory is unlikely to continue to increase at the rate it has in the recent past. Rather, it is likely that white Catholics will continue to accumulate assets much like Mainline Protestants, making the two groups increasingly similar. Alternatively, if recent Catholic attitudes toward work and money reflect their working-class past, it is possible that increasing numbers of Catholics will move into the highest levels of the wealth distribution. If Catholics continue to excel in education, for instance, they will continue to gain occupational prestige and to adopt attitudes toward work and money that are similar to MPs or Jews who are more likely to have pro-accumulation attitudes.

Mobility in Progress? Conservative Protestants May Be Changing

Throughout this book, I have discussed CPs as an important group of related denominations that are quite similar on many dimensions of SES, including wealth. In particular, CPs tend to have relatively low SES. CPs are worth examining more closely because this is a large and growing group of denominations and because some of the evidence I presented in prior chapters suggests their position in the wealth distribution might be changing. In this section, I begin by exploring the processes that account for the relatively low SES position CPs have occupied, including a brief summary of the family, education, and work processes that I have addressed already and a new discussion of saving and accumulation patterns. I then discuss the prospects for upward mobility for this group and speculate about future patterns.

First, CPs have tended to have unique education, family, work, and income patterns that have predisposed them to low wealth. Like white Catholics, CPs tend to come from relatively disadvantaged families. I showed this using descriptive statistics in Chapter 2, and multivariate models I presented earlier in this chapter confirm these patterns. In particular, recall the logistic regressions shown in Table 6.1. The findings in that table show that, like white Catholics, CPs had parents with low educations and have been relatively unlikely to ever inherit, controlling for many other factors that influence family SES. Recall that this table is a multivariate version of tables presented in Chapter 2 and is similar to Tables 5.9 and 5.10 but with omitted categories for religion selected to focus on CPs (and white Catholics). Also, like white Catholics, CPs were relatively disadvantaged on other measures of well-being in childhood, including family income and other resource measures, not shown here to conserve space.

Educational attainment, fertility, and marriage processes have tended to keep wealth low for CPs as they enter and move through adulthood. Members of CP churches have a history of completing somewhat less education, particularly advanced degrees, than those from other faiths. Some have argued that this pattern reflects a conflict in cultural orientation between CPs beliefs and the approaches of secular schools and universities that propagate secular humanist values (Sikkink 1999) and promote scientific investigation rather than acceptance of divine truths (Darnell and Sherkat 1997). Family behaviors have also predisposed CPs to low wealth. CPs have tended to have children relatively early (Pearce 2010) and to have large families (Lehrer 1996; Marcum 1981, 1986). Moreover, because they tend to value a relatively traditional division of labor (Ellison and Bartkowski 2002; Gallagher and Smith 1999), CP women have tended to participate in paid work outside the home at low rates, particularly when their children are young (Lehrer 1995). Although CPs are similar to white Catholics on important family background measures, CPs have not had the rapid increase in SES over their adult lives. Most research, including the results I present in this book, shows that CPs have been relatively low on many measures of adult wealth. The findings I presented in Chapters 4 and 5 largely confirm this pattern.

Second, CPs have unique saving and accumulation patterns that have limited wealth accumulation. Saving from current income and resulting asset growth are perhaps the best predictors of total adult wealth. In fact, discussions of the behaviors that affect wealth usually imply that these behaviors affect saving even if the connection is not explicit. CP education, family, and work behaviors will reduce the availability of funds to save. There may also be an intergenerational effect on saving for CPs. People learn to save from their parents and other family members (Chiteji and Stafford 1999, 2000), and a large majority of CPs remain affiliated with their childhood religion as adults or return to their childhood religion after a brief departure (Roof 1989; Sherkat 1991). As a result, saving is likely to have been low in prior generations of CPs for the same demographic reasons that it is low in current generations. As these patterns cumulate across generations, they will reduce active saving in each generation, and the resulting low wealth will diminish asset transfers across generations. Finally, CPs are unlikely to marry people of other religions and thus

TABLE 6.4. *CPs and Asset Growth: Multilevel Growth Models of Asset Growth Rate, 1985–2004*

	Estimate	Standard Error
White Conservative Protestant (CP)	2.44*	1.05
Year*White Conservative Protestant (CP)	− 4.00***	.75
Black Conservative Protestant (BP)	14.20*	7.01
Year*Black Conservative Protestant (BP)	− 9.40***	.71
Year	5.77***	1.22

Notes: Data are from the 1979–2004 NLSY. Sample size is 4,369. Dependent variable is yearly asset growth. In models 3 and 4, black refers to black non-CPs. Standard errors are in parentheses. Models include 6,111 respondents or 73,332 (6,111*12 years) observations. Also controlled but not displayed are gender, age, nonreport of income, region of residence, and immigrant status for respondent and parents.
$^+$p < .1 *p < .05 **p < .01 ***p < .001.

unlikely to expand their repertoire of skills and strategies by marrying someone with a different tool kit (Kalmijn 1991; Thornton 1985).

Table 6.4 uses a unique type of multivariate model to explore how saving and accumulation vary by religion, with a focus on CPs. To model asset growth (Table 6.4), I used NLSY data and multilevel growth models (Singer 1998). These models allow me to isolate the effect of religion on the growth in asset values over time during adulthood (1985 through 2004). I estimated these models in SAS Proc Mixed. The general structure of the multilevel growth models is the same as the net worth models that I presented in previous chapters, but the growth models treat both the intercept and the slope as random effects. This is equivalent to interacting specified individual-level effects with time (year). These models facilitate studying asset accumulation by providing estimates of the effects of covariates on both the initial value and the growth rate of the dependent variable (with other effects controlled). I included measures of (1) religion and (2) an interaction between religion and time. The interpretation is: (1) the effect of religious background on the initial (1985) value of net worth, other covariates controlled, and (2) the effect of religion on the growth rate of net worth (between 1985 and 2004), other covariates controlled.[1]

The results presented in Table 6.4 provide evidence that CPs accumulate assets during adulthood slower than people from other religious

[1] The White's test was significant, and the Ordinary Durbin-Watson indicated first-order autocorrelation. I corrected using the estimator option and assuming an AR(1) process.

backgrounds with otherwise comparable demographic traits. The model
shown in this table indicates that those raised in CP families start their
adult lives (using 1985 as the base) with more assets than their other
demographic characteristics would predict ($\beta = 2.36$), but that they accumulate assets significantly slower during adulthood than the omitted category ($\beta = -4.00$). Separate models, not shown, separate the effects
for CPs and BPs and show that both start with relatively high wealth in
1985 and accumulate slowly. In both asset growth models, I control for
growth over time by all groups by including a measure of year, and the
estimate for the time variable is significant and positive in both models.
Yet even with these strict controls, the CP effects are very strong and
highly significant.

It is also possible to look at how religious mobility (changes in religion
over time) affects wealth for CPs as a way to underscore the importance of
religion. I have proposed elsewhere (Keister 2008) that if religion affects
wealth, there should be different relative effects for those who: (1) were
CP in both childhood and adulthood, (2) left CP churches after childhood
(apostates), and (3) became CPs as adults. All three groups should have
low wealth compared to MPs and white Catholics who were never CP.
I argued that it is likely that those who were CP in both childhood and
adulthood will have the lowest wealth because long-term affiliation is
likely to reinforce the values and behaviors that reduce wealth. I showed
that all three groups of CPs have relatively low wealth. I also showed that
those who remained affiliated with CP denominations between childhood
and adulthood had the lowest wealth of the three groups, suggesting that
the continuous (or renewed) effect of exposure to CP values has the
strongest effect on adult wealth. Although religious mobility varies by
race (Sherkat 1991), I found no significant difference between white and
black CPs in the effect of religious mobility on wealth in exploratory
analyses. I acknowledged that these findings do not provide conclusive
evidence of a causal relationship between religion and wealth, but they
are consistent with the patterns that should emerge if there is a direct
effect of religion on net wealth ownership of other individual and family
influences.

Although most of my evidence suggests that CPs still have a wealth
disadvantage, there is some evidence that this might be changing. CPs
have tended to have education levels, fertility and marriage patterns,
and work and income patterns that are consistent with low wealth; the
descriptive evidence I presented in Chapters 2 and 3 show that the gap

between CPs and MPs/white Catholics on many of these determinants of wealth ownership is not as pronounced as previous research has reported it to be (Keister 2008; Lehrer 2009). Moreover, the descriptive statistics from Chapters 4 and 5 show that most measures of real and financial wealth are lower for CPs than for MPs and white Catholics, but again the gap is not as pronounced as previous research demonstrated it was in the 1990s and early 2000s (Keister, 2008; Lehrer 2004a; Lehrer 2010). The multivariate models show that once other factors are controlled, CPs do have significantly less wealth than MPs and white Catholics, but the descriptive statistics are close enough to raise questions about future patterns.

What is happening? Are the gaps really closing and, if so, are all CPs changing? That is, are there differences across the various groups that comprise the very large group of churches I call CP? There are certainly important doctrinal differences among the groups; if church doctrine affects attitudes and orientations toward education, family, work, and money, there might be within-group differences (i.e., within the CP group). However, there is simply very little of this variation within the data. Extensive data exploration and analyses (not shown) indicate that CPs are much more similar to each other than to other groups on nearly all the measures I discuss in this book. Providing detailed breakdowns by type of CP offers almost no additional information.

Are the gaps really closing? Two patterns have emerged in the scholarly literature recently, which provide reason to imagine the gaps might be closing. First, research on elites provides a small kernel of evidence suggesting change might be occurring. Specifically, Lindsay (2008) explores whether there is an increase in CPs in the power elite (he uses the term Evangelicals, but we are largely talking about the same group of people). He conducted interviews with 360 elite informants, including former U.S. presidents and other very influential people, and supplemented these interviews with archival and ethnographic data designed to investigate whether there has been change in this group and, if change has been occurring, the mechanisms that account for it. Lindsay finds that CPs (Evangelicals) have indeed become more prominent in the power elite in recent decades (Lindsay 2008). He proposes the change has largely been a top-down process involving social networks and identity formation among elites. One caveat is that Lindsay proposes that this change occurred in the absence of growth of self-professed members of CP churches. Unfortunately, other data suggest that there has been important growth in CP church membership and the percentage of Americans affiliated with CP churches. Although this does not negate Lindsay's findings, it does suggest that a more nuanced interpretation is in order.

A second area of research that provides support for the notion that there might be change in the standing of CPs is work on the growth of megachurches. Megachurches are those with more than 2,000 attendants at weekly services; average weekly attendance in a recent survey of these large churches was more than 3,500 (Thumma 2005; Thumma and Travis 2007). Although very large churches have been around for decades, CPs' membership in these large churches has more than doubled in the recent past (Thumma 2005; Thumma and Travis 2007). Megachurches have proliferated across denominations, including CP denominations (Chaves 2006). There is some concentration of megachuches in certain regions, including the west, southeast, and south-central states, but every state has at least some very large churches (Thumma 2005; Thumma and Travis 2007). Most important here, there is some evidence that members of megachurches affiliated with CP denominations have relatively high SES (Thumma 2005; Thumma and Travis 2007). One implication of this could be that CPs have become more well-off on measures such as education, income, and wealth. However, others have argued that membership is increasingly concentrated in large churches regardless of denomination (Chaves 2006). This does not imply that CPs are not getting wealthier; it simply raises questions about whether there is something special about megachurches that is attracting higher SES members. This is another question on which additional research will provide more insight than I am able with current data. Moreover, future changes in megachurch membership will help clarify the nature of SES trends that are obscured now perhaps because the changes are in their early stages.

We saw in Chapter 4 that CPs are still relatively unlikely to be wealthy; that is, they are unlikely to be in the top 10 percent of the wealth distribution. However, their representation in this group is higher than it was in previous years, providing some evidence that there has been change either among people who are CPs or in the type of person who becomes a member of a CP denomination. Table 6.5 provides detailed profiles of the wealthy and not-so-wealthy to highlight the factors that are correlated with membership in position in the wealth distribution. Consistent with the strategy I used in Chapter 4, I define the wealthy as those in the top 10 percent of the NLSY wealth distribution and not rich as those in the other 90 percent of the distribution. For the entire sample, about 18 percent of the rich have ever inherited, and 73 percent are married.

TABLE 6.5. *Who Are the Rich?*

	All Respondents		White Catholic		CP		Hispanic Catholic	
	Not Rich	Rich	Not Rich	Rich	Not Rich	Rich	Not Rich	Rich
Ever inherited	9.1	18.6	9.5	17.7	8.6	12.5	1.5	7.1
Married (%)	70.0	84.5	73.0	83.3	73.6	92.5	66.8	78.5
Education (years)	13.7	15.5	13.8	15.3	13.4	15.0	13.0	14.7
Age first birth	25.4	29.0	26.5	29.3	24.5	27.4	24.3	27.5
Net worth ($1,000)	112.8	744.9	153.7	743.7	94.6	668.0	99.8	754.5
No home debt	17.2	15.9	13.6	15.1	19.3	23.9	19.4	9.0
Raised CP (%)	27.6	16.5	0.0	0.0	77.4	78.8	0.0	0.0
Raised Catholic (%)	34.1	36.4	100	100	0.0	0.0	100	100

Notes: Data are from the 1979–2004 NLSY. Sample size = 4,369. Religion was measured in 2000. Rich refers to respondents who report net worth in the top 10% of NLSY wealth holders in 2004; not rich refers to respondents who are in the other 90%. Net worth is median and is in 2004 dollars. No home debt refers to the percent of respondents who do not have mortgage debt.

The typical rich person has more than fifteen years of education and is twenty-nine years old. The typical rich respondent has a net worth of more than $700,000, and only 16 percent have home mortgages. In contrast, 9 percent of the nonwealthy respondents have inherited, and 70 percent are married. These respondents have fewer than fourteen years of education and are somewhat younger (twenty-five years old) than their wealthy counterparts. Their net worth is slightly more than $112,000, and they are somewhat more likely to have home debt. White Catholics are relatively typical of NLSY respondents on many of the demographics included in Table 6.5. However, consistent with my discussion in the first part of this chapter, nonwealthy white Catholics are wealthier than the average NLSY respondent. In contrast, wealthy white Catholics are no wealthier than the typical rich respondent. I discuss Hispanic Catholics in more detail later in this chapter.

Most important for the current discussion is a profile of wealthy CPs. Table 6.5 shows that wealthy CPs are less likely than the typical wealthy NLSY respondent to have inherited, and are much more likely to be married. Wealthy CPs are typical of other wealthy respondents in their education levels and are slightly younger than average. Both wealthy and nonwealthy CPs have lower net worth than the typical respondent in each group; both groups of CPs are also more likely than the average respondent to have home debt. There is no significant difference between wealthy and nonwealthy CPs in the likelihood that they were raised CP; however, consistent with my discussion throughout this book, both groups were highly likely to be raised in CP families. An alternative strategy for assessing CP wealth that would allow direct exploration of changes in membership in CP churches and their effects would be to update the analyses I described earlier that compared the wealth of those who were CPs in both childhood and adulthood, left CP churches after childhood, and became CPs as adults. Unfortunately, the data to update this are not available. There are plans to update the religious affiliation questions on the NLSY, but so far the new data on religion have not been collected. This will be an important task for future research to explore.

Finally a brief note on the relationship between religion and politics is in order. The focus of my research is religion and economics; I deliberately do not include politics to the extent possible so as to provide enough breadth regarding the relationship between religion and wealth. As a result, when I talk about conservatives, I am referring to religious conservatives, as I noted in Chapter 1. However, I frequently receive questions about the relevance of politics to the patterns I study, and admittedly, contemporary political developments may be relevant to a discussion about upward wealth mobility among CPs. Alliances between conservative religious groups (that tend to include moderate- to low-SES people) and conservative political groups (that tend to include high-SES people) might be part of the reason that CPs appear wealthier now than they did in the past. Again, however, we do not currently have the data to ascertain the extent to which political alliances are affecting the composition of CPs and the SES of members of CP denominations. On a related note, I also receive many questions about how CP orientations toward money inform the formation of religious-political alliances and their implications. Some observers have raised questions about whether allegiances between religious and political conservatives violate the apparent economic self-interest of many of those who are involved because of their religious beliefs. The alliances often suggest that religious values prevail over economics in the formation of the alliances and the subsequent political decision making of many alliance members. My findings might help explain this behavior. CPs accept that material possessions belong to God, and people are managers of those possessions. I showed that, as a result, CPs tend to seek divine guidance in making important decisions, avoid excess accumulation, and favor using money to support religion. These same values may influence CP political alliances and voting. That is, CPs may seek advice from religious leaders in making important political decisions, and they may accept that accumulating excess national wealth is less important than promoting other interests (e.g., right to life, traditional marriage). Finally, the political alliances that CP churches join often support using federal funds to support religious causes. If CPs value using their money to support God's work, it would not be surprising that these alliances are appealing to them. Of course, my results do not address these issues, but future research might usefully explore whether there is merit to this extension of my findings.

Potential for Mobility: Hispanic Catholics and Assimilation

Hispanic Catholics might seem like the least likely group to include in a chapter on wealth mobility, but as the subtitle suggests, this is a group that has the potential for upward mobility. Studies of groups that have already experienced upward wealth mobility are rare because there are so few groups that have moved up in the wealth distribution noticeably and in a time frame that allows observation. Even rarer – nonexistent, to the best of my knowledge – are discussions of any sort of groups that may be starting the process of upward mobility. Yet observing a group that has (perhaps!) just begun the mobility process could be useful because it could highlight in a unique way the factors that initiate mobility, and understanding the origins of upward mobility has implications for both basic research and practical questions of well-being.

Are Hispanic Catholics poised to move up in the wealth distribution? Prior research showed Hispanic Catholics to be soundly situated at the bottom of the wealth distribution and many of the other distributions of traits that affect wealth. Research on the distribution of wealth and wealth accumulation showed that Hispanic Catholics and BPs were relatively even in their holdings of total net worth and most of the components of net worth (Keister 2000a, 2005, 2007). Research on family processes, educational attainment, income and wages, and job processes also showed Hispanic Catholics to be relatively disadvantaged (Glass and Jacobs 2005; Lehrer 2000, 2004; Steen 1996). Although there is no question that Hispanic Catholics are still disadvantaged on most of these measures compared to other religious groups, some of the evidence I presented in previous chapters of this book suggested that something may be changing. Although their income is still quite low, Hispanic Catholics have wealth that is significantly higher than BPs, and the difference between Hispanic Catholics and BPs is growing. Consider, for example, Table 4.2.

Only 4.8 percent of Hispanic Catholics in the NLSY and 6.7 percent in the HRS are in the top 10 percent of the wealth distribution (see Table 4.2) compared to 10.6 percent of all NLSY and 27.5 percent of all HRS respondents. Yet only 0.8 percent of BPs in the NLSY and 5.7 percent of BPs in the HRS are in the top 10 percent of the wealth distribution, suggesting that Hispanic Catholics are slightly better off financially than BPs, particularly in the younger NLSY sample.

What factors might enable upward wealth mobility for Hispanic Catholics? Recall the data presented in Table 6.5, the profile of wealthy respondents to the NLSY. Like most respondents of any religious affiliation, rich Hispanic Catholics (i.e., those in the top 10 percent of the wealth distribution) are more likely to have inherited than those who are not rich (i.e., in the other 90 percent of the distribution). There is also a significant difference in marital status between rich Hispanic Catholics and others. More than 78 percent of the wealthy Hispanic Catholics are married, compared to 66.8 percent of their less wealthy counterparts, suggesting that the marriage premium I have been discussing throughout the book is an advantage to Hispanic Catholics compared to, for example, BPs who are likelier to be never married or divorced. Wealthy Hispanic Catholics are also likelier to have postponed fertility than those who are not in the top of the wealth distribution, suggesting that family size is a potential stumbling block for this group that has historically been characterized by early fertility and large family size. Wealthy Hispanic Catholics had their first child, on average, at age 27.5, and the typical nonwealthy Hispanic Catholic had a child at age 24.3. Somewhat surprisingly, there is no significant difference between wealthy Hispanic Catholics and other members of the same ethno-religious group in educational attainment. However, evidence not included in this table suggests that those Hispanic Catholics who do acquire education above a high school degree do postpone fertility and limit their family size. Consistent with a group that is still situated relatively low in the wealth distribution, both wealthy and nonwealthy Hispanic Catholics have net worth lower than the typical respondent (all respondents). Consistent with other evidence I have presented, Hispanic Catholics are not nearly as wealthy as white Catholics. Notably, however, wealthy Hispanic Catholics are wealthier than wealthy CPs. This is an important first sign of upward mobility. It is not a guarantee that group is moving or will continue to move up, but evidence that the tail of the Hispanic Catholic wealth distribution extends beyond that of the CP wealth distribution is suggestive of an important change.

TABLE 6.6. *Hispanic Catholics: Evidence of Mobility?*

	Base Model		Add Education, Family	
	Estimate	Standard Error	Estimate	Standard Error
Catholic, Hispanic	16.15***	8.79	14.67*	10.86
Catholic, white	33.17***	4.88	17.00*	6.01
Mainline/Liberal Protestant (MP)	13.21***	6.44	7.86*	5.14
Jewish	195.66*	42.17	71.03*	45.85
Other religion	−9.54	23.65	−41.95	61.76
No religion	25.39	12.76	21.12	31.99
Fertility				
Age at first birth	–	–	−1.24**	.74
Number of children	–	–	−.32	6.44
Number of children (square)	–	–	−.47	1.23
Marriage				
Ever married	–	–	7.31	17.04
Number of marital changes	–	–	−4.10	5.50
Both Catholic	–	–	9.13	13.62
Education				
College degree	–	–	1.31	42.35
Advanced degree	–	–	−5.25	29.85
Financial resources				
Family income (log)	–	–	10.21**	4.08
Two−earner household	–	–	.68**	.24

Notes: Data are from the 1979–2004 NLSY. Sample size is 4,369. The omitted category for religion is CPs and BPs. Also controlled but not displayed are other childhood family income, childhood family structure, parents' education, parents' work status, (full time, part time, unemployed), parents' immigration status, a dichotomous indicator that the respondent did not report childhood family income, gender, age, other marital statuses and education levels, and region of residence.
*p < .05 **p < .01 ***p < .001.

Table 6.6 repeats the multivariate models of total family net worth that I have discussed previously, but this version of the model highlights how Hispanic Catholics (the test group and first religious group included in the table) compare to CPs and BPs (the omitted category). The results show that, controlling for just basic demographics and family background traits, Hispanic Catholics have significantly greater wealth than CPs and BPs. The second model adds education and family behaviors to the base model. As we would expect, the effect of being Hispanic

Catholic is slightly weaker in the second model, but it is still positive and significantly different from zero. The second model also shows that age at first birth and total family income are the two factors that are important for Hispanic Catholics and account for the reduction in the religious effect for this group. A couple of important caveats are in order. First, sample sizes for Hispanic Catholics for these descriptive and multivariate analyses are sufficient (more than 1,000) for making inferences, but this is still a relatively small group. Moreover, the composition of this group changes continuously as new immigrants enter the United States. My sample does not provide sufficient numbers to explore within-sample differences (e.g., between those with Mexican versus other Latino origins), although there is reason to suspect there are important differences. Future research might usefully address these questions. There are also non-Catholic Hispanics who could provide a useful comparison and insight into the relative importance of ethnicity and religion. Again, my sample is not large enough to adequately address this question, but additional growth in the Hispanic population in the United States will no doubt make this possible in the future. These basic analyses also suggest other questions that future research might explore, using updated data as it becomes available: Are Hispanic Catholics on par with CPs? Is one group moving faster than the other? Who is moving down to allow these groups to move up, if they are indeed experiencing upward mobility?

Rising Tides or Trading Places?

I have spent this entire chapter talking about upward mobility, but I have not specifically addressed an important underlying question. That is, do the changes and potential changes we see in wealth ownership reflect rising tides (i.e., all groups ascending together) or groups trading places? The notion that rising tides lift all boats suggests that it is possible for everyone to be better off over time. That is, when economic conditions are generally improving – as they typically have in the United States despite occasional and sometimes severe recessions – it is possible that nearly everyone will be better off as time passes. Alternatively, the changes we see might reflect groups trading places. That is, it might be that when white Catholics moved up, others moved down in the distribution. Trading places can occur without the downwardly mobile group decreasing their wealth ownership, of course, because a distribution implies a finite *and relative* set of positions.

Some of the growth in wealth that I detect in my analyses undoubtedly reflects rising tides, because the time frame in which I study these groups was a time of extreme growth for nearly all groups. What I am unable to do with the data I have available is to explore what happens to these groups when the economy declines. However, an important natural experiment is currently underway that will make this sort of analysis not only possible but also unavoidable. The extreme recession of 2008 and beyond will factor into future analyses of wealth ownership whether researchers want to study it or not. For those who are so inclined, the recession will provide an interesting and important setting in which to study the processes of rising (and declining) tides compared to changes experienced by individual groups.

At the same time, because the time period I study was a period of growth and many of the groups I study benefitted from this growth, I can be somewhat confident when I say that some of the changes I study reflect changes in relative position. The case of white Catholics is an important example. White Catholics have clearly garnered more wealth in the past decade; at the same time, the wealth of MPs – an important comparison group for white Catholics – has grown but not nearly as quickly. Analyses that I did not include here, comparing the accumulation rates for white Catholics and MPs, show that, controlling for other background and demographic factors, white Catholics in the NLSY have accumulated assets more quickly than MPs in recent years. My sample sizes are a bit small, but the data suggest that Episcopalians are the one MP group for whom wealth has continued to grow at a rate comparable to that of white Catholics. Jews are another important comparison group for white Catholics. As white Catholics have moved up, surpassing MPs in wealth ownership on some measures, Jews have maintained a relatively firm, high position in the wealth distribution. That is, there is no evidence that Jews have moved down. The precarious (and potential) nature of mobility for CPs and particularly Hispanic Catholics makes it more difficult to address whether any group is moving down as (or if) these groups are beginning to move. Current data suggest that BPs are solidly at the bottom of the wealth distribution, but beyond that, it is impossible to ascertain who, if anyone, will move as CPs and Hispanic Catholics adjust their positions. This is yet another question that future research will be better able to address.

Wealth mobility is an important process underlying wealth inequality. However, researchers have paid relatively little attention to wealth mobility, at least in part, because it is so rare. In this chapter, I took advantage of the unique opportunity created by Roman Catholics in recent decades to study the relationship between religion and wealth mobility. I isolated non-Hispanic whites raised in Roman Catholic families and explored the factors that have accounted for their changing position in recent decades. I also proposed that CPs and Hispanic Catholics may be experiencing a bit of upward mobility as well. Because the mobility process has just begun for these groups, my discussion for these groups was largely speculative. In the next chapter, I continue to discuss the conditions and circumstances that make some groups unique. As it was in this chapter, my objective is to use the experience of particular groups to better understand the more general processes that account for wealth accumulation and inequality.

7

Notable Achievement

Just as wealth mobility (Chapter 6) provides important clues about the financial strategies and processes that account for wealth ownership, so does consistent achievement. The findings that I report throughout this book – and other available research – show that Mainline Protestants, Jews, and Mormons/LDS in the United States have achieved high levels of financial success that are worth additional attention. As I have mentioned briefly, Mainline Protestants have historically had high SES and have occupied positions of power in the United States. A historic advantage certainly contributes to their current well-being, but I explore how and why these denominations have maintained their advantage. There is also evidence that Jews have attained notably high levels of well-being; this achievement has become evident in the results I present throughout this book, and these are consistent with the small number of other empirical works that have explored the contributing factors (Burstein 2007; Chiswick 1986, 1993; Lehrer 2009). It appears that human-capital acquisition, family behaviors and processes, and other issues related to ethno-religious particularity, marginality, and social capital contribute to Jewish achievement. Educational attainment is high among Jews, fertility rates are low, rates of female employment when children are young are low, and wealth appears to follow. I explore the magnitude of the Jewish advantage and address some of the possible explanations for the achievement of this group.

Finally, Mormons/LDS are also unique in ways that might be instructive. Mormons/LDS tend to be religiously conservative, but unlike other CPs, they tend to have high levels of educational attainment. Mormons/LDS have relatively high fertility rates (similar to other CPs) and low rates of female employment when children are young (similar to Jews). High homogamy levels reinforce these influences to create a distinctive set of patterns that might be useful in understanding the religion-wealth relationship. In this chapter, I explore these patterns and ask whether there is an LDS/Mormon wealth advantage as well.

Mainline Protestants: A History of High SES

The results I presented throughout this book provide evidence to support the relatively advantaged position that Mainline Protestants have held in the United States since colonial times. I found that MPs come from higher-SES families, attain higher levels of education themselves, and have slightly above-average rates (and higher than those of CPs and BPs) of being married, remaining childless, postponing fertility, and otherwise exhibiting educational and family behaviors that contribute to wealth accumulation. Tables 5.9 and 6.1 showed that MPs were more likely than other groups to have highly educated parents (MPs and white Catholics were the reference group) even controlling for other traits that explain educational attainment. Table 5.10 showed that MPs are more likely than others to inherit (again MPs and white Catholics were the reference group), controlling for other determinants of inheritance.

I also found that adult MPs have occupational and income advantages and orientations toward work and money that also predispose them to having higher wealth. MPs are more likely than the general population and particularly more likely than CPs and BPs to be in managerial and professional occupations, to have high household income, to have high individual income for both men and women, and to be comparatively unlikely to report that religion affects their career choices and financial decision making. Consistent with the findings in the first part of the book, I then reported in Chapters 4 and 5 that MPS do indeed have relatively high net worth, real assets, and financial assets. Table 5.11 showed that MPs have higher wealth than others (again using MPs and white Catholics as the reference group). Notably, however, Table 6.3 shows that the MP wealth advantage is reduced by adding educational attainment to the multivariate model, suggesting that human capital acquisition is a critical part of the reason MPs have high wealth.

The findings I have been discussing are comparable to findings from other relatively recent research that shows MPs have advantages on many SES measures (Park and Reimer 2002; Smith and Faris 2005). Unlike some other recent works including Smith and Faris (2005), however, I

TABLE 7.1. *Detailed Protestant Groups: Wealth Measures*

	Net Worth	High Net Worth (%)	Real Assets	Financial Assets
Mainline/Liberal Protestant (MP)	$146,000	14.2	$202,672	$60,000
Presbyterian	$201,800	17.3	$219,000	$61,500
Episcopalian	$174,000	20.8	$225,000	$104,000
Methodist	$139,320	15.3	$182,000	$55,000
Lutheran	$137,000	10.4	$202,000	$53,200
All Respondents	$99,500	10.6	$155,000	$40,000

Notes: Data are from the 1979–2004 NLSY. Sample size = 4,369. See Tables 4.1 (net worth and real assets), 4.2 (high net worth), and 5.1 (financial assets) for values and details. Total n = 4,369. Net worth, real assets, and financial assets are medians and are in 2004 dollars. High net worth is more than $600,000 (i.e., approximately the top 10 percent of the NLSY net worth distribution). MP denominations include only moderate and liberal groups. See Chapter 1 for details.

have not yet discussed variations by specific denominational types within the large MP group. Smith and Faris argue that there are likely to be important within-group variations in educational attainment and income for MPs that result from important historical and theological differences across the major denominations. Consistent with this expectation, they provide analyses using the General Social Survey, which show some MP groups have performed better than other groups on these SES measures. In particular, they find that members of Unitarian, Episcopalian, Presbyterian USA, and UCC churches rank relatively high on SES measures.[1] Using standard SES measures such as college completion, total education, household income, occupational prestige, and a composite SES measure, they find that these and other MP groups score relatively high. In Smith and Faris's analysis, MP groups also appear to have improved in standing more than other groups.

Using NLSY data, I find a similar basic ranking of MPs by denomination, suggesting that the basic SES structure of the NLSY is consistent with the GSS. However, the differences by denomination are not pronounced enough in the NLSY, nor are the differences across MP groups significant enough to report within-group differences for MPs on each measure I addressed in this book. There are, however, some MP groups that stand out on key wealth measures to warrant a brief discussion. Table 7.1 shows how four MP groups compare to all MPs and to the

---

[1] Smith and Faris find that other MP groups also have high SES, but these denominations perform particularly well on all measures included in their study.

total NLSY sample. In this table, I report wealth by adult religion and include measures of net worth, high net worth, real assets, and financial assets. The measures for MPs (all) and all respondents are consistent with those reported in Tables 4.1 (net worth and real assets), 4.2 (high net worth), and 5.1 (financial assets) for values and details. Net worth, real assets, and financial assets are medians and are in 2004 dollars. High net worth is a percentage. I highlight the wealth holdings of Presbyterians, Episcopalians, Methodists, and Lutherans, using only MP groups where there are both MP and CP denominations that share these names.

Table 7.1 shows that Presbyterians and Episcopalians have particularly high total net worth, with Episcopalians having slightly higher real assets and financial assets than Presbyterians. The net-worth difference reflects differences in liabilities that I do not show here. Lutherans and Methodists also have high net worth compared to other MPs and to the total sample, although they own slightly less wealth than Presbyterians and Episcopalians. Lutherans have notably high real assets but low financial assets. Indeed, Episcopalians stand out among these groups in their holdings of financial assets, making them more comparable on this measure to Jews than to other MPs (see the next section of this chapter).

The important conclusion about MPs is that even though there is some variation across MP denominations in attainment, these groups are very similar to each other – and different from more conservative Protestant denominations – on important measures of SES. In most detailed analyses of Protestant denominations since the 1970s and 1980s, MPs have outpaced CPs on important measures of SES. My own detailed explorations of the data sets I use and other data sets that include education, occupational prestige, income, wealth, and related information by detailed Protestant denominations (not included in this book, to save space) suggests that MP denominations "hang together" remarkably well and are consistently and significantly higher than CP denominations, as they have been throughout U.S. history. Smith and Faris (2005: 101) also conclude that there has been little change since the 1960s and 1970s in the structure of inequality. They note that the "structure of interreligious inequality that Rook and McKinney [1987] mapped in the 1970s and 1980s continues to hold" and that there has been "much more continuity than change in the system of inequality" in the interceding decade. This consistent and clear MP advantage, combined with the high degree of internal similarities across MP denominations, is the reason I have not provided detailed measures for particular Protestant groups throughout this book.

Perhaps a more interesting and important question is: What factors account for the enduring advantage enjoyed by members of MP denominations? An important part of the reason MPs enjoy an attainment advantage is historical. A complete history of religious stratification in America is beyond the scope of this book, and indeed, others have already done a fabulous job outlining and explaining how religious stratification developed and progressed since colonial times (Davidson 1994, 2008; Davidson and Pyle 2011; Davidson, Pyle, and Reyes 1995). However, a limited discussion of past stratification patterns and the role history played in creating and perhaps maintaining wealth stratification today is warranted. Historical accounts convincingly demonstrate that religious stratification was well established in colonial times. As Davidson and Pyle (2011) point out, 95 percent of those who signed the Declaration of Independence and 75 percent of those attending the Constitutional Convention belonged to Anglican, Congregational, or Presbyterian churches. Other Protestant denominations, such as Baptists, that had more adherents at the time were virtually unrepresented at these important events that demonstrated both rank and power at the time. Others have provided complimentary evidence that wealth ownership was highly concentrated during colonial times. In particular, there is evidence that the top 1 percent of wealth owners held approximately 13 percent of wealth (Beeghley 2005). In major cities at the time, again, Anglicans, Congregationalists, and Presbyterians were overrepresented among the elites (Baltzell 1964). There is also some evidence that Quakers were overrepresented in certain cities, including Philadelphia (Tolles 1948). During the 1800s, the U.S. religious landscape changed dramatically (Davidson and Pyle 2011). Many new groups emerged (e.g., Mormon/LDS, Christian Church/Disciples of Christ), others divided along racial and regional lines (e.g., Methodist Episcopal Church – South separated from Methodist Episcopal Church, Southern Baptist Convention was formed), several existing groups grew dramatically during this century (e.g., Baptists, Methodists), and others benefitted from immigration (e.g., Catholics, Jews). Yet during these same one hundred years, more than one-half of those serving as President of the United States were either Episcopalian or Presbyterian (Davidson and Pyle 2011), and members of these same religious groups continued to be overrepresented among the nation's top wealth holders in an increasingly unequal wealth distribution (Gregory and Neu 1962). During the 1900s, of course, there continued to be considerable changes in the religious composition of the country, and the distribution of wealth ebbed and flowed, returning to nineteenth-century extremes in the 1980s and 1990s

(Keister 2005). Most important for this discussion, however, is that the certain MP denominations – Episcopalians, Presbyterians, and, to a lesser extent, Congregationalists – continued to be overrepresented among top wealth holders and in positions of power.

What factors caused this early and lasting divide along religious lines and the MP advantage that continues today? Some groups were able to establish themselves in important positions because they arrived in the colonies first, but the fact that the same groups have maintained their positions over time is harder to explain. Davidson and Pyle (2011) argue that conflict theory can explain the long-standing advantage that MPs enjoy as part of a more general, and ingrained, ranking of religious groups. They argue that laws, ideologies, and customs that favored elites ensured that these groups, including elite religious groups, were more likely than other groups to occupy positions of power. Moreover, once certain groups were in power, they had incentives to reify laws and to promote organizations that would ensure that they would stay in power. Consistent with this approach, Davidson and Pyle tend to focus on the presence of MPs in positions of power, including their roles as Presidents of the United States and as heads of universities.

There is certainly some truth to the conflict perspective on religious stratification, and Davidson and Pyle do a thorough job outlining the evidence supporting their ideas. It is clearly the case that being the first to arrive in the new world and not having to overcome the challenges associated with assimilating that later arrivals contended with was an important advantage. Sociologists have also provided ample and convincing evidence that groups who are in powerful positions will take measures, however unconscious, to maintain that power. Often notions about the types of people who are capable of leading important organizations and the way occupations should be stratified by race, gender, and religion are conveyed in schools and by organizations through their curricula, procedures, and requirements for advancement that most members of the organizations take for granted. Davidson and Pyle point to schools as an important component of the process by which some groups establish and maintain power, suggesting that elite, often private, schools trained generations of leaders and excluded others who might otherwise have been upwardly mobile.

However, it is always difficult to provide empirical support for arguments explaining stratification that rely on the notion of collusion among members of some groups to exclude members of other groups from positions of power. Moreover, there is very strong evidence, even in Davidson and Pyle's own accounts of historical processes, that the indirect (including intergenerational and demographic) and direct (those that operate through religious beliefs) processes that I propose in this book are an essential part of the reason MPs have maintained their advantages. Education is definitely an important part of the explanation. As my own findings here and the findings of large numbers of other scholars show, religion affects family and individual orientations toward education and the completion of schooling. Parents transmit their religious beliefs and their orientations toward education, which are often intertwined, to their children. Similarly, religion and intergenerational processes can affect orientations toward marriage, fertility, and related family behaviors. These contribute – at the individual and family levels – to SES. The direct effect of religious beliefs regarding attainment – beliefs that are reinforced by membership in religious groups and participation in religious services – also lead directly to attainment. Prior research has shown that MPs consistently exhibit orientations and behaviors consistent with high achievement. Moreover, and perhaps most strongly, if the institutionalized structure of inequality theorized by conflict theorists were the only process at play, Jews and white Catholics would never have gained the advantages they did. I discussed the upward mobility of white Catholics in Chapter 6, showing that demographic processes and unique beliefs contributed to their upward mobility. I will provide additional detail regarding Jewish achievement in the next section. The important point here is that both groups would have continued to be disadvantaged if institutionalized inequality were the sole – or even primary – determinant of wealth position.

Jews: Notably High Achievement

Levels of Achievement

Levels of socioeconomic achievement among American Jews are particularly high, and scholars are beginning to describe and to make attempts at explaining this extraordinary success. The estimates I have included in this book document this achievement, and I have hinted at some of the potential explanations in other chapters. In this section, I draw attention to the degree to which Jews are exceptional and offer some ideas about the reasons for this notable position. Median annual household income is much higher for Jews than it is for members of other religious groups, and Jews are much less likely than members of other religious groups to experience poverty. Table 7.2 uses NLSY data, first reported in

TABLE 7.2. *Jews Compared to Other Groups: Adult Household Income*

	Median Household Income	Below poverty line (%)
Jews compared to:		
White Conservative Protestant (CP)	$31,825	− 8.7
Black Conservative Protestant (BP)	$66,731	− 26.6
Mainline/Liberal Protestant (MP)	$20,019	− 4.0
Catholic	$18,706	− 6.4
White	$13,962	− 4.0
Hispanic	$46,814	− 18.8
Other religion	$38,346	− 11.2
No religion	$39,012	− 10.7
All Respondents	$31,825	− 9.9

Notes: Data are from the 1979–2004 NLSY. Sample size = 4,369. See Table 3.7 for values and details.

Table 3.7, to highlight the degree to which median annual household income for respondents reporting that they are Jewish (in adulthood) exceeds the median for members of other religious groups. For example, Table 3.7 reported that median household income for Jews was $93,423 in 2004 (using 2004 dollars); that table also reported that median household income for CPs was $61,598 in that year. Table 7.2 reports the difference between those two medians as "Jews compared to: White Conservative Protestant (CP)." That is, Table 7.2 reports that the difference is $31,825. A positive value indicates that the Jewish median (or percentage in the case of poverty in Table 7.2 and other measures in subsequent tables) exceeds the value for the comparison group; a negative value indicates that the Jewish value is lower than the value for the other group. I use a similar strategy for Tables 7.3 through 7.5. In each case, I note below the table which chapter and which table of this book contain the original information.

Indeed, as Table 7.2 summarizes, Jewish median annual household income exceeds the median for all other households by a considerable amount. Jewish households have median income that exceeds the typical NLSY household income by more than $31,000. I already mentioned that Jewish households have income that exceeds CP household income by the same large margin. The difference between Jewish and MP households is not as extreme, but the Jewish advantage is still greater than $20,000. The difference between Jewish households and BP or Hispanic Catholics is particularly notable. Jewish household income exceeds BP household

TABLE 7.3. *Jews Compared to Other Groups: Median Net Worth and Real Assets*

	Net Worth (median)	High Net Worth	Financial Assets (median)
Jews compared to:			
White Conservative Protestant (CP)	$341,100	40.0	$206,000
Black Conservative Protestant (BP)	$400,700	46.0	$231,500
Mainline/Liberal Protestant (MP)	$277,500	32.6	$179,000
Catholic	$289,000	33.1	$181,000
White	$267,500	30.9	$180,000
Hispanic	$372,000	42.0	$220,000
Other Religion	$358,000	34.2	$219,600
No Religion	$365,800	36.2	$209,000
All Respondents	$324,000	36.2	$199,000

Notes: Data are from the 1979–2004 NLSY. Sample size = 4,369. See Tables 4.1 (net worth), 4.2 (high net worth), and 5.1 (financial assets) for values and details. High net worth refers to having more than $600,000 in net worth, or being in approximately the top 10 percent of wealth holders. Table 4.2 reported percentages of households in the high-wealth category; this table reports the difference between those percentages.

income by more than $66,000; and the Jewish median exceeds the Hispanic Catholic median by more than $46,000. There are similarly large gaps between Jewish households and other households in the percentage below the poverty line. Again, the summary provided in Table 7.2 refers to the data originally included in Table 3.7, in which I reported that none of the Jewish households in the sample I used reported income that would qualify them as below the poverty line. Given that at least some members of each other group that I study were living in poverty, it is not surprising that Jewish households are less often in poverty compared to all other groups. Consistent with the other data I have presented, the gaps between Jewish households and BP and Hispanic Catholic households are particularly extreme. These findings are consistent with other research that shows Jews have a relative advantage in both personal earnings and total household income. Burstein (2007) summarized research dating to the early 1970s that showed Jews' relative earnings or income exceeds that of Protestants (in most research MPs and CPs have been considered together) by up to 246 percent and white Catholics by up to 243 percent; the more recent evidence also suggests that these differences hold in newer, more specialized data sets (Chiswick and Huang 2008).

The Jewish wealth advantage is equally large. Table 7.3 summarizes the differences between Jewish household wealth and the household wealth of

other religious groups, using three measures that I originally discussed in
Chapters 4 and 5. First, I compare Jewish households to other households
on median net worth. Median household net worth for Jewish respondents, first reported in Table 4.1, is $423,500. The difference between
Jewish households and CP households is $341,100, and the difference is
particularly high when Jews are compared to BPs or Hispanic Catholics.
Mainline Protestants and Catholics, the two groups with relatively high
net worth, still each have notably less net worth on average than Jewish
households. Table 7.3 also compares households on the percentage in
approximately the top 10 percent of wealth holders. I originally reported
these patterns in Table 4.2 and noted that households with more than
$600,000 in net worth are in the top 10 percent of wealth holders.
Table 4.2 reported percentages of households in the high-wealth category. Table 7.3 reports the difference between those percentages. For
Jewish households, 46.8 percent are in this high-wealth category; that
is a difference of about 40 percentage points compared to CP households, 46 percentage points compared to BPs, and 42 points compared to
Hispanic Catholics. The gap is not quite as large when Jewish households are compared to MP and white Catholic households, although the
difference between the percentages still exceeds 30 in both cases.

Finally, Table 7.3 compares Jewish and other households on median
financial assets. Jewish respondents reported household financial assets
that averaged $239,000 (Table 5.1), which exceeds the median of all
other respondents (summarized in Table 7.3) by considerable margins.
Once again, the gaps reported in Table 7.3 are most extreme when Jewish households are compared to BP and Hispanic Catholic respondents.
Multivariate results included in Tables 5.11 and 6.3 showed that these
results do not change when a long list of other determinants of net worth
are controlled. What is perhaps most amazing is that these multivariate
results – and comparable results published in other research (Burstein
2007; Keister 2005; Lehrer 2004b, 2009) – are statistically significant
even with very small sample sizes because the magnitude of the effect is
very large. Some also try to attribute these remarkable differences to the
high incomes and wealth of those living in urban areas; the argument
usually hinges on the idea that Jews are overrepresented in large, high-
income cities like New York City. In reality, there are large populations
of Jews in many geographic areas in the United States just as there are
wealthy people of all faiths living throughout the United States. Sampling
techniques and weighting of data further ensures that Jews are represented appropriately in the data I use. In addition, in the multivariate

models I present in this book and elsewhere, I control for urban residence to hold constant the effect of living in a city for all groups (Keister 2003, 2005, 2008). In additional sensitivity tests (not shown), I also explore the effect of removing from the data or focusing exclusively on Jews living in New York City (a process that requires using nonpublic geo-coded data from the NLSY) and other urban areas. I find the effect of being raised Jewish and being Jewish as an adult on family background, income, and wealth are as strong (or stronger) when certain groups are either studied in isolation or excluded.

There is also evidence that Jews compare favorably to other religious groups in occupational attainment. I explored issues related to work in Chapter 3 and showed that Jews tend to be in high-prestige management occupations more often than other people. I do not repeat that information here, to conserve space, but the Jewish occupational attainment advantage is remarkable enough to warrant a brief mention. Burstein (2007) summarizes findings of other research that draws on various data sources and shows that since the 1960s, Jews are much more likely to be in upper nonmanual/ white-collar/professional/managerial occupations than Protestants (including Episcopalians), Catholics, and/or all non-Jews.[2] Consistent with these occupational differences, researchers have shown that Jews have considerably higher occupational prestige scores than members of other religious groups (Burstein 2007; Smith and Faris 2005). As Smith and Faris (2005) show using the GSS, Jewish occupational prestige scores are nearly 4 points higher than Episcopalians', nearly 10 points higher than Catholics, and 10.5 points higher than for other non-Jews.

A final measure of the Jewish SES advantage that has appeared in research since the 1960s and that underscores the indicators I have summarized so far in this section is representation in the Marquis *Who's Who* (the *Who's Who*). The *Who's Who* is a listing of names and biographies of leaders and other influential people that has been compiled since 1899 and that has become a standard reference for understanding which individuals and groups are in positions of power. It is not surprising that in the early part of the twentieth century, Jews appeared on this list much less frequently than other Americans and even less frequently than those with British backgrounds. As I addressed in Chapter 4, leadership positions were filled almost exclusively by those with affiliations to

---

[2] Naturally researchers define occupations differently. The summary I give here refers to some of the occupational types highlighted in previous research.

Protestant – nearly always Mainline Protestant – churches. However, by the 1970s, Jews were more than 2.5 times as likely as all Americans and more than twice as likely as the British to be on the list. By the mid-1990s, the gap between Jews and others on the *Who's Who* had grown even larger. In the 1990s, Jews were 4.5 times as likely as other Americans and nearly 6 times as likely as the British to be represented (Burstein 2007; Lieberson and Carter 1979; McDermott 2002). This is consistent with evidence and my note in Chapter 4 that Jews have become better represented in both the national and local elite circles (Davidson 1994; Davidson, Pyle, and Reyes 1995; Zweigenhaft and Domhoff 1982, 2006).

As with all religious groups, there are important within-group differences for Jews in SES and in the behaviors and processes that lead to achievement. I have not addressed differences across Jewish denominations previously in this book because samples are too small in the data sets I use and because I need reliable information on wealth to address my questions. One potential alternative data set that I have considered using is the National Jewish Population Study (NJPS). The NJPS is a unique data set that contains relatively large samples of Jews and that others have used to explore denominational comparisons in Jewish educational attainment and income (Hurst and Mott 2006). Some have used these data quite effectively to show subgroup differences in earnings, particularly among men (Chiswick and Huang 2008). Unfortunately, wealth information in these data are not sufficient to use them to supplement my analyses. In addition, there are some questions about the reliability of the data. For example, Hurst and Mott (2006) use the NJPS to study SES differences for Orthodox, Conservative, Reform, and "other" Jews. They operationalize religious affiliation as religious upbringing and provide a detailed exploration of cross-denominational patterns of social relations, family behaviors, and SES outcomes. They find that Jews raised as Orthodox are less likely than those raised as Conservative and Reform to complete college degrees, with relatively consistent patterns for men and women. However, Hurst and Mott also find that men raised as Orthodox Jews consistently report having higher adult earnings than other Jews, whereas there is no denomination difference for women raised Jewish (see the next section for more on Jewish educational attainment). The authors acknowledge that these findings are ambiguous regarding Jewish success and suggest that the relationships might be curvilinear. Of course, it is also possible that there are reporting issues with the data or that sample sizes are not large enough even in this specialized data to clearly identify within-group differences for Jews. For these reasons, I have opted not to

TABLE 7.4. *Jews Compared to Other Groups: Family Background*

	Parents' Income (median)	Father Had a BA (%)	Mother Had a BA (%)	Ever Inherited (%)
Jews compared to:				
Conservative Protestant (CP)	$19,300	10.7	29.6	34.9
Black Protestant (BP)	$26,000	14.4	31.4	60.2
Mainline/Liberal Protestant (MP)	$15,000	1.1	24.0	20.3
Catholic	$23,400	4.8	28.4	32.5
White	$17,500	3.0	27.5	26.1
Hispanic	$27,000	13.3	32.2	58.2
Mormon/LDS	$20,000	8.3	32.4	35.3
Other religion	$16,500	3.8	17.3	13.8
No religion	$21,000	6.5	25.2	34.6
All Respondents	$18,000	6.3	27.3	33.0

Notes: Data are from the 1979–2004 NLSY. Sample size = 4,369. See Table 2.2 for values.

rely on the NJPS for my own analyses, but I will refer to some of the other interesting patterns found in these data in later parts of this chapter.

Explaining Jewish Achievement

There are many potential explanations for the extraordinary achievement of Jews.[3] Not least among those explanations is high-achieving families of origin. Prior generations of American Jews may have been underrepresented in leadership positions and may not have enjoyed the extraordinary levels of financial well-being that I described in the last section. However, today's adult Jews are very likely to have been born to high-achieving parents and to enjoy all the benefits that result from an advantaged family background. Table 7.4 summarizes the level of advantage enjoyed by Jewish respondents to the NLSY. Recall that respondents to this survey were between the ages of fourteen and twenty-two in 1979; that is, these are adults who are currently in their prime working years. Table 7.4 is similar to the tables I discussed earlier in this chapter: It compares Jews to members of other religious groups, highlighting the gap between the groups. Parents' financial resources, including their income, are an important measure of well-being in childhood, and the first column in Table 7.4 compares parents' income for Jews and others, using income

---

[3] The explanations I discuss are the reputable, social-scientific reasons. I borrow this language from Burstein (2007: 214) who makes this important distinction to "exclude genetic explanations and those proposed by anti-Semites."

from the first NLSY survey year and data that first appeared in Table 2.2. Jewish respondents had parents with notably higher incomes than all other respondents, and the difference was again particularly high between Jews and Hispanic Catholics and BPs.

Parents' education is another important indicator of family background, and the fathers of today's adult Jews were much more likely than other fathers to have completed a bachelor's degree. The difference in father's education between Jews and MPs is minimal and not significant, and the Jewish–white Catholic difference is only marginally significant. There is a striking difference again in father's education between Jews and Hispanic Catholics/BPs. Perhaps the most striking pattern in this table is in the column comparing mother's education across groups. Consistent with other research that shows Jewish women achieve relatively high levels of education, the gap between Jews in the NLSY sample and others in mother's education is remarkable. In the generation that included the mothers of NLSY respondents, it was still rare for women to complete a college degree. Not so for Jewish women. In Chapter 2, I noted that more than one-third of Jews in the NLSY had mothers with bachelor's degrees; Table 7.4 underscores the point that this puts Jews at least 17 percentage points and up to 33 points ahead of other respondents. Given that highly educated mothers tend to have highly educated, high-performing children, this gap is likely an important part of the story of Jewish attainment.

Naturally, inheriting parents' wealth has critical advantages for attainment. The final column in Table 7.4 shows the Jewish advantage in receiving inheritances. Jews are very likely to receive an inheritance at some point in their lives (again, see Table 2.2 for details); most importantly, Jews are dramatically more likely than members of other religious groups to receive an inheritance, with gaps ranging from 13 percentage points (compared to those in the "other religion" category) up to more than 60 points (compared to BPs). Chapters 5 and 6 included results of multivariate models (Tables 5.9 and 6.1) that show these advantages remain even controlling for other determinants of family background.

Human-capital acquisition is another very important part of the story of Jewish achievement. Some would include educational attainment and other forms of human capital with income and wealth as measures of achievement (i.e., some would include them in the previous section of this chapter). Human capital certainly is an essential measure of achievement. Of course, human capital is also an important explanation of other forms of achievement, including income and wealth. Regardless of where

TABLE 7.5. *Jews Compared to Other Groups:*
Educational Attainment

	Years of Education	Has Advanced Degree (%)
Jews compared to:		
White Conservative Protestant (CP)	2.8	22.7
Black Conservative Protestant (BP)	3.3	29.2
Mainline/Liberal Protestant (MP)	1.7	13.9
Catholic	2.4	22.4
White	2.0	21.1
Hispanic	3.5	27.0
Mormon/LDS	2.2	25.3
Other religion	1.1	8.2
No religion	3.3	23.9
All Respondents	2.4	20.9

Notes: Data are from the 1979–2004 NLSY. Sample size = 4,369. See Table 2.5 for values.

human capital fits in the big picture, Jewish educational attainment is quite remarkable, and an emphasis on education and human-capital acquisition has been important in Jewish communities for centuries. As Burstein (2007: 215) points out, Rabbinic Judaism placed a premium on knowledge of Jewish law and very strongly encouraged education for children. As a result, as early as the eleventh and twelfth centuries, "most Jews had some basic literacy and a significant number of them, as merchants and scholars, had acquired higher levels of education and learning" (Botticini and Eckstein 2005).[4]

Table 7.5 summarizes the Jewish advantage in educational attainment, drawing on data from Table 2.5. The first column shows that Jewish respondents to the NLSY, with 16 years of total education on average, had 2.4 more years than the typical respondent, 3.3 more years than BPs, and 3.5 more years than Hispanic Catholics. The difference in total years of education between Jews and other high-achieving groups – such as MPs and white Catholics – is not that stark. However, comparing respondents on completion of advanced degrees shows that Jews have a human-capital advantage even over these other high achievers. Table 7.5 shows that the gap between Jews and other groups in the percentage of NLSY respondents finish an advanced degree ranges from

---

[4] Cited in Burstein (2007:215).

8 points (comparing Jews to those in the "other religion" category) to nearly 30 points (comparing Jews to BPs and Hispanic Catholics).

This gap is consistent with that identified in other research, dating to the early 1980s; Barry Chiswick (1983, 1986, 1988, 1993), in particular, has provided detailed evidence that human capital is an essential part of the achievement for American Jews. Burstein (2007) provides an excellent summary of this and related research on human capital. Having highly educated parents – particularly mothers with relatively high levels of education – and coming from families that are otherwise financially secure provides part of the explanation for high educational attainment among Jews. In addition, some have proposed that Jewish culture tends to be characterized by a pro-education orientation, further contributing to high levels of human-capital acquisition, including education (Burstein 2007; Hurst and Mott 2006).

Family behaviors and processes, particularly fertility behaviors, are also an important part of the explanation of Jewish achievement. Table 2.8 compared groups on three important fertility measures: the percentage of the group having any children, age at first birth, and total number of children born. The table showed that Jews are somewhat more likely than most others to have children (i.e., somewhat less likely to remain childless), but the differences are slight. However, that table highlighted that Jews tend to have children somewhat later in life and to have fewer children. I have not replicated the results here, to conserve space. In addition to having relatively low fertility, rates of female employment when children are young are relatively low in Jewish families (Chiswick 1986; DellaPergola 1980). There is evidence that all contemporary Jewish denominational groups are relatively gender-egalitarian (Hurst and Mott 2006). These patterns create high levels of home investment in both male and female children. Ultimately, investment in child quality contributes to high levels of human-capital acquisition and relatively high returns on educational investments for both men and women, although there are some gender differences across Jewish denominational groups in the degree to which gender and human capital are related (Chiswick 1988, 1993; Hurst and Mott 2006; Lehrer 1999). Because fertility rates are low, the dilution of material resources transferred in the form of inheritance is low and strains on resources in the adult family are minimal. High rates of homogamy among Jews also suggests that the influence of these demographic traits is likely to be enhanced by marriage to a person with a similar propensity for attainment (Kalmijn 1991; Lehrer 1998).

Jewish particularity has also been offered as an explanation for high achievement. Although this explanation is difficult to measure or test empirically, it deserves attention because it appears in much of the literature on Jewish achievement, and some aspects of the argument seem to hold empirically when they can be tested with data (Burstein 2007; Hurst and Mott 2006). Burstein (2007) is one scholar who points to particularity as an important part of the explanation for Jewish success, noting that the importance of education in Jewish life is an important component of this explanation. Burstein agrees with other scholars who also point to aspects of Jewish faith that emphasize mutual assistance and this-worldly pursuits as traits leading to success. Mutual assistance refers to the importance of in-group support through self-help organizations maintained in the Diaspora (Burstein 2007). A focus on this-worldly pursuits includes an emphasis on financial pursuits (e.g., saving, owning, giving, loaning) that lead directly to financial outcomes (Bonder 2001; Burstein 2007; Featherman 1971; Lehrer 2004a).

An orientation toward this-worldly activities likely manifests itself in many of the behaviors and processes I have already discussed, including human-capital acquisition, work and occupational advancement, and income. It is also likely to influence approaches to saving and investing that affect wealth directly. In Chapter 4, I showed that NLSY respondents who were raised in Jewish families were notably more likely to follow a financial path that involved acquiring financial assets early in life: Approximately 33 percent of those raised Jewish followed this path, compared to 4 percent of all respondents and 2 percent of those raised CP, 1 percent of those raised BP or Hispanic Catholic, 8 percent of those raised MP, and 5 percent of those raised Roman Catholic (see Table 4.5). Similarly, I showed in Chapter 5 (Table 5.1) and summarized earlier in this chapter (Table 7.3) that the median value of financial assets owned by Jewish respondents to both the NSLY and the HRS exceeds those of the total samples and of every other religious group by a large margin. Given that financial assets – which tend to involve more financial risk and greater returns than real assets – are more likely to lead to wealth accumulation, it is likely that this characteristic of Jewish investing contributes to success in wealth accumulation.

Another potential explanation for Jewish achievement that arises in scholarly discussions and that is difficult to explore systematically is marginality. That is, it is possible that the role of Jews as a marginalized group in many societies has contributed to high SES. Burstein (2007) appropriately observes that this issue is less about Jews and more about the relationships Jews have with their traditional ethnic communities and with other, usually western, societies and groups that dominate those societies. There is a great deal of scholarship on the stress placed on individuals who attempt to maneuver multiple contexts of this sort and the strategies people and groups use to overcome the challenges of being members of multiple groups. Burstein (2007: 224, fn 3) relays the story of Robert K. Merton, the renowned sociologist, who was born Meyer Schkolnick and changed his name to avoid anti-Semitism that permeated higher education and that he feared would prevent him from advancing in the discipline. There is voluminous literature on assimilation that I will not be able to review here that deals with issues of marginality and includes important works on Jewish assimilation (Alba 2005; Alba and Nee 2003).

Another potential explanation for Jewish success is self-selection of immigrants. That is, there is some chance that immigrants – in this case Jewish immigrants – have higher education levels and higher earning potential (i.e., as a result of unmeasured personality and other traits such as intelligence and motivation) that coethnics who do not immigrate do not possess. This issue has attracted considerable research attention because it is both important to understanding the relative success of immigrant groups and because it should lend itself to being addressed empirically. Unfortunately, there is considerable debate regarding the degree to which self-selection affects achievement levels, including among Jews. Patterns of self-selection have been studied intensely in relation to labor market assimilation of immigrants, and evidence regarding self-selection has been used to understand subsequent changes in skills. An interesting recent study explores the role of self-selection in earnings assimilation among Jewish immigrants from the former Soviet Union to the United States and Israel (Cohen and Haberfeld 2007). In this study, Cohen and Haberfeld use census data from the United States and Israel to compare educational attainment and earnings assimilation of Jews who immigrated between 1968 and 2000. They argue that both the United States and Israel welcomed immigrants from the former Soviet Union with few restrictions between 1968 and 1989, making this a natural experiment for understanding self-selection processes. Cohen and Haberfeld find that immigrants to the United States have higher education and experience significant earnings increases more rapidly in their new country than those who immigrated to Israel. They find that self-selection accounts for these findings. I do not present results in this book that directly explore the potential for selection bias in education, income, and wealth for Jews. However, the multivariate models I use control for country of origin for both respondents and their parents. Additional data exploration demonstrates that there is no significant difference between SES levels of NLSY respondents born in the United States and SES levels of those born in other countries. Regardless, the role of selection bias in explaining Jewish achievement is worthy of future study.

The final potential explanation for Jewish success that warrants additional study is the role of social networks. In other words, it may be that Jews have unique social networks that encourage and facilitate achievement. As I will discuss in more detail in Chapter 8, data on social networks are still limited, and reliable data on both social networks and wealth are even rarer (I am not aware of a data set that contains reliable information on both). Yet the NJPS does have information on social networks and Jews, and a recent study provides preliminary evidence that networks might have some effect on attainment (Kadushin and Kotler-Berkowitz 2006). Kadushin and Kotler-Berkowitz explore how social networks and organizational memberships among American Jews are related to philanthropic behavior, religious behavior, and other outcomes. Most interesting here is the effect on financial behavior, particularly philanthropic activities. There is a strong tradition of charitable giving among American Jews (as I noted in Chapter 3 in relation to Table 3.12), and Kadushin and Kotler-Berkowitz (2006: 479) note that the "lore of fundraisers holds that money is raised mainly through personal and organizational contacts." Consistent with this, they find that Jews of all denominations give generously, controlling for household size, education, age, and other contributing factors. Most importantly, the effect of social networks and formal organizational members on giving among Jews is extremely strong. In the words of the authors, their table showing the effects of networks and organizational associations on giving to Jewish causes "shows the strongest joint effects of information networks and formal membership we have thus far encountered" (Kadushin and Kotler-Berkowitz 2006: 479). This is an influential study that provides valuable preliminary evidence regarding the importance of religious social networks to financial outcomes. It does not provide a definitive statement about Jewish achievement but it does suggest that future research will be useful to explore these questions in more detail.

LDS: Unique among Conservative Protestants?

Another small group that deserves additional mention is the Church of Jesus Christ of Latter-Day Saints, which goes by the nickname Mormons (I use the short term LDS/Mormon henceforth). The name Mormon comes from the *Book of Mormon*, a historical text published in 1830 by Joseph Smith, Jr., founder of the Mormon/LDS church, which records God's interactions with early Americans.[5] The King James version of the Bible is used by Mormons/LDS as an essential scriptural work.

Although I include all Mormons/LDS in the same category in my discussion and analyses, there are important denominations with different histories and beliefs (ReligionFacts 2010). The Church of Jesus Christ of Latter-Day Saints (i.e., The Church of Jesus Christ, or the LDS) claims the most members and is a continuation of the "Rocky Mountain Saint" branch of Mormonism. The Community of Christ (once known as the Reorganized Church of Jesus Christ of Latter Day Saints) has the second-largest membership among the Mormon denominations and continues the "Prairie Saint" movement. This group disavows the term Mormon because of its association with polygamy and because it is not true to the original name of the church (ReligionFacts 2010). There are many other, smaller Mormon faith groups as well, including the Aaronic Order, the Apostolic United Brethren, the Church of Christ (Fetting/Bronson), the Church of Christ (Temple Lot), and the Restoration Church of Jesus Christ of Latter-Day Saints. Membership ranges from slightly more than 2,000 to more than 11 million (ReligionFacts 2010). These may sound like large numbers, but the population of Mormon/LDS as a percentage of the U.S. population remains quite small. As a result, survey data sets typically include relatively small numbers of Mormon/LDS members, making quantitative analyses difficult. Sample sizes in the data sets I use prohibit analysis of more detailed subgroups, and I refer broadly to members of all Mormon churches as Mormon/LDS. I also use the term Mormons/LDS when I reference other published research even if the authors used other terminology; I do this to be consistent in this document and because the definition of Mormon used in the other published work that I reference is consistent with my own definition (i.e., inclusive of all subgroups).

In Chapters 1 and 2, I included separate estimates for Mormons/LDS in my tables because I had large enough sample sizes to expect that the estimates were reasonable approximations of population averages. Moreover, on the measures I included for Mormons/LDS, I was able – in most cases – to verify that the estimates were consistent with other data on this group. Most importantly, I included separate estimates for Mormons/LDS when possible because my analyses of various data sets and other

---

[5] The full name of the text is *The Book of Mormon: An Account Written by the Hand of Mormon upon Plates Taken from the Plates of Nephi.*

published research suggest that Mormons/LDS are unique among Conservative Protestants. In Chapter 1, I showed that Mormons/LDS have relatively strong religious convictions compared to the entire GSS sample and comparable to CPs, and Mormons/LDS participate in religious activities more than the total sample similar to members of most CP denominations.[6]

In Chapter 2, I showed that Mormons/LDS have unique family patterns. In particular, Mormons/LDS come from large families and tend to have somewhat large families of their own (Table 2.8), patterns that may reduce status attainment, including wealth ownership. This is consistent with research that uses other data and shows that Mormons/LDS have significantly higher total fertility relative to MPs, CPs, and Catholics, particularly for couples in homogamous unions (Lehrer 2009). However, my estimates of family formation using the NLSY (not shown) are also consistent with other published research showing that patterns of union formation and marital stability among Mormons/LDS may negate the family-size effect. For example, Lehrer (2009) shows that Mormons/LDS are notably unlikely to enter informal or cohabiting relationships, and Lehrer and Chiswick (1993; Lehrer 2009) show that Mormons/LDS have relatively stable marriages. That is, they find that for religiously homogamous couples, the probability of divorce within 5 years of marriage ranges from 0.13 to 0.27, with homogamous Mormon/LDS unions having the lowest risk of union dissolution (Lehrer and Chiswick 1993; Lehrer 2009). They also find that there is no significant difference in stability for MPs, CPs, Catholics, and Jews in religiously homogamous unions. Given the importance of marriage in generating status attainment and wealth accumulation, Mormons/LDS might indeed have an advantage.

In addition, I showed in Chapter 2 that although Mormons/LDS come from relatively low-income families, their fathers attained higher levels of education than CPs (Table 2.2). The level of educational attainment for the fathers of Mormon/LDS respondents was not remarkably different from the sample average, but it was also – quite importantly – not lower than other groups. In contrast, the mothers of Mormon/LDS respondents did have relatively low education levels compared to most other groups (BPs reported mothers with lower education levels). Table 2.5 also points to an important change: for NLSY respondents themselves (today's

---

[6] Mormons/LDS are typically not included with other CPs because they are unique in many ways, but they are considered Protestants and they do tend to otherwise fit the definition of Conservative, including accepting the Bible as the literal Word of God.

working adults), total educational attainment for Mormon/LDS respondents was a bit higher than the sample average. It was not dramatically higher, nor was the difference statistically significant. But the difference in means (between Mormons/LDS and members of other religious groups) is best interpreted with the standard deviation as well. The standard deviation (average difference from the center) for Mormons/LDS was notably lower than the standard deviation for other groups. This suggests that higher educational attainment is more normal – or there are fewer people at the extremes – for Mormons/LDS than for other groups. Of course, the means also reflect small sample sizes for Mormons/LDS, which complicate interpretation and underscore the importance of careful interpretation of these findings. These means are consistent with estimates of age-specific cohort levels of educational attainment available in other data sets, suggesting that they are believable, but it is still important to exercise caution in interpreting them. Given the strength of family background, particularly father's education, and a person's own education in predicting wealth ownership, these findings suggest that there might be some difference between Mormons/LDS and other CPs.

Although the educational differences I report in early chapters are not profound, they are important, at least in part, because they are consistent with what scholars of Mormon culture suggest might be a more general movement toward emphasizing educational attainment and particularly advanced degrees. In the early history of the Mormon/LDS church, there was considerable ambivalence toward education, particularly advanced education, as secular education is likely to breed skepticism of conservative church beliefs (Arrington 1969; Cummings 1982; Mauss 1984). In the 1920s and 1930s, however, the Mormon/LDS church began to recognize that "churches need loyal intellectuals" (Mauss, 1984:440) and began to provide funding for advanced education of select scholars outside Utah (Arrington 1969; Mauss 1984). At that time, observers report that the orientation of church officials and official doctrine changed in important ways, becoming more accepting and encouraging of learning at all secular universities and extending this thinking to both men and women (Arrington 1969; Mauss 1984). However, as I will discuss more later in the chapter, it was several more years before the real inclusion of women in thinking about education took hold (Arrington 1969; Mauss 1984).

Moreover, recent efforts by Mormon/LDS Church leaders have focused on promoting education even more strongly than those in the early twentieth century and have included explicit efforts to increase education levels and to generate scholars who are members of the church. The Mormon/LDS church now has an extensive secular education emphasis, including, but not at all limited to, its Brigham Young University in Provo, Utah. In addition, the Mormon/LDS church started the Perpetual Education Fund in 2001, a program designed to provide low-interest loans to college students, which are intended to increase education levels and to continue to fund generations of scholars as repayments are used to fund new recipients of the funds (Church of Jesus Christ of Latter Day Saints 2010). Official church publications report having made more than 10,000 loans through the Perpetual Education Fund as of the end of 2010 (Church of Jesus Christ of Latter Day Saints 2010). Although there is little scholarship particularly focusing on educational attainment of Mormons/LDS, the evidence that we do have (including my own estimates from the NLSY and GSS) suggest that education levels are relatively high for Mormons/LDS. There is also some evidence that younger generations of Mormons/LDS are more likely than their parents to pursue advanced degrees, consistent with the church's recent push for education. Unfortunately, sample sizes for Mormons/LDS are small and limit the reliability of multivariate analyses of available data.

One pattern that is beginning to emerge in available data is that Mormon/LDS women are increasingly likely to pursue educations; men still exceed women in total education and in obtaining advanced degrees, but gender differences in this generation compared to those in previous generations of Mormons/LDS (see earlier discussion) are less pronounced. For all respondents, both men and women complete an average of 13.7 years of education.[7] Male Mormon/LDS respondents report an average of 14.5 years of education (significantly higher than the sample average), whereas female Mormon/LDS respondents report 13.8 years (consistent with the sample average). For all respondents, 13.5 percent of males complete advanced degrees, whereas 14.3 percent of females earn some sort of post-bachelor degree. A notable 16.2 percent of male Mormon/LDS respondents receive advanced degrees, whereas only 11.6 percent of Mormon/LDS women earn advanced degrees. This difference demonstrates that there are still important gender differences among Mormons/LDS, but again, the differences, particularly in total education, are less extreme than they were in previous generations.

---

[7] My estimates from the 2004 NLSY. Total $n = 4,369$.

Education levels for Mormon/LDS NLSY respondents are also high compared to other religious groups. For males, Mormons/LDS have 14.8 total years of education, whereas CPs have 13.1 years, BPs have 12.5 years, white Catholics have 13.8 years, and Hispanic Catholics have 12.5 years. Male Mormons/LDS even exceed MPs in total education: Male MPs have an average of 14.3 years of education. Jews – the groups I discuss earlier in this chapter as high achievers – are the only groups to outpace Mormons/LDS, with males completing 16.5 years of education. Similar patterns are true for advanced degrees for males. More importantly, similar patterns hold for female Mormons/LDS compared to females from other groups. Female Mormons/LDS outpace female CPs, white Catholics, and Hispanic Catholics in total education; they also outpace female CPs and Hispanic Catholics in earning advanced degrees. Differences among female Mormons/LDS, white Catholics, and MPs are not significant. The lower-than-average Mormon/LDS likelihood of obtaining an advanced degree (compared to the full sample) almost exclusively reflects high levels of obtaining an advanced degree by female Jews. These patterns suggest that there are important attainment differences for both male and female Mormons/LDS when SES is measured as education.

Patterns in educational attainment for both male and female Mormons/LDS suggest that – because education is such a strong predictor of wealth – the net worth of Mormons/LDS may well be higher than that of other groups. There is certainly likely to be a generational difference in attainment as education opportunities have improved considerably for current adult Mormons/LDS relative to their ancestors. The educational patterns I summarize also suggest that it is important to use caution when reading qualitative accounts of Mormon/LDS, which tend to be common given limited samples in quantitative data sets. A notable example of qualitative work on female Mormons/LDS negotiation of the educational process starts with the premise that the patriarchal Mormon/LDS church seeks to maintain gender inequality and explores why female Mormons/LDS pursue education and suggests that females would not pursue educations (Mihelich and Storrs 2003). This is flawed on both points. As I have noted, the Mormon/LDS church does promote education for both genders, and both genders pursue education. The authors were surprised to learn that Mormon/LDS women were not critical of the church and ultimately spent most of the article justifying female Mormon/LDS education attainment as part of motherhood (Mihelich and Storrs 2003). Given that the sample consists of twenty undergraduates from a northwestern university (both authors were at the University of Idaho), the factual statements of the article are inconsistent with data from representative samples, and the fact that one author is a former Mormon/LDS-turned-professor underscores the importance of extreme caution in internalizing such "research." Normally I would not have mentioned flawed work, but I raise this issue in relation to Mormons/LDS because a great deal of published research on this group is qualitative, often by necessity, and difficult to interpret because of its reliance on small samples (Mauss 1984).

What, then, do we know about Mormon/LDS attainment? Family processes and education levels lead observers to speculate that Mormons are likely to have high incomes and wealth. Indeed, those are the conclusions I would draw from the conceptual model that has guided my work in this book. I would expect Mormons/LDS to have relatively high incomes and wealth. It is likely that their pro-family orientation would also predispose them to homeownership prior to owning financial assets, but their education levels would make them willing to invest in financial assets as well. It is also likely that charitable giving would be high among Mormons/LDS because of their combined religiosity, education levels, and (likely) high incomes and wealth. Unfortunately, however, small sample sizes for Mormons/LDS in most major data sets make it very difficult to make more general statements about attainment than I have made here. Sample sizes for Mormons/LDS on most income and wealth measures in the NLSY were fewer than thirty subjects, and I stopped separating them after the second chapter of this book. Other survey data sets that have information on income, wealth, and religion such as the PSID, also have small samples for Mormons/LDS (Ottoni-Wilhelm 2010). One strategy that researchers often use is to sample Mormons/LDS. This can be effective and has added to our understanding of this important group (Mauss 1984), but it is challenging to compare Mormons/LDS to other groups with an exclusively Mormon sample. Future research may be better able to draw conclusion about attainment for this group.

The issue of a small sample size also underlies my decision to include Mormons/LDS in my discussion of high-achieving groups rather than in the previous chapter on mobility. They are likely to be high-achieving, even though I cannot show it with income and wealth measures. Yet, this is also a group that is probably upwardly mobile, suggesting that it would not have been out of step to include them in Chapter 6. I could have included them in either discussion; however, I relied heavily on multivariate models to discuss mobility in Chapter 6, and that would have been impossible to do with Mormons/LDS, given sample sizes. I ultimately decided to include them in this chapter, together with Jews, who are also a small and high-achieving group, for consistency in both topic and method.

8

A Truly Complex Relationship

I acknowledged at the start of this book that the relationship between religion and material well-being is complex, and that it is challenging to describe it completely. One issue that contributes to the difficulty is data limitations. Modern data is certainly far superior to the data that early social scientists used to explore the effects of religion on attainment and other intermediary processes, yet modern data are not perfect. Often we have strong empirical evidence that part of a causal chain holds, but no empirical evidence to support another part of that same chain, making it difficult to show that the chain is valid. For example, in the first part of this chapter, I discuss religiosity. There is reliable empirical evidence that the strength of a person's religious convictions is at times more important than religious affiliation in accurately predicting some of the family processes that affect wealth attainment. However, modern data do not allow us to connect religiosity with both family processes and attainment outcomes, making it difficult to say with confidence whether there is a connection between these processes.

In this chapter, I introduce ideas and hypotheses regarding the relationship between religion and wealth that I cannot test well enough with existing data for me to include additional analyses. The ideas and gaps I address are all very likely to be part of the reason that religion and wealth are related, but data and related limitations force me to leave these ideas untested. I will continue to explore empirical evidence, but I will rely on evidence from other sources and speculate about patterns that are likely to operate in real social settings but that current data cannot support. Readers might want to take this chapter as a call to explore the open questions that each section raises. I address a range of issues, including some processes that originate in childhood, some that are strictly adult processes, and others that occur over time. The topics that I address here appear throughout Figure 1.1. Discussing them together allows me to complete the conceptual picture to some extent but is not a comprehensive coverage of all other factors that affect the relationship between religion and material well-being.

Religiosity

I have focused largely on religious affiliation up to this point, but commitment to religion or religiosity can also affect attainment. Religiosity is usually measured as the strength of religious beliefs or participation in religious activities either publicly or privately, and its origins are the subject of important research attention. Religiosity can affect intergenerational and demographic processes, network connections, and orientations toward work and money that affect well-being across the life course. Religiosity heightens the effects of affiliation that I have discussed so far: Those who are more committed to a particular denomination or set of beliefs are likely to experience more intense effects of those beliefs on the demographic, human capital, work, and financial processes that lead to attainment. Imagine, for example, the CP who is strongly committed to her religious beliefs, studies church teachings daily, and attends religious services twice weekly where her already strong beliefs are reinforced by exposure to additional information that is consistent with her foundational belief system. This person is more likely than a person who is CP in name only to possess the demographic, human capital, and financial traits that have emerged throughout this book as typical of CPs. Religiosity can also have a generally positive effect on well-being, including human-capital acquisition, health, and other attainment-related outcomes. Empirical tests of the relationship between religiosity and the processes that produce attainment have generated mixed results, perhaps, as Evelyn Lehrer has argued, because the underlying mechanisms may exert countervailing influences on attainment-related outcomes (Lehrer 2010). That is, the increased intensity of affiliation on attainment for those who are more religious may be counteracted, in some cases, by the corresponding general improvement in well-being. This confusion may also be further muddied by the potential that unusually high religiosity may be associated with extreme beliefs and behaviors that reduce well-being (Lehrer 2009).

There are also important challenges involved in measuring religiosity that make testing related ideas – and arguably in evaluating existing tests of such ideas – challenging at best. Measures of frequency of participation in religious activities, no matter how detailed or carefully collected, do not necessarily capture the true nature or strength of beliefs. For example, a young father who attends religious services at the request of his wife who hopes to set a good example for their children may appear to be religious but, in fact, may have little understanding or commitment to the teachings of the church he attends. Another challenge is spuriousness. For instance, religious people may also be more conscientious about working hard (and saving money) than their less religious counterparts because they possess some personality trait that leads to both behaviors (religiosity and hard work). In this case, it is the personality trait that causes both religiosity and hard work, rather than religiosity causing hard work. More particular empirical challenges have also plagued research on religiosity. For instance, if there is a nonlinear relationship between religiosity and attainment, using dichotomous measures of attendance to capture religiosity makes it nearly impossible to identify and specify the true, underlying relationship. Using continuous measures offers some improvement, but even these have their challenges. Finally, data sets that currently contain information on wealth outcomes, including the data sets I use in this book, do not contain reliable measures of religiosity. For these reasons, I do not include separate empirical estimates of the association between religiosity and wealth. As data improve and more data sets begin to include reliable wealth information, researchers will be able to fill this gap and estimate more accurately than I am able to do the important role of religiosity in the creation of wealth.

Related to religiosity and the content of religious beliefs are issues and processes related to the amazing variety of religious approaches that characterizes the United States, as well as the contemporary clash of religious ideas that results from an ethos of religious tolerance. These important questions that I mentioned in Chapter 1 are beyond the scope of this book. Yet the origin of beliefs and the role of aggregate processes in generating and maintaining those beliefs deserve a bit more mention. Just as it is difficult to measure religiosity, it is extremely difficult to empirically test ideas about the origin of religious beliefs and the role that interactions among religious groups play in that process. Future research might be better able to speak to the role of these important issues in creating wealth ownership, but unfortunately they remain beyond the scope of this book.

Charitable Giving

We know a good deal about charitable giving from both academic research and foundations interested in increasing giving, and giving the importance of philanthropy in the ideas of some of history's greatest thinkers. Yet we know surprisingly little about how giving is related to wealth ownership. In Chapter 3, I noted that charitable giving refers to gifts of money and time and that the box in Figure 1.1 labeled "charitable giving" illustrates the influence of human capital, work, religion, and adult traits and processes on charitable giving. Chapter 3 also addressed both general trends in charitable giving and variations across religious groups in giving, particularly in giving to religious organizations. Indeed, philanthropy has been a concern for hundreds of years, figuring centrally in the writings of Aristotle, Aquinas, Ignatius, Luther, Calvin, and others (Schervish and Whitaker 2010).

General trends, and particularly trends by religious affiliation, are important components of the processes I describe in this book. More important, however, is the link between charitable giving and wealth. Figure 1.1 suggests that charitable giving has a direct effect on wealth, but how exactly does charitable giving affect wealth? It might seem that there is a straightforward connection, but in reality the relationship is somewhat complex. For example, it is possible that charitable giving, including tithing and other forms of giving to religious organizations, decreases wealth. After all, saving can be considered the resources that remain from income after consumption, including tithing. It is even possible to argue that gifts of time could decrease wealth because of the opportunity costs associated with that time (e.g., a person could be working for income rather than volunteering, and that income would increase the person's wealth). Alternatively, however, it is possible that charitable giving increases wealth because it is an investment in a social network that can assist the contributor during difficult financial times (see further in this chapter for more discussion of this issue). Investments of both time and financial resources in social capital can have substantial long-term positive effects on net worth.

Unfortunately, reliable data connecting charitable giving with wealth outcomes are not currently available. There is excellent data showing how giving varies across faiths, including showing unique patterns for the groups I discuss and for smaller groups such as Muslims (Smith 2010). Yet data that allow a connection between giving and wealth are not available. The most effective strategy for making a connection is the one I have used in this book. I first demonstrated religious variations in orientations toward charitable giving and in actual giving (Chapter 3). I then showed that these patterns are consistent with charitable giving being a net wealth reducer (Chapters 4 and 5). This method leaves more room for error than an ideal analysis that directly connects giving with wealth; future research using data that do not yet exist will certainly be able to make this connection.

Social Capital and Network Traits

Social capital and network traits are certainly very important components of the relationship between religion and SES. *Social capital* refers to the individuals to whom a person is connected. *Network traits*, or network structure, are characteristics of the set of a person's social relations. In Figure 1.1, social capital is included with both family/social background and with adult family and friends. This underscores the importance of social relations at all points in the life course. Network traits are included as a pathway. As the other pathways do, network traits affect both transitions from childhood to adulthood and those that occur within adulthood. I discuss these two together because there is clearly an overlap, but the two concepts are distinct enough to label differently in Figure 1.1. Individuals are important and can provide influence and direction, and the overall structure of a person's social relations tends to be an important determinant of the direction taken during the life course. I discuss the two in Chapter 8 because of data limitations. That is, contemporary data sets that have reliable information on wealth do not have reliable social network information; likewise, data sets with reliable social network information do not currently have reliable wealth data. This is changing, and future research will be able to draw a more certain connection. For now, I am only able to speculate on what is likely an important piece of the picture.

Sociologists have shown that social capital and network traits affect a large number of behaviors and processes, including attainment (Bearman, Moody, and Stovel 2004; Haynie 2001; Moody 2004). Children learn how to approach education, work, and financial decision making, including saving and avoiding debt, from their parents and others with whom they are associated (Cavalli-Sforza 1993; Chiteji and Stafford 1999, 2000; Keister 2008). Parents and teachers affect children's perspectives on education and work through the structuring of children's activities at home (Lareau 2002, 2003) and in the classroom (Willis 1981). Parents' jobs and their attitudes toward those jobs also convey class-based information to children that have the potential to affect socioeconomic attainment (Kohn 1976; Kohn and Slomczynski 2001; Kohn et al. 2000). Parents and other adults also convey information about saving and investing that affects how children approach money. Financial literacy is learned, and people who are not exposed to positive lessons regarding financial literacy may be at a disadvantage in accumulating wealth.

Religious-based social capital is likely to matter as much as other types of social capital. Religious-based social networks have been a focus in sociology since the early days of the discipline (Durkheim 1954 [1912]; Simmel 1905; Sombart 1911; Weber 1930), and scholars have recently begun to explore the modern significance of these connections. There is some evidence that religion-based networks improve outcomes such as emotional and physical health and promote health, life satisfaction, psychological coping, and positive behaviors among adolescents (Ellison 1991; Ellison, Gay, and Glass 1989; Ellison and Levin 1998; Krause et al. 2001; Levin 1994; Smith 2003b). Although much research focuses on the positive implications of social capital and network traits, there are also potentially negative effects. It is even possible that religion-based social networks can have negative effects. For example, there is evidence that religion-based social networks can reinforce negative attitudes, orientations, and behaviors. In addition, people do not simply happen upon their social relations, and recent research suggests that some religious groups deliberately restrict their social ties in a way that can be detrimental. CPs, for example, tend to have relatively narrow or consolidated social networks, populated largely by others from similar faith communities (Sherkat 2009; Smith 2003a; Welch, Sikkink, and Loveland 2007), and consolidated social networks can have a detrimental effect on education-related outcomes such as verbal ability (Sherkat 2009). Prior research has not explored whether this pattern varies across CP groups, but it is likely that there are differences comparable to the differences in educational attainment that have been shown for CP subgroups (Beyerlein 2004).

How does religion-based social capital and network traits affect attainment? The positive, self-reinforcing nature of religion-based social relations can improve attainment for groups in which most members have high levels of education, income, and wealth. For example, members of religious groups in which others have accumulated significant assets are more likely to learn the skills needed for wealth accumulation. These contacts might also provide information and financial resources that lead to wealth ownership. In contrast, faiths in which the majority of social contacts are asset-poor may pass along skills that inhibit saving and wealth accumulation. Poor saving habits, excess consumption, the accumulation of large amounts of debt, and other problematic behaviors can be passed along as easily as positive behaviors. Closed social networks may exacerbate any direct, negative effect that faith has on attainment.

Is there likely an effect of religion-based social capital and network traits on wealth accumulation? Yes, but it is impossible to explore this empirically. Social capital, religion-based and other, is likely to affect wealth both directly and through other forms of attainment. Social connections affect human capital, work, job traits, and income. These feed into wealth accumulation. Social connections are also likely to affect wealth directly: Friends and family might provide start-up capital for a business, pay off student loans, contribute a down payment for a home or other real estate, or provide emergency funds during difficult financial times. To the extent that members of churches and denominations are similar in SES, social relations are likely to reinforce financial well-being. Researchers have discussed religious human capital (i.e., the capital that accumulates through participation in religious activities with other people) and have shown that this capital can have important positive effects on many outcomes, including financial well-being and physical and mental health (Iannaccone 1998; Lehrer 2009). The mechanisms here are the same as those that drive the relationship between religiosity and well-being. Unfortunately, however, data limitations make it impossible for me to test these ideas empirically.

Investing in Religion

A unique set of questions related to social capital and network traits has to do with the role of religion as an investment. That is, investments (financial or social) in religious organizations and networks of people connected by religious beliefs may be an investment with potential financial implications. In all cases, social connections made through religious organizations have the potential to yield financial or other material benefits. At the extreme, it might be better for some people to invest in religious organizations than in traditional financial organizations. Imagine, for example, that a family that is struggling financially has a modest amount to save at the end of some months. The family could either put the money in a savings account (or other investment) or donate it to their church or synagogue. The money saved in a traditional financial instrument might never amount to enough to cover a significant financial need; whereas, under some circumstances, the investment in human capital the family gains by investing financially and personally in the religious organization might pay off more dramatically when the family needs assistance. At first, this may seem far-fetched, but my own preliminary research suggests that investing in religious organizations may indeed be beneficial to a large number of families. Using a combination of quantitative data analysis, simulation modeling, and in-depth qualitative interviews, I find that for approximately 15 percent of Americans, most of whom are CP, BP, or Hispanic Catholic, investing in church has a larger present value than investing in savings accounts; for approximately 10 percent of the population, the investment in church is likely to outpace investments in the stock market (Keister in progress). This research is preliminary, but it can be illustrated by a case from my in-depth interviews with members of a Hispanic Catholic church in a medium-sized western city. One family that was heavily invested, both personally and financially, in the church discovered that their child needed braces during the time I was working in the area. They did not have sufficient savings to pay for the braces, but when their fellow church members learned of the need, the other families collected enough money to pay for the braces. The more important discovery I made here was that this was the norm for how this church – and similar churches in the area – handle their member's financial needs.

Gender and Intermarriage

Wealth is a family possession; that is, wealth tends to be owned jointly by both partners to a marriage, and decisions about the allocation of resources tend to be made jointly when two adults share ownership of assets. For this reason, I have treated wealth as a household concept throughout the book and have largely discussed religion as a household trait as well. What this means practically is that I treat unmarried people the same as married people and that I assume that married people share the same religion, typically the religion of the head of household or respondent. I will address gender issues briefly here because they tend not to be particularly important in understanding the connection between religion and wealth, as I will explain later in the chapter. I will spend a little more time addressing the related issue of intermarriage (i.e., marriage between two people of separate faiths) because this issue is potentially more important to understanding how religion affects wealth.

First, the relationship between gender and wealth ownership is a bit difficult to study because the role of gender is obscured in married couples, and married couples are an important segment of the U.S. population. Research that tries to isolate gender issues often focuses on unmarried women and men (never married, divorced, widowed) and compares them to married couples (Chang 2010; Yamokoski and Keister 2005). This research tends to find that single mothers and fathers – but particularly mothers – are economically disadvantaged in wealth ownership in comparison to married couples. To some extent, finding that single people have less wealth than married people is obvious: After all, married couples join assets, and in most cases the sum of the individual estates exceeds that of either individual. Because I address the importance of marriage in creating wealth in detail in Chapter 2, I will not revisit the topic here. However, it is important to point out that analyses not reported here show that gender does not affect the religion-wealth relationship once other factors are controlled. In particular, education and work status appear to diminish any independent effect of gender or single parenthood on the religion-wealth relationship. Admittedly, detailed data on gender roles in financial decision making in married couples and/or data that shows whether and how married couples own assets independently might show that there is, in fact, a role for gender in understanding how religion affects wealth. Unfortunately, available data do not currently allow for such fine-tuned analyses.

Second, religious intermarriage has more potential than gender for aiding in understanding how religion affects wealth. Religious intermarriage is becoming more common, and researchers have made considerable progress documenting trends in interfaith marriage. Among the important findings coming from this literature is evidence that those who live in areas where the concentration of coreligionists is low are more likely to intermarry (Lehrer 1998, 2009). There is also evidence of detailed trends in intermarriage, including evidence that the number of marriages between CPs and MPs is declining, whereas the number of marriages between CPs and Roman Catholics and those between CPs and people with no formal religious affiliation are increasing (Hout, Greeley, and Wilde 2001). What is important here is that when family members have different religious affiliations and beliefs, they may be more likely to have divergent perspectives on financial decision making. Imagine, for example, a CP married to a Catholic. If the couple retain their religious affiliations (i.e., neither converts to the other's faith), it is possible that on matters such as tithing, the couple will be at odds. In this example, the CP may prefer to use a portion of the couple's income to make contributions to a church, whereas the Catholic may not share the sense that this is an important or worthwhile use of resources. Questions such as this about what happens when people with different religious beliefs marry could provide insight into the relationship between religion and wealth. For instance, which person's values dominate financial decision making in interfaith couples? Or do couples merge their religious beliefs in some way to create a unique financial strategy? This is likely to affect wealth ownership to the extent that there is a direct effect of religious orientations and values on financial decision making.

Assessing the effect of interfaith marriage on wealth requires very specialized data. The ideal data would contain detailed information on both spouses' religious background and adult religious affiliation (and beliefs if possible). The ideal data would also need to contain information about wealth outcomes and the financial decision making that leads to those outcomes. For example, the data would contain information about who makes financial decisions for the family, who is considered the owner of particular assets (e.g., does one person own a pension plan because their employer makes this plan possible?), and how these decisions change over time. Even with the ideal data, analyses would also be cumbersome because the possible combinations of religious pairs grow large quickly. Imagine, for example, the data showed that CP-MP couples have unique financial decision making and wealth patterns and that the data also showed important differences within CP denominations. Creating and understanding the detailed differences would require both very large samples and careful analysis.

Is interfaith marriage likely to matter for understanding how religion and wealth are related? Yes, preliminary analyses suggest that interfaith marriages have somewhat unique wealth accumulation patterns. For instance, CPs who marry Catholics tend to have higher wealth than CPs who marry other CPs or who marry people from other religious groups. Unfortunately, because the specialized data I describe earlier do not exist, these are very preliminary results. Perhaps most important for my current study is the fact that interfaith marriages are on the rise, but same-faith marriages dominate the data I use. The role of interfaith marriage is likely to increase in importance over time; hopefully data availability will improve at the same time, allowing researchers to explore this important question more completely.

Health

One of the most vibrant areas of research in the scientific study of religion is the exploration of the relationship between religion and health and mortality outcomes. Interest in – and debate surrounding – the religion-health connection has grown in recent years across a large number of social science and medical disciplines. There is evidence of an association between religious affiliation and participation and various measures of physical and mental health (Musick, 2010). In particular, research has shown that religious participation is associated with improved lifestyle behaviors (e.g., decreased use of alcohol, improved diet, appropriate exercise), use of health care, improved immunity, and reductions in circulatory ailments, stroke, cancer, and other diseases (Chatters 2000; Ellison and Levin 1998). Similarly, religious participation is associated with improved coping, decreased depression, an improved sense of meaning in life, and overall better mental health (Chatters 2000; Hackney and Sanders 2003). There is also evidence that religion, particularly religious involvement, is associated with lower adult mortality, perhaps particularly for women, married couples, and the highly educated (Ellison and Levin 1998; Hummer et al. 2010; Rogers, Krueger, and Hummer 2010). Researchers have also demonstrated that there are unique patterns of morbidity and mortality by race/ethnicity and religion (Chatters 2000; Ellison et al. 2010). Specifically, there is evidence of unique patterns of health and well-being among Mormons/LDS, Adventists (Ellison and Levin 1998; Heaton 2010), and Jews (Heyman 2010).

Although the literature on religion and health is voluminous, there is still considerable debate over whether there is a clear, causal relationship between religion and health outcomes and about the exact nature of the relationship. There is also some evidence that religion can have negative effects on health. For example, in some extreme cases, religious beliefs and affiliation with certain religious groups can encourage self-care, promote inappropriate use and delays in using health care, and encourage exclusive treatment by untrained clergy (Chatters 2000). However, the association between religion and health is quite robust and continues to emerge in new analyses, new data, and in research in disciplines that were previously not concerned over a religion connection. There are many excellent reviews of the literature on religion and health, and indeed volumes have been written that explore the nuances underlying the association (Chatters 2000; Ellison and Hummer 2010; Ellison and Levin 1998). I will not attempt to review the literature here, but rather will consider the implications for these patterns for understanding attainment and wealth accumulation.

There are at least three reasons that religion might affect health and well-being (Chatters 2000; Lehrer 2009). First, religious teachings can encourage healthy behaviors. Religious services and other activities often contain messages regarding healthy lifestyle choices, health-related resources, and other information that can encourage and support efforts of members to stay healthy. There are also potentially positive psychological benefits of participating in religious activities. The mental health benefits of religious affiliation and participation likely reflect the positive side effects of religious involvement. Finally, supportive, healthy social networks associated with membership in religious-based organizations and participation in religious services and activities can reinforce healthy behaviors and improve well-being.

There is very little research connecting health – either physical or mental – and wealth accumulation, but health certainly matters for the processes that lead to wealth ownership and likely matters for the accumulation of assets, too. Physical and mental health is positively related to educational attainment both early in life and over the entire life course. Health is also positively related to time in the labor force, hours worked in any job, career advancement, and occupational prestige and satisfaction. As a result, health can affect income streams, the availability of funds to save, the accumulation of net worth, and related outcomes such as retirement behavior (French 2005). I do not include separate estimates linking religion and health, and I also do not include estimates linking health and wealth because both relationships are well established in the literature. However, the connection is important and health is certainly part of the complex set of processes that link religion with wealth accumulation.

Nonstandard Work

One unique career path that has become more common and that deserves additional attention is nonstandard work. Nonstandard work is any employment relationship that does not follow the traditional pattern of an employee working full time for a single organization and spending the typical forty hours per week in the workplace. Nonstandard work refers to part-time, casual-status, temporary, and contract work. In addition, self-employed people, those holding multiple jobs, and people who work primarily from home are usually considered nonstandard as well. Nonstandard work is often referred to as contingent work because the relationship is conditional on a range of preferences, needs, and demands from both the worker and the employer. There is evidence that a large and growing segment of the American workforce spends large portions of their working lives in nonstandard jobs (Houseman 2001a; Kalleberg and Reynolds 2000; Tilly 1996).

The rise in nonstandard work arrangements dates to at least the 1970s when workers began to desire and to demand more flexibility in their work schedules and the time they spent in the workplace (Houseman 2001b; Kalleberg 2000). Increasing numbers of married women, single mothers, and older workers were willing to work but preferred jobs that were part time, temporary, or otherwise allowed flexibility not typical of traditional jobs. At the same time, firms began to demand more flexible, adaptable workers in order to remain competitive in a changing global economy and as technological advancements began to alter the nature of production in many industries (Cappelli 1999; Lee 1996).

The implications of nonstandard work for workers and employers are mixed, and because there are both advantages and disadvantages, it is challenging to estimate the outcomes empirically. Nonstandard workers usually have flexibility in scheduling, freedom to terminate one job without giving up the entire income, and opportunities to evaluate employers before committing to a long-term relationship. However, many nonstandard workers receive relatively low compensation and limited benefits (e.g., insurance, pensions, unemployment) compared to their traditionally employed counterparts. Highly educated, white, male nonstandard workers appear to be an exception; this group appears to be able to parlay nontraditional positions into relatively high wages and may even receive generous benefits in some cases. There are also mixed benefits of nonstandard work for employers, and these typically mirror the pros and cons faced by workers. Employers may benefit from lower costs and greater flexibility that result from their limited commitment to nontraditional workers. However, there are benefits to having a workforce that is trained and prepared to respond immediately to workplace demands; having to identify and perhaps train nonstandard workers can be costly and time-consuming.

There is reason to suspect that nonstandard work arrangements vary by religious group. Indeed preliminary estimates (conducted by the author) using the NLSY and the Panel Study of Income Dynamics suggest that there are important differences. However, there is continued controversy about how nonstandard employment relations and career paths affect workers (Appelbaum 1992; Blank 1998; Callaghan and Hartman 1991), and data connecting religion, nonstandard work, and wealth are limited. For these reasons, I reserve this discussion for Chapter 8 rather than discuss it as a well-established set of findings in Chapter 3. I am also unwilling to include empirical estimates here that connect religion, nonstandard work, and wealth because the data are not reliable.

As nonstandard work becomes more common and more data become available, researchers may want to explore whether nonstandard work does intercede between religion and attainment.

Entrepreneurship

Entrepreneurship is another work pattern worthy of mention. There is evidence that entrepreneurs are wealthier than the average American. There is also evidence that entrepreneurs become wealthy by starting businesses rather than having more wealth from the start (Keister 2005; Kim, Aldrich, and Keister 2004). It is also likely that there are differences by religious affiliation in entry into entrepreneurship. The decision to become an entrepreneur reflects family background processes, human capital and educational status, and other intergenerational and demographic processes, many of which are included in Figure 1.1. Given that religious beliefs also affect orientations toward work, it is likely that there is a direct effect of religion on decisions regarding self-employment. Studying entrepreneurship requires specialized data, because those starting businesses are difficult to identify and sample; including enough entrepreneurs and comparable others in a data set is extremely challenging and expensive. Without specialized data of this sort, estimates of self-employment are precarious at best. The Panel Study of Entrepreneurial Dynamics (PSED) is a particularly useful data set for studying business start-ups because it includes large samples of nascent entrepreneurs as well as detailed financial, demographic, and background information about the respondents, which are useful in understanding what factors affect the process of business start-ups. Unfortunately, other data sets that contain information on religion and wealth have limited data on business start-ups, and the PSED has no information about religion. Again, future research could usefully explore whether entrepreneurship matters to an understanding of how religion and attainment are related.

Saving

Saving from current income refers to identifying a portion of household financial revenues that will be retained rather than consumed. Saving naturally has a very strong, positive, significant effect on wealth accumulation. The effect is so strong that I have included a separate box in Figure 1.1 for saving, including measures such as whether a household saves or not, the percent of income saved, and the total amount saved.

This box might also include the financial vehicles in which money is saved and whether saving is deliberate or forced (as in by employers). The figure shows that income, human capital, work, family, and other adult behaviors and processes affect saving; in turn, saving leads directly to total wealth ownership. In Chapters 4 and 5, I explored religious differences in asset allocation as well as differences between working-age and postretirement strategies for distributing assets across various instruments. In Chapter 6, I addressed and modeled asset accumulation patterns, focusing on CPs, to explore whether CPs have unique saving behavior. In the Chapter 6 analyses, I was able to isolate and examine growth (and decline) in overall wealth levels over time. Other researchers have used similar strategies in the absence of data on active saving (Hurst and Ziliak 2006). Both strategies shed some light on active saving from current income, but both sidestep the core issue to some extent. Ideally, I would be able to construct empirical models that use saving as the dependent variables. In particular, it would be ideal to model whether households save or not, the percentage of their income saved, and the total amount saved; that is, it would be ideal to model the concepts I include in the box labeled saving in Figure 1.1.

If I were able to model saving directly, it is likely that I would find important differences by religious group that reflect the processes I have described throughout this book. We know from other research on saving that intergenerational and demographic processes influence saving. As I have noted, people learn to save from their parents; saving also increases with human capital, marriage, and income. Family size and divorce tend to decrease saving. Sociologists and economists have identified many of these patterns and have explored how policy changes and related external shocks influence saving (Hurst and Ziliak 2006). Because these patterns vary by religion, it is likely that there are religious differences in saving. In Chapter 5, I also demonstrated that there are differences by religious affiliation in orientations toward money and saving; and in this chapter, I discuss the importance of network traits and social capital and note that there are established religious differences in both. Again, these variations are likely to translate into religious differences in active saving. Being able to model saving explicitly would be particularly helpful for understanding how orientations translate into wealth ownership.

Unfortunately, data limitations again prevent me from constructing models that relate religious affiliation (or participation) and saving. The greatest challenge to any model of saving is measuring the dependent variable. Saving is a difficult concept to capture in survey data and extremely difficult to isolate in data collection that does not involve a survey. Removing consumption from total income is a strategy, but it does not necessarily follow that all nonconsumed income is saved, nor are data on religion and consumption particularly compelling, as I discuss later in the chapter. The Survey of Consumer Finances – a data set I use elsewhere in this book – does include information on saving, but as the experts who collect those data admit, measuring saving is challenging (Kennickell 2009). Given the number of ways households can set aside income, it is startlingly difficult to isolate what counts as saving and what does not, even with what seems like nearly complete data on household financial decision making. As financial vehicles proliferate and rules governing the use of these vehicles become more complex, it becomes increasingly difficult to segregate saving. Imagine, for example, income that is put in pretax health savings accounts or employer-sponsored pension plans. There are tax implications, savings that are lost because they are not spent (as in health savings accounts), and savings that are matched (as in employer-sponsored pension savings). Each employer tends to have some unique rules regarding these vehicles as well, which further complicates measures of saving. An added roadblock for my research is that the data sets that include information on saving, such as the Survey of Consumer Finances, do not include information on religion. As a result, modeling the relationship between religion and saving is something that will have to happen when data are available.

Consumption

It is a basic economic fact that income is either saved or spent. Although income receives a great deal of attention from sociologists, and income and saving receive the attention of economists, the other piece of the equation – consumption – is frequently downplayed or overlooked entirely. Marketing researchers pay closer attention to consumption patterns than social scientists given the obvious monetary incentives involved in marketing. However, marketing research rarely includes religion in its discussions; a notable exception is Hirschman's work from the 1980s on religious affiliation and consumption processes (Hirschman 1983). Her research drew on social-scientific understanding of the relationship between religion and SES, but little has been done to update the work in recent decades. As Zukin and Maguire (2004) point out, there are at least three reasons that consumption has not played a central role in the conversations of academic social scientists: (1) consumption is a very large topic that crosses theoretical approaches; (2) it is often taken for granted because it meets our basic needs, including needs for food and shelter; and (3) the study of consumer behavior has traditionally been left to applied sociologists and psychologists (and, we might add, marketing researchers). Yet consumption habits and patterns are likely central to understanding wealth accumulation and attained wealth status.

We know from the research that has been done on consumption that many of the factors that affect saving also affect consumption, including economic, social, and cultural processes. Economic issues naturally matter: Total income, income sources, projections about future income, and related processes affect whether people consume basic goods and what kinds of goods they consume. Social processes also matter. People are influenced by those around them, by advertising, by desires to create a social image, and other processes that involve interactions with others in what and how much they consume (Zukin and Maguire 2004). It also has become clear that culture affects consumption (Bourdieu 1984). Bourdieu's (1984) notion of cultural capital, for example, highlights how people use consumer goods and the process of consumption to create social status. Consumption, in turn, has a direct effect on wealth accumulation because income that is consumed cannot be saved, invested, or otherwise used to generate wealth.

Bourdieu's argument that culture is central to understanding consumption suggests that there is reason to believe there are differences by religious affiliation and religious belief in consumption patterns. There is also strong, current empirical evidence of important variations in consumption by religion (Park and Baker 2007). Park and Baker use the Baylor Religion Survey to show how class, demographic behaviors and processes, and religion affect consumption, particularly consumption of religious paraphernalia. The outcome in this work – religious purchases – suggests that there is going to be an effect of religious beliefs, but the underlying message that culture matters is clear in the findings.

Why should religion matter for consumption? First, there are likely indirect effects of religion on consumption that originate from intergenerational and demographic processes. For example, we learn to consume from our parents and others we encounter throughout our lives, and adult family size and marital status affect our basic needs and consumption preferences. Second, there is likely to be a direct effect of religious belief on consumption. For instance, if my religious beliefs suggest that God owns my money, and I am a manager of that money, I might approach consumption in a way that is different from the person who does not hold this belief.

Ideally, then, I would include information about consumption in my analyses of religion and wealth. Unfortunately, data on religion and consumption is very limited. The NSLY and PSID include basic consumption information, but a thorough analysis of consumption behaviors requires specialized data that are not available in either of those data sets. The Baylor Religion Survey served the purposes of Park and Baker, but those data do not include sufficient sample sizes or information on wealth to connect religion, consumption, and wealth. The Consumer Expenditures Survey is a unique and incredibly rich source of data on consumption, but it does not include information on religion. Again, future research will usefully expand the discussion that I start here by including analyses of the role the consumption plays in connecting religious beliefs to wealth accumulation.

Financial Literacy

Financial literacy is a component of human capital, and it is a very important component in a discussion of wealth attainment. In Figure 1.1, I include financial literacy with other types of human capital, but it is worthy of a separate, albeit brief, discussion. Financial literacy is the ability to understand personal financial decisions and to make informed decisions with at least basic knowledge about the potential costs and benefits associated with those decisions. Financial literacy includes skills necessary to understand how financial resource management changes over time in response to economic conditions and life-course stage. A financially literate person is able to read and understand information regarding a variety of real assets, financial assets, and liabilities. Basic understanding of risk, statistical probabilities, and compound interest is also part of financial literacy.

Specific elements of financial literacy range dramatically from understanding the functioning of the economy and participants in the economy to knowledge of particular financial instruments and investment options. For example, basic financial literacy includes understanding that deposits in government-insured (i.e., insured by the Federal Deposit Insurance Corporation [FDIC]) member banks are guaranteed up to $250,000. The FDIC was created by the Glass-Steagall Act of 1933 and was intended to prevent bank runs of the sort that occurred during the Great Depression. Understanding that savings and checking accounts held in most U.S. banks are, indeed, protected is an essential piece of information that can affect a household's general financial strategy and their accumulation of assets. Similarly, understanding how to buy a home, including how to obtain a mortgage, is a component of financial literacy that can have important implications for wealth accumulation. Other components of financial literacy include knowing how to make decisions regarding pension plans in the workplace, how to select and manage a credit card, when to hold investments versus selling them, whether there is true risk involved in an investment and how great the risk is, and when and how to seek help making financial decisions.

The relationship between financial literacy and wealth accumulation is relatively straightforward. The relationship is positive: Those with greater knowledge of financial issues tend to accumulate assets more quickly. More precisely, there is likely a curvilinear relationship; that is, there is a threshold beyond which additional knowledge produces decreasing amounts of gain. The mechanism underlying this relationship is also fairly transparent: Making informed decisions regarding finances facilitates movement toward greater wealth, the direction most people prefer to go. As I mentioned in Chapter 2, financial literacy tends to increase with levels of formal education, and empirical evidence shows that as education increases so do decisions that facilitate wealth accumulation. More highly educated people save more, begin saving earlier in life, invest in relatively high-return assets, and accumulate lower levels of debt that does not yield greater wealth (e.g., consumer debt as opposed to business debt or student loans).

Does financial literacy vary by religion? There is reason to suspect that it does: Financial literacy tends to increase with formal education, and I have already shown that there are significant differences in human-capital acquisition by religious affiliation. Perhaps more importantly, a great deal of financial literacy is gained during secondary education. Because differences in educational attainment by religion are particularly noticeable in completion of levels of education beyond high school, it is likely that differences in financial literacy by religion are pronounced. Unfortunately, current data sets do not contain information on religious affiliation, financial literacy, and wealth accumulation. Future researchers will hopefully be able to address this issue more thoroughly.

Risk Preferences

A special topic that may in part result from financial literacy and that deserves some additional attention is risk preferences. Throughout this book, particularly in Chapters 4–6 when I discussed religious variation in wealth ownership, I alluded to the role that risk preferences play in determining saving behavior. I have discussed the potential for risk preferences to affect the allocation of assets across asset types (i.e., high-risk and low-risk assets), and I mentioned (Chapter 4) that there has been very little exploration of religious affiliation and belief correlated with risk tolerance. *Risk tolerance* is the degree of uncertainty that individuals prefer – or that they can tolerate – in financial decision making. Risk tolerance usually refers to the psychological or emotional impact a negative change in portfolio value has on an investor: A person with a high risk tolerance is able to handle more fluctuation in portfolio value than a person with a low risk tolerance. Economists have done a great deal of work defining risk tolerance and its opposite: risk aversion. There is evidence that risk tolerance varies with age, education and other forms of human capital, gender, family size, and financial goals (Chetty 2007; Halek and Eisenhauer 2001; Hayashi 2005; Nielsen 2005). For example, a retired person with a fixed income will typically have a lower risk tolerance than a young person with no family and many years of work ahead in which losses in asset value can be regained.

One exception to my note that there has been little effort to understand how religious affiliation or belief correlates with risk tolerance is a paper by Martin Halek and Joseph Eisenhauer (2001). In this paper, Halek and Eisenhauer use insurance data to estimate detailed demographic differences in risk tolerance and aversion, including religious differences. At first glance, the paper's findings suggest no role for risk tolerance in understanding variations by religious affiliation in wealth, because the authors find that there is no effect of religious affiliation on risk tolerance controlling for other demographic traits including age, education and other human capital, gender, marital status, number of children, race, immigrant status, employment status, occupation, and history of depression/drinking. However, the data analysis used in this paper has problems that shed considerable doubt on the religion finding. The authors use life insurance purchases in the Health and Retirement Survey as a proxy for risk tolerance, a measure that has disadvantages. They also use a single data point (1992), so their results address risk at a single point in time rather than accumulation over time. Most problematic are the religion measures: The authors control for Protestant, Catholic, and Jewish, with all other groups as the omitted category. As I have shown throughout this book, there are clear differences within Protestant and Catholic groups in family, educational, work, occupational, and saving behaviors.

There is reason to conjecture that there are real differences by religious affiliation and belief in risk tolerance. First, because it is well known that risk tolerance varies with other demographic traits (see earlier discussion) and because it is well known that many of these demographic traits also vary with religion, it is likely that there is an indirect effect of religion on risk tolerance via these other demographic processes. Second, there is likely to be a direct effect of religious affiliation and belief on risk tolerance given variations in conceptions of this-world and other-world states, the role of deity in affecting the well-being in those states, and the ability of people to intercede in the divine's plans. Consistent with the existence of a direct effect of religious affiliation and belief on risk tolerance, I have shown that orientations toward work and money vary significantly by religious affiliation. In turn, it is likely that risk tolerance has a significant effect on wealth outcomes. Risk tolerance affects family and human capital processes, labor market behaviors and processes, portfolio behavior, and saving; these have clear, established effects on wealth accumulation. Indeed, a well-developed literature, primarily in economics, has shown that there are also important interactions among these demographic and financial processes. For example, there is evidence that marital shocks (marriage, divorce) lead to reallocation of assets to less risky instruments, buying a house increases risk aversion and leads to consumption changes for a short period, and employment shocks (job loss, job changes) can affect risk tolerance in different ways, depending on the nature of the shock.

Providing equally compelling tests of the relationships among religious affiliation, religious beliefs, risk tolerance, and wealth outcomes requires specialized data. For example, survey data could be used if it includes detailed religion information, wealth outcomes, and detailed information on risk tolerance. The risk tolerance information would ideally include both self-reported tolerance for risk and measures that assess risk without clearly indicating this as their purpose. The HRS data that I have used in this book and that Halek and Eisenhauer (2001) used in more limited form includes the necessary religion and wealth information, but it is difficult to assess risk well using these data. I have repeated Halek and Eisenhauer's exploration of life insurance purchases using detailed religious categories, and my preliminary results suggest that this single change affects the results sufficiently to suggest that further exploration of a religious effect on risk is worthwhile. I do not report these findings because using life insurance purchases is a much-less-than-ideal way to measure risk. To the best of my knowledge, there are no other survey data available that contain all the necessary information (religion, wealth, demographic controls) and reliable risk tolerance measures. Future research may be able to fill this gap.

Downward Mobility

I devoted an entire chapter to discussing the relationship between religious affiliation and wealth mobility, but my discussion focused almost entirely on upward mobility. Naturally, any movement of one group upward implies either changing group boundaries or the downward mobility of another group. I offered a limited discussion of changing boundaries, rising tides versus changing positions, and related issues in Chapter 6, but I have not addressed the issue of downward mobility in much detail. Indeed, downward mobility receives very little attention from social scientists, including sociologists. Perhaps our fascination with the wealthy and a collective mentality that generally prefers accumulating assets to losing them is at play here. Whatever the reason, there have been relatively few systematic studies of downward mobility in the social sciences. In the 1960s and 1970s, researchers discussed the downward mobility of some groups, largely out of an effort to understand trends in poverty and to identify groups that were at risk of entering the ranks of the poor. This type of research is still relatively common today. For example, a recent paper using PSID data assesses whether there are racial differences among women in the causes of downward mobility from white-collar jobs (Wilson 2009). Consistent with previous work in this area, this paper shows that African-American women are quickest to experience downward mobility, followed by Hispanic women. White women are the slowest to move down from their white-collar jobs. Also consistent with other research in this tradition, religion does not play a role in the processes described in this work.

Research on mobility, including work that explores the determinants of downward mobility, has largely focused on income, because reliable data on wealth have historically not been available. Once large-scale data sets – such as the NLSY, HRS, and PSID – were established enough to provide evidence of trends in wealth mobility, it began to attract research attention. The empirical evidence from this emerging field shows detailed trends in mobility, including by religion and consistent with the patterns I showed in Chapter 6. In addition, empirical work on wealth mobility has shown that there is more *individual and household* wealth mobility – both upward and downward – than we would expect by chance

(Keister 2005). That is, there is enough movement of individuals and groups both up and down in the wealth distribution to explain the patterns. Moreover, many of the logical predictors of upward mobility also predict downward mobility, albeit in the opposite direction: Family size, marital shocks, human-capital and education acquisition, labor market shocks, and financial crises are among the most important causes of mobility (Keister 2005).

Despite the growing availability of data on the wealth mobility, research on the downward wealth mobility of entire groups, including religious groups, is still rare. This absence of empirical evidence largely reflects the newness of wealth data generally and the infrequency of noticeable movement of entire groups. Of course, the upward mobility of white Catholics suggests some movement, and I discussed these implications in Chapter 6. There are also potential future implications of the movement of CPs and Hispanic Catholics. As I argued in Chapter 6, there are reasons to suspect that these groups might experience some degree of upward wealth mobility in coming years. If these groups move and if their movement in the wealth distribution does not reflect a general upward trend in wealth values, some other group or groups will necessarily be displaced. Future research will usefully explore which groups become relatively worse off and which stagnate. Of course, it is also possible for changing group boundaries – as in boundaries among Protestant groups – to create a complete rearrangement of the structure of wealth ownership by religious groups. But again, this is an empirical issue that future research will have to sort out.

This chapter was part acknowledgment that the relationship between religion and well-being is a complex relationship that cannot be completely or definitely described in any study, and part call for future research to continue to clarify the details of this important relationship. I addressed a series of important issues that are very likely to be part of the religion-wealth relationship but that I am not able to evaluate empirically with as much accuracy as I would like given the current state of data. My hope is that this information invigorates research on this critical question and its various subquestions, ensuring that we ultimately understand the role of religion in wealth ownership, and its absence, more fully than is now possible.

9

How Much Is Enough?

When asked how much is enough, John D. Rockefeller is said to have replied, "just a little bit more." This might be an urban legend, but the sentiment is something most people understand. Indeed, most people respond to survey questions about how much income or wealth they need with similar answers: usually slightly more income than they currently receive and slightly more wealth than they currently own. The definition of slightly more varies a bit, but the underlying emotion is the same: I am not quite there. Personal finance books – both textbooks and books targeting popular audiences – rarely address the issue of a stopping point. The message tends to be the same across these books, and it usually focuses in some way on how more accumulation is better. The message in scholarly writing on income and wealth, including some of my own research and perhaps even this book, is remarkably similar. More accumulation of income or wealth is usually better, no matter the starting point. The message across these sources is something akin to Sophie Tucker's message when she is reported to have said "I've been rich, and I've been poor. Believe me, rich is better." There is no question that having income and wealth offers important advantages, including occupational and educational advantages, reduced fear of financial crises, personal and family security, comfort, and the knowledge that one's heirs will be taken care of. As I addressed in Chapter 1, the benefits of wealth ownership in particular are tremendous, and the fact that a large percentage of the U.S. population has virtually no wealth can be troubling.

However, even though wealth and income have advantages, more is certainly *not* always better. Moreover, most people recognize this. I teach a class at Duke called "Getting Rich," and the students provide wonderful examples of how, when they are confronted with hard questions about whether more is always better, most people will agree that there are nuances that complicate the issue. What do you have to do to get more? What are the trade-offs in terms of occupational conditions, family life, and other opportunity costs? On the first day, most students say they signed up because they want to be rich. It is what I expected, and it is the reason I called the class Getting Rich (I also wrote a book called *Getting Rich*, about wealth mobility, and the class does deal with wealth accumulation and mobility, so the title was not entirely a gimmick). In the course, we explore how markets function; we read and debate theories of accumulation, mobility, and inequality; we study personal finance, including buying a home and other real estate, investing, and planning for retirement; and we meet with several very wealthy people (e.g., entrepreneurs, business people, hedge fund managers, etc.) to understand how they got rich, what they think rich is, and what they would do differently had they another chance. Students write essays throughout the semester on the meaning of wealth, the functioning of markets and investment instruments, creating personal financial plans, charitable giving, pension plans, estate planning, and ultimately, on their conception of how much is enough.

One important effect of addressing the issue of wanting wealth and income in regular conversations in a classroom is that the students usually become tired of it. By the end of the semester, they have a metered approach. I do not lead them to this new position; on the contrary, I continue to lead classes on the details of how people become wealthy, how to plan for their personal financial futures, how to navigate market fluctuations, and related topics. Yet the students usually stop exclaiming that they want to be rich. Rather, they write about the pros and cons of wealth ownership, the importance of financial security balanced with exciting work and satisfying family life, and they acquire the skills to know how to have enough. They also write a final essay on "how much is enough." I force them to write about that topic, but most of them are ready to take a more moderate stance than they did at the start of the class. Inevitably, they say that, given their personal values and motivations, they do not want tremendous wealth, and they can support that claim with a well-argued and developed financial plan that will get them enough. Even still, the measures they identify are probably beyond what most of them will achieve (even for motivated graduates of Duke University).

Perhaps more importantly for this book, questions about how much is enough underscore the important direct effect religious beliefs have on wealth accumulation. Deciding how much is enough is complicated. Some people are clearly over the threshold by external, objectives standards (i.e., it is hard for most people to imagine that Bill Gates' fortune of more than $26 billion is not enough). For most people, however, enough is more elusive. The elusiveness of the end point can also create challenges for understanding the processes that lead to wealth accumulation, including the role of religion. The primary complicating factor relates to the fact that a decision *not to* accumulate can look like an *inability to* accumulate. For example, if a person decides she has enough wealth, quits her job, and stops saving (assuming she has not reached retirement age), we might guess that she is unable to save or not interested in investing. If we do not have sufficient data, we might conclude that something about her – her gender, education, job status – motivate her lack of saving. We would be missing the important point that she has decided she has enough and is actively not saving. However, religion is a somewhat different issue because most religious beliefs say something about how much is enough. Indeed, the fact that most religions say something about enough underscores the important role that religion plays in determining wealth ownership.

These are the questions I explore in this final chapter. First, I ask how much is enough. I ask how much we really need, and I address objective attempts to identify needs and to establish thresholds. I also discuss the role of uncertainty and the simplifying assumptions used to determine the point at which one has enough. As part of this discussion, I briefly address the related issue of whether wealth creates happiness. Determining how much is enough inevitably leads to questions about the trade-offs, and happiness (however it is defined) is an important part of the trade-offs. I conclude with a general recapping of the arguments and findings contained in this book, particularly as they relate to having enough, and I address the very important role that values, orientations, and the related issue of culture played in the story I have told. A final caveat: in this chapter, I do not attempt to adjudicate between decisions not to accumulate and the inability (whether derived from personal or structural factors) to accumulate. I provided some related empirical evidence in Chapter 3 when I discussed values and orientations toward work and money. But I do not have decisive data linking religion to decisions to accumulate (or not to accumulate). Future research, perhaps using experimental data more effectively, may clarify this issue. My intention is simply to highlight an important question related to accumulation and to which religious teachings are often directed.

How Much Do You Really Need?

Asking how much is enough implies that there is an objective number at which a person, or a family, has sufficient income and wealth and does not need more of either. It is the point at which most people would consider themselves rich or independently wealthy. For most people, that is the point at which they would, at least at first, say that they have enough. Financial planners spend considerable time trying to identify this number, both for general reference purposes and for particular clients. The answer typically involves some combination of income and wealth at which paid work is no longer necessary. The goal is often calculating estimated retirement needs to ensure that savings and investments are sufficient to cover expenses when a person no longer works, usually at or around age sixty-five. However, the same general approach can identify a point (i.e., a financial level) prior to retirement when it is possible to live without income from paid work. I will refer to this as postretirement and include both normal and early retirement. The first step is to identify all the necessary annual expenses, including housing and home maintenance, taxes, health care, clothing, groceries, basic utilities, payments on debt, transportation, childcare and other costs related to children such as education, insurance, emergency cash, and all other necessities. It is also useful to estimate expenses that are not essential to living but that most people would want to be able to enjoy, including travel, recreation and entertainment, dining out, charitable giving and tithing (though some might consider these expenses necessary), leaving an inheritance, consumer goods, nonessential utilities such as cable and cell phone extras, and real luxuries such as a second home, vehicles in addition to those that cover basic transportation needs, spa treatments, and the like. It is also necessary to factor in inflation and to realize that costs are very likely to continue to grow over time even if a person does not make lifestyle changes. Second, it is necessary to estimate sources of funds to cover these expenses. For retirees, Social Security retirement benefits may be part of the equation. Estimated employer pension benefits (whether defined benefit or defined contribution) are also available postretirement at limited or no cost, or can be available preretirement, often at a substantial cost (e.g., early-withdrawal penalties). Other savings would need to cover the remainder of costs.

Consider a simple example of a person estimating necessary retirement needs in today's dollars. Annual postretirement costs are usually estimated at 70–80 percent of preretirement costs; therefore, a person making about $44,000 a year before retirement would need to plan to have about $35,000 in annual income to cover postretirement costs (Garman and Forgue 2010). That person is likely to receive about $13,000 in Social Security retirement benefits and an employer pension of about $6,000 in current dollars, assuming average saving and benefits for today's workers (Garman and Forgue 2010: chapter 17). For this example, total expenses ($35,000) minus total income ($13,000 plus $6,000) leaves a $16,000 gap that would need to be filled by other saving. Assuming this person saved this much, he would have enough to retire.

Unfortunately, this type of calculation becomes complicated quickly by challenges associated with estimating expenses and income, uncertainty about the future, and confusion about what to include in a calculation of this sort. Estimating expenses can be particularly difficult. The 70–80 percent (the figure used to estimate the proportion of preretirement income needed postretirement) assumes minimal debt, and indeed many financial planners will advise people to have virtually no debt if they plan to retire (Garman and Forgue 2010). This includes having no mortgage debt – in other words, owning a home outright. There are also challenges associated with predicting the future of expenses, income, and other factors that affect how much a person needs to live. For example, it is difficult to estimate how costs will change over time. Inflation is not predictable, and business cycles can affect the value of goods in unexpected ways. Another complication is estimating the amount of income that investments will produce. Market fluctuations and unpredictable investment returns create challenges to estimating how much saving is enough. Uncertainty about life expectancy, unanticipated medical expenses, and other emergencies further complicate the calculation. Add to this limited financial literacy, fear about risks that may not be real (e.g., fear of medical crises that are unlikely), and other fears about not being able to cover basic needs, and things get even more complicated very quickly.

In addition to problems associated with estimating costs and anticipating future changes, changing standards or standards that are impossible to achieve make the concept of how much is enough even more difficult to estimate. For many people, as they accumulate assets, their expectations about what constitutes a necessity changes. It might be that twice-yearly vacations, including expensive accommodations, are not considered necessary for those at the bottom of the wealth distribution. However, for those at the top who may enjoy frequent travel, expensive trips may seem essential. There are those who are so wealthy, it is clear they have enough and for whom accumulation becomes a game (Frank 2007). Though their numbers are growing, they still represent only a small portion of the population. At the other end of the spectrum are those who will never have enough because circumstances and their own decision making combine to keep their wealth low. Having enough for these people is also close to impossible, but for very different reasons. One thing all these people have in common is that having enough is an elusive goal, and more usually appears better.

Of course, there are people who have decided that they do have enough and may not be attempting to accumulate additional assets. John Bogle is an interesting example of a person who has (publicly in his case) acknowledged that he has enough and does not need more. Bogle founded the Vanguard Mutual Fund Group and is President of the Bogle Financial Markets Research Center. He is also the author of the book *Enough: True Measures of Money, Business, and Life*. In this book, Bogle acknowledges that he has never been among the wealthiest people in the country, despite his position as founder and former CEO of one of the largest mutual fund companies in the country. He says, "I have never played in that billion-dollar-plus major league; nor, for that matter, even in its hundred-million-dollar-plus minor league. Why not? Simply because as the founder of Vanguard, I created a firm in which the lion's share of the rewards would be bestowed on the shareholders of the truly *mutual* mutual funds that compose the Vanguard Group" (Bogle 2009: 234). Bogle goes on to say that Vanguard operates on an at-cost basis, making their net income essentially zero. His own wealth is largely held in a tax-deferred retirement plan to which he continues to contribute and which he invests in relatively low-risk mutual funds. He attributes both his wealth and his confidence that he has enough to his thrifty (Scottish) genes, thrifty values, and low-risk investment strategies (Bogle 2009).

But then, as Bogle suggests, it is not just about the money; deciding how much is enough involves deciding what it means to be happy, and that is difficult. When I give talks about wealth, someone in the audience inevitably asks whether money leads to happiness. The answer is: it depends. It depends largely on what money means, but more importantly it depends on what it means to a person to be happy. And this complicates things further. A recently released Gallup World Poll using data from 155 countries collected between 2005 and 2009 and representing 96 percent of the world's population showed that "life evaluation, or life satisfaction, rises with personal and national income (Gallup World Poll 2010)." The Gallup Poll found what many have suspected and what researchers have been able to surmise from other data as well. Presumably this relationship reflects the mechanisms we would expect to connect financial well-being with satisfaction. As financial resources increase, consumption, the satisfaction of desire, prestige, security, and even power tend to increase.

What was unique about the Gallup Poll was that it was able to look directly at both life satisfaction (i.e., feeling that your life is generally going well) and the day-to-day positive and negative feelings that people experience. Prior research has largely been restricted to looking at whether financial well-being (typically defined as income) affects life satisfaction. This research has found that income does increase *satisfaction*, but there has been little evidence of a correlation between income and life *enjoyment*. It is important to point out that both the Gallup Poll and other research rely on information about income rather than wealth; however, given that there is a positive (albeit modest) correlation between income and wealth, it is likely that these same studies would have found a positive correlation between wealth and happiness. Studies looking directly at the relationship between wealth and income are rare because data are scarce. Even using income as a proxy for wealth has created considerable debate. Some of the debate relates to a degree to which moving out of poverty (or the difference between those in poverty and the rest of the population) accounts for most of the correlation.

There is also debate about whether any of the related empirical findings are simple correlations, or whether there is a causal relationship between financial well-being and happiness. The causation issue is extraordinarily difficult to determine here, same as it tends to be in much of social science. For example, even if there is a correlation at the national level between financial well-being and happiness, it is extremely difficult to control for the large number of factors at various levels of aggregation that account for that correlation. Social psychological research investigates much more precise differences across individuals, but it is even difficult to make certain causal statements using that research because both financial well-being and happiness may be influenced by similar background and genetic effects (Schnittker 2008). New research attempts to address this (and related questions) by using twins to study the relationship between happiness and success (including financial success) by eliminating the influence of genetics. The results are promising, suggesting that there may indeed be an independent (positive) effect of success on happiness

(Schnittker 2008). Again, however, a weak point of this research is in defining both financial well-being and happiness. Given that it is this difficult for researchers to determine whether wealth and happiness are related, it is no surprise that individuals find it difficult to know whether more wealth will make them happier. Some conclude that more must be better; others – like Bogle – decide that enough is enough.

Religion and Having Enough

What role, then, does religion play in conceptions about how much is enough? It is likely that religion is an important determinant of ideas and related decisions regarding having enough for both those who continue to accumulate and those who may have stopped accumulating (either consciously or unconsciously in either case). I argued in Chapter 1 that religious affiliation and beliefs affect wealth outcomes both indirectly and directly. The indirect connection occurs through religion's effect on intergenerational and demographic behaviors and processes such as education and educational attainment, marriage behavior, fertility, work, and job processes and the timing and ordering of each of these processes. I also argued that religion can affect wealth by shaping network connections. Because each of these intergenerational, demographic, and network behaviors and processes affects wealth, there is an indirect religion-wealth relationship. Each of these intergenerational, demographic, and network behaviors and processes also affects conceptions of how much is enough, creating another link between religion and wealth. For example, attaining additional education or having children may alter conceptions about how much wealth a person needs. To the extent that religion affects these other processes, it may also affect wealth outcomes.

The stronger link between religion and conceptions of enough-is-enough is likely through what I have referred to as a direct link, or the effect religious beliefs have on orientations and values of various sorts. I have argued that religious beliefs affect orientations toward work, saving, investing, and related financial processes. Part of the mechanism through which this happens is often via ideas about how much is enough. For example, Christians refer to Paul's words regarding contentment in discussions about material possessions: "And God is able to bless you abundantly, so that in all things at all times, having all that you need, you will abound in every good work" (2 Corinthians 9:8). For Christians, an ideal goal is an authentic relationship with God, a source of contentment that transcends material want. Other religious traditions have similar ideas, and of course, the relative weight of such passages varies with denomination even within broad faith groups. Yet the underlying connection is the same: Religion affects conceptions of enough-is-enough (i.e., contentment, satisfaction), and these affect wealth. Of course, religious beliefs also can affect definitions of happiness and conceptions of how to attain satisfaction in life, and these may affect when people determine they have enough. Each of these additional, powerful connections between religion and accumulation highlights the very important role that religion plays in determining wealth ownership.

Conclusions

Not only did I propose that religion matters for wealth accumulation, but I also provided very strong empirical evidence to demonstrate that the two are closely related. In Chapter 2, I began by exploring the intergenerational and demographic processes through which religion directly affects wealth. I showed patterns by religion in family background, including parents' income, education, wealth (by exploring inheritance), immigrant status, and childhood family structure. I also showed patterns by religion in educational attainment, marital status, and fertility. In Chapter 3, I broadened the exploration of indirect processes and began to explore the direct connection between religion and wealth by isolating how work, income, and orientations toward work and money vary by religious affiliation. I showed that there is some variation in work behaviors by religious affiliation in work behaviors – most notably when men and women are separated – and occupation. Differences by religion were even more pronounced in earnings, including earned income and government transfer payments. Even stronger still were relationships between religious affiliation and orientations toward work and money.

Important patterns in SES by religious affiliation began to appear by the end of Chapter 3 and as I explored wealth ownership patterns directly in Chapters 4 and 5. To summarize briefly: white Catholic, MPs, and particularly Jews generally had intergenerational and demographic patterns consistent with high SES, including small family sizes, high educational attainment, high-SES occupations, and high incomes. These same groups reported orientations toward work and money that are conducive with wealth accumulation. In contrast, Hispanic Catholics, CPs, and particularly BPs demonstrated patterns consistent with lower SES, including larger family sizes, lower educational attainment, low-SES occupations, low incomes, and orientations toward work and money that would reduce accumulation. These patterns were borne out in Chapters 4 and 5, in which I looked directly at patterns in wealth ownership by religious affiliation. In these chapters, I looked at total net worth and disaggregated it into its components, including total real assets, total financial assets, various types of real and financial assets, and liabilities. I looked at how the percentage of people in high-wealth and low-wealth categories varies by religious affiliation, and at the relationship between religion and accumulation trajectories over time. The patterns in wealth ownership that I showed in Chapters 4 and 5 followed clearly from the intergenerational/demographic patterns and orientations that I described in prior chapters. Indeed, the patterns of wealth ownership by religion were even clearer than any of the patterns I showed prior (with the possible exception of income, a close relative of wealth). Perhaps most importantly, the religious patterns in wealth ownership were very clear in multivariate regression results (Chapter 5) that allowed me to explore the relative importance of various influences on religion. The bottom line was that – net of a very large number of other behaviors and processes – there is a remarkably strong relationship between religious affiliation and wealth ownership.

I then isolated certain religious groups and explored their wealth accumulation patterns more closely in Chapters 6 and 7. In Chapter 6, I addressed upward and potential upward wealth mobility, focusing on white Catholics, CPs, and Hispanic Catholics. White Catholics have already been upwardly mobile, and my investigation in Chapter 6 demonstrated that factors such as changing educational attainment, family size, and female labor force participation have led to increasing levels of wealth ownership for this group in recent decades. I showed that CPs have been relatively poor, owning little wealth and accumulating at low rates, but that there is some evidence that this group may be changing and becoming wealthier. I also looked briefly at Hispanic Catholics and focused on some very preliminary evidence that this group might also be experiencing the very early stages of upward mobility. The speculative discussions were, of course, preliminary, but they are suggestive of important patterns that may become clear in future decades and that underscore the constantly changing nature of the religion-wealth relationship. In Chapter 7, I looked more closely at two religious groups that have established patterns of high achievement – MPs and Jews – and addressed both within-group patterns and potential reasons for this achievement. I argued that there is relatively strong consistency across MP groups in SES, including wealth, and addressed the historical, demographic, and other patterns that contribute to this. For Jews, I showed how extremely different their SES is compared to other groups. My discussion was consistent with other recent evidence on Jewish achievement and highlighted the degree to which Jews have succeeded on most SES measures. I concluded this chapter with a bit more speculation, this time centered on Mormons/LDS. This relatively small (but growing) religious group is religiously conservative but has some potential to be distinct in their wealth accumulation. I addressed this issue briefly and discussed the data issues that make it challenging to provide definitive information about their wealth accumulation with available empirical evidence.

The relationships that I proposed and explored empirically in this book relied on concepts, theoretical mechanisms, and ideas about the interaction of social processes that originate with status attainment and life course approaches to social behavior. The status attainment model – still the standard in research on stratification and inequality – provided the basic structure for my discussions of how intergenerational and demographic processes interact with adult behaviors and processes to create personal and family well-being. The life course perspective contributed ideas and structure for thinking about changes that occur in individual lives over time. This approach treats lives as coherent entities that derive their structure and meaning from various antecedent-consequent linkages. Life course research is the source for my treatment of lives as trajectories that include important turning points that can provide information about the directions people move over time.

Although ideas from the status attainment and life course schools of thought provided the foundation for my discussions, there was much more to what I proposed and to what I found with my empirical investigations then either of these approaches offers independently. That is, this book is much more than a simple status attainment or life course approach to understanding wealth. First, my approach is unusual because it merges thinking from both of these important and influential schools of thought. The two work well together, particularly in studying stratification outcomes, but researchers do not usually draw on both simultaneously. More importantly, my work explored concepts and relationships that neither status attainment nor life course research has tackled previously. Notions of culture, including measures of religion and religious beliefs, seldom enter discussions in either camp. Similarly, it is still rare for sociologists to study wealth and wealth accumulation, including sociologists who draw on status attainment or life course ideas, although studies of wealth have become more common than they were even a decade ago.

Perhaps the most important contribution of this book is the statement it makes about culture and the role that culture plays in producing behaviors and outcomes. Culture has largely been considered by sociologists as a collection of ideas that are used to rationalize choices but that do not themselves lead to behaviors (Swidler 1986). The toolbox or repertoire approach to understanding culture is important and has, as a result, been influential in sociology. Yet it leaves open the question of whether elements of cultural orientation, and the values associated with cultural orientation, act as motivators of behavior. Studies of religion are more likely to include the concept of values and orientations (and the beliefs they produce), but research connecting values to outcomes is still limited and often viewed with skepticism given the association of values with functionalism (Hitlin and Piliavin 2004; Vaisey 2009). More current research is beginning to show that cultural ideas may both justify and motivate behavior (Vaisey 2009), but data on cultural orientations is rare and connecting these orientations to behaviors is challenging.

Religious beliefs and values are an important part of culture, and what I showed was that these beliefs and values are indeed important motivators of the behaviors that lead to a critical component of well-being: wealth ownership. I was able to show descriptive relationships between religious affiliation and the behaviors and processes that we know lead to wealth ownership. I was even able to show very strong connections between religious affiliation and wealth. My descriptive results showed that religious affiliation and wealth are related. More importantly, I was able to show that changes in religious affiliation correspond predictably with levels of wealth ownership, and I was able to show that even with a very large number of other behaviors and processes controlled, religious affiliation is associated very strongly with wealth ownership in multivariate models. I do have to make some assumptions, largely because data connecting religious values and wealth are still limited. But my assumptions are relatively modest. The implication is that having a religious affiliation implies holding certain values and orientations – including values regarding work and money – which explain the remaining religion effect in these multivariate models of wealth. In other words: I control for everything (possible) that affects wealth ownership, including religion. Because the other processes that should explain why religion matters (e.g., education, fertility, marriage behavior) do not make the religion effect insignificant, the remaining religion effect is extremely an effect of religious values. I bolster this claim with evidence from other data, which shows a strong connection between religious affiliation and the very values and orientations that are likely to cause the effect.

Culture is widely accepted as an important explanation of social and economic processes, but it is notoriously difficult to measure and to incorporate in empirical research. Although measuring religious beliefs comes with its own inherent challenges, measuring and quantifying religious beliefs is perhaps more possible than measuring and quantifying other aspects of culture. My hope is that this book brings us a bit closer to understanding how cultural orientations lead to economic behaviors.

Appendix

Multivariate Model Details

In Chapters 5 and 6, I included multivariate regression models of various outcomes related to wealth ownership using the 1979–2004 NLSY. I use data prior to 1985 to create background variables; and I use data from 1985–2004 to create other measures including dependent variables. For all models, I created pooled cross-section time series data with the 1985–2004 data; collection of wealth information began in 1985 when the youngest respondents were in their twenties. In the multivariate models, person-years is the unit of analysis, allowing me to take advantage of the longitudinal nature of the data. The data included one observation per respondent per year, and both the dependent and independent variables were able to vary yearly for each respondent. Table 5.9 includes logistic regression models of father's and mother's educations. The dependent variable is whether the respondent's biological father (model 1) and biological mother (model 2) had a bachelor's degree or more. Table 5.10 includes a model of another dichotomous outcome: whether or not the respondent has ever received an inheritance. Because the outcome in each of these models is dichotomous, I use logistic regression to estimate the models. Tables 5.9 and 5.10 use the full NLSY sample; Table 6.1 repeats these logistic models for white, nonimmigrant respondents to the NLSY who reported religion as Roman Catholic in 1979. Otherwise the models are identical.

Table 5.11 includes Generalized Least Squares (GLS) models of total household net worth. GLS is a likelihood-based general linear regression that I chose to use because the White's Test for heteroskedasticity was significant, and the Ordinary Durbin-Watson Test (D-W) for first-order autocorrelation was significantly different from two. Because the Ordinary D-W was significant, it was not necessary to use the General D-W for high orders of autocorrelation (Greene 2003). Practically, I used SAS Proc Mixed to estimate the models using the estimator option to correct for heteroskedasticity following Diggle, Liang, and Zeger (1994) and assuming an AR(1) structure in correcting for autocorrelation. I omitted several outliers, but the omission did not affect the results. Tables 6.3 and 6.6 repeat these models but vary the omitted variable for the religion measure to highlight wealth accumulation processes for various religious groups.

To model asset growth (Table 6.4), I used NLSY data and multilevel growth models (Singer 1998). These models allow me to isolate the effect of religion on the growth in asset values over time during adulthood (1985 through 2004). I estimated these models in SAS Proc Mixed. The general structure of the multilevel growth models is the same as the net worth models described earlier, but the growth models treat both the intercept and the slope as random effects. This is equivalent to interacting specified individual-level effects with time (year). These models facilitate studying asset accumulation by providing estimates of the effects of covariates on both the initial value and the growth rate of the dependent variable (with other effects controlled). I included measures of 1) religion and 2) an interaction between religion and time. The interpretation is: 1) the effect of religious background on the initial (1985) value of net worth, other covariates controlled, and 2) the effect of religion on the growth rate of net worth (between 1985 and 2004), other covariates controlled. Again, the White's test was significant, and the Ordinary Durbin-Watson indicated first-order autocorrelation. I corrected using the estimator option and assuming an AR(1) process.

Works Cited

Abbott, Andrew and Alexandra Hrycak. 1990. "Measuring Resemblance in Sequence Data: An Optimal Matching Analysis of Musicians' Careers." *American Journal of Sociology* 96:144–85.

Alba, Richard. 2005. "Bright vs. Blurred Boundaries: Second-Generation Assimilation and Exclusion in France, German, and the United States." *Ethnic and Racial Studies* 28:20–49.

Alba, Richard D. 1981. "The Twilight of Ethnicity among American Catholics of European Ancestry." *Annals of the American Academy of Political and Social Science* 454:86–97.

Alba, Richard and Victor Nee. 2003. *Remaking the American Mainstream: Assimilation and Contemporary Immigration.* Cambridge, MA: Harvard University Press.

Alcorn, Randy C. 2003. *The Law of Rewards: Giving What you Can't Keep to Gain What You Can't Lose.* Carol Stream, IL: Tyndale House Publishers.

———. 2005. *The Practice of Tithing as the Minimum Standard for Christian Giving (sermon notes).* Gresham, OR: Eternal Life Ministries.

Ammons, Samantha K. and Penny Edgell. 2007. "Religious Influences on Work-Family Trade-Offs." *Journal of Family Issues* 28:794–826.

Altonji, Joseph G., Todd E. Elder, and Christopher R. Taber. 2005. "Selection on Observed and Unobserved Variables: Assessing the Effectiveness of Catholic Schools." *Journal of Political Economy* 113:151–84.

Alwin, Duane. 1986. "Religion and Parental Childbearing Orientations: Evidence for a Catholic-Protestant Convergence." *American Journal of Sociology* 92:412–20.

Alwin, Duane F. and Jacob L. Felson. 2010. "Religion and Child Rearing." Pp. 40–60 in *Religion, Families, and Health: Population-Based Research in the United States*, edited by C. G. Ellison and R. A. Hummer. New Brunswick, NJ: Rutgers University Press.

Appelbaum, Eileen. 1992. "Structural Change and the Growth of Part-Time and Temporary Employment." Pp. 1–14 in *New Policies for the Part-Time and Contingent Workforce*, edited by V. L. duRivage. Armonk, NY: Sharpe.

Arrington, Leonard J. 1969. "The Intellectual Tradition of the Latter-Day Saints." *Dialogue* 14:119–29.

Baltzell, E. Digby. 1964. *The Protestant Establishment: Aristocracy and Caste in America*. New York: Random House.

Bartkowski, John P. and Christopher G. Ellison. 1995. "Divergent Perspectives on Childrearing in Popular Manuals: Conservative Protestants vs. the Mainstream Experts." *Sociology of Religion* 56:21–34.

Bearman, Peter and Hannah Brückner. 1999. "Promising the Future: Abstinence Pledges and the Transition to First Intercourse." *American Journal of Sociology* 106:859–912.

———. 1989. *Family Size and Achievement*. Berkeley, CA: University of California Press.

Bearman, Peter S., James W. Moody, and Katherine Stovel. 2004. "Chains of Affection." *American Journal of Sociology* 110:44–91.

Beeghley, Leonard. 2005. *The Structure of Social Stratification in the United States*. Boston: Allyn and Bacon.

Beyerlein, Kraig. 2004. "Specifying the Impact of Conservative Protestantism on Educational Attainment." *Journal for the Scientific Study of Religion* 43:505–18.

Blake, Judith. 1981. "Family Size and the Quality of Children." *Demography* 18:421–42.

Blank, Rebecca M. 1998. "Contingent Work in a Changing Labor Market." Pp. 258–94 in *Generating Jobs: How to Increase Demand for Less-Skilled Workers*, edited by R. B. Freeman and P. Gottschalk. New York: Russell Sage Foundation.

Blau, Peter and Otis D. Duncan. 1967. *The American Occupational Structure*. New York: Wiley.

Bogle, John C. 2009. *Enough: True Measures of Money, Business, and Life*. Hoboken, NJ: Wiley.

Bonder, Rabbi Nilton. 2001. *The Kabbalah of Money: Jewish Insights on Giving, Owning, and Receiving*. New York: Shambhala.

Borjas, George J. 1999. *Heaven's Door: Immigration Policy and the American Economy*. Princeton, NJ: Princeton University Press.

———. 2000. *Issues in the Economics of Immigration*. Chicago: University of Chicago Press.

Botticini, Maristella and Zvi Eckstein. 2005. "Jewish Occupational Selection: Education, Restrictions, or Minorities?" *Journal of Economic History* 65:1–26.

Bourdieu, Peter. 1984. *Distinction: A Social Critique of the Judgment of Taste*. Translated by R. Nice. Cambridge, MA: Harvard University Press.

Brimmer, Andrew F. 1988. "Income, Wealth, and Investment Behavior in the Black Community." *American Economic Review* 78:151–5.

Bryk, Anthony S., Valerie E. Lee, and Peter B. Hollan. 1993. *Catholic Schools and the Common Good*. Cambridge, MA: Harvard University Press.

Bucks, Brian K., Arthur B. Kennickell, Traci L. Mach, and Kevin B. Moore. 2009. "Recent Changes in Family Finances from 2004 to 2007: Evidence

from the Survey of Consumer Finances." *Federal Reserve Bulletin*, http://www
.federalreserve.gov/pubs/bulletin/2009/pdf/scf09.pdf.

Bucks, Brian K., Arthur B. Kennickell, and Kevin B. Moore. 2006. "Recent
Changes in U.S. Family Finances: Evidence from the 2001 and 2004 Survey of
Consumer Finances." *Federal Reserve Bulletin*, http://www.federalreserve.gov/
pubs/bulletin/2006/financesurvey.pdf.

Burstein, Paul. 2007. "Jewish Educational and Economic Success in the United
States: A Search for Explanations." *Sociological Perspectives* 50:209–28.

Call, Vaughn R.A. and Tim B. Heaton. 1997. "Religious Influence on Marital
Stability." *Journal for the Scientific Study of Religion* 36:382–92.

Callaghan, Polly and Heidi Hartman. 1991. *Contingent Work: A Chart Book on
Part-Time and Temporary Employment*. Washington, DC: Economic Policy
Institute.

Cantril, Hadley. 1943. "Educational and Economic Composition of Religious
Groups." *American Journal of Sociology* 48:574–9.

Cappelli, Peter. 1999. *The New Deal at Work: Managing the Market-Driven
Workforce*. Cambridge, MA: Harvard Business School Press.

Caskey, Richard. 1994. *Fringe Banking: Check-cashing Outlets, Pawnshops, and
the Poor*. New York: Russell Sage Foundation.

Cavalli-Sforza, L. Luca. 1993. "How Are Values Transmitted?" Pp. 305–318 in
The Origin of Values, edited by M. Hechter, L. Nadel, and R. Michod. New
York: Aldine de Gruyter.

Center, for Philanthropy. 2003. "Center for Philanthropy Panel Study."

Chang, Mariko Lin. 2010. *Shortchanged: Why Women Have Less Wealth and
What Can Be Done About It*. New York: Oxford University Press.

Chatters, Linda M. 2000. "Religion and Health: Public Health Research and
Practice." *Annual Review of Public Health* 21:335–67.

Chaves, Mark. 2006. "All Creatures Great and Small: Megachurches in Context."
Review of Religious Research 47:329–46.

Chaves, Mark and Sharon L. Miller. 1999. *Financing American Religion*. Walnut
Creek, CA: AltaMira Press.

Chetty, Raj and Adam Szeidl. 2007. "Consumption Commitments and Risk Preferences." *Quarterly Journal of Economics* 122:831–77.

Chiswick, Barry R. 1983. "The Earnings and Human Capital of American Jews."
Journal of Human Resources 18:313–36.

———. 1986. "Labor Supply and Investment in Child Quality: A Study of
Jewish and Non-Jewish Women." *Review of Economics and Statistics* 68:
700–703.

———. 1988. "Differences in Education and Earnings across Racial and Ethnic
Groups: Tastes, Discrimination, and Investments in Child Quality." *Quarterly
Journal of Economics* 103:571–597.

———. 1993. "The Skills and Economic Status of American Jewry: Trends over
the Last Half-Century." *Journal of Labor Economics* 11:229–242.

Chiswick, Barry R. and Jidong Huang. 2008. "The Earnings of American Jewish
Men: Human Capital, Denomination, and Religiosity." *Journal for the Scientific Study of Religion* 47:694–709.

Chiteji, Ngina S. and Frank P. Stafford. 1999. "Portfolio Choices of Parents and Their Children as Young Adults: Asset Accumulation by African-American Families." *American Economic Review* 89:377–80.

———. 2000. "Asset Ownership Across Generations." *Jerome Levy Institute Working Paper*.

Church, of Jesus Christ of Latter-Day Saints. "Official Website of the Church of Jesus Christ of Latter-Day Saints." Accessed October 26, 2010, http://lds.org/?lang=eng.

Cohen, Bernard P. 1988. *Developing Sociological Knowledge: Theory and Method*. Belmont, CA: Wadsworth Publishing Company

Cohen, Yinon and Yitchak Haberfeld. 2007. "Self-Selection and Earnings Assimilation: Immigrants from the Former Soviet Union in Israel and the United States." *Demography* 44:649–68.

Cohen-Zada, Danny and William Sander. 2008. "Religion, Religiosity, and Private School Choice: Implications for Estimating the Effectiveness of Private Schools." *Journal of Urban Economics* 64:85–100.

Coleman, James S. 1990. *Foundations of Social Theory*. Cambridge, MA: Harvard University Press.

Coleman, James S., Thomas Hoffer, and Sally Kilgore. 1982a. "Achievement and Segregation in Secondary Schools: A Further Look at Public and Private School Differences." *Sociology of Education* 55:162–82.

———. 1982b. "Cognitive Outcomes in Public and Private Schools." *Sociology of Education* 55:65–76.

Coleman, John A. 1993. *One Hundred Years of Catholic Social Thought*. Maryknoll, NY: Orbis Books.

Collins, Randall. 1997. "An Asian Route to Capitalism: Religious Economy and the Origin of Self-Transforming Growth in Japan." *American Sociological Review* 62:843–65.

Conley, Dalton. 1999. *Being Black, Living in the Red: Race, Wealth and Social Policy in America*. Berkeley, CA: University of California Press.

Cummings, Richard J. 1982. "Quintessential Mormonism: Literal-Mindedness as a Way of Life." *Dialogue* 15:92–102.

D'Antonio, William V., James D. Davidson, Dean R. Hoge, and Katherine Meyer. 2001. *American Catholics: Gender, Generation, and Commitment*. Walnut Creek, CA: Altamira Press.

D'Antonio, William V., Dean R. Hoge, and James D. Davidson. 2007. *American Catholics Today: New Realities of Their Faith and Their Church*. Lanham, MD: Rowman and Littlefield.

Dahl, Robert A. 1961. *Who Governs? Democracy and Power in an American City*. New Haven, CT: Yale University Press.

Darnell, Alfred and Darren E. Sherkat. 1997. "The Impact of Protestant Fundamentalism on Educational Attainment." *American Sociological Review* 62:306–15.

Davidson, James D. 1994. "Religion among America's Elite: Persistence and Change in the Protestant Establishment." *Religion and Democracy* Winter: 419–40.

———. 2008. "Religious Stratification: Its Origins, Persistence, and Consequences." *Sociology of Religion* 55:419–40.

Davidson, James D. and Ralph E. Pyle. 2011. Ranking Faiths: *Religious Stratification in America*. New York: Rowman and Littlefield.

Davidson, James D., Ralph E. Pyle, and David V. Reyes. 1995. "Persistence and Change in the Protestant Establishment, 1930–1992." *Social Forces* 74:157–75.

DeBerri, Edward P. and James E. Hug. 2003. *Catholic Social Teaching: Our Best Kept Secret, Fourth Edition*. Maryknoll, NY: Orbis Books.

DellaPergola, Sergio. 1980. "Patterns of American Jewish Fertility." *Demography* 17:261–73.

Demereth, Nicholas Jay. 1965. *Social Class and American Protestantism*. Chicago: Rand McNally.

Domhoff, G. William. 2006. *Who Rules America? Power and Politics, Fourth Edition*. New York: McGraw Hill.

Downey, Douglas B. 1995. "When Bigger Is Not Better: Family Size, Parental Resources, and Children's Educational Performance." *American Sociological Review* 60:746–61.

Durkheim, Emile. (1954 [1912]). *The Elementary Forms of Religious Life*. New York: Free Press.

Dynan, Karen E. 1993. "The Rate of Time Preference and Shocks to Wealth: Evidence From Panel Data." *Board of Governors of the Federal Reserve System Working Paper Series, Number 134*.

Edgell, Penny. 2006. *Religion and Family in a Changing Society*. Princeton, NJ: Princeton University Press.

Ellison, Christopher G. 1991. "Religious Involvement and Subjective Well-Being." *Journal of Health and Social Behavior* 32:80–99.

Ellison, Christopher G. and John P. Bartkowski. 2002. "Conservative Protestantism and the Division of Household Labor among Married Couples." *Journal of Family Issues* 23:950–85.

Ellison, Christopher G., David A. Gay, and Thomas A. Glass. 1989. "Does Religious Commitment Contribute to Individual Life Satisfaction?" *Social Forces* 68:100–23.

Ellison, Christopher G. and Robert A. Hummer. 2010. *Religion, Families, and Health: Population-Based Research in the United States*. New Brunswick, NJ: Rutgers University Press.

Ellison, Christopher G., Robert A. Hummer, Amy M. Burdette, and Maureen R. Banjamins. 2010. "Race, Religious Involvement, and Health: The Case of African Americans." Pp. 321–48 in *Religion, Families, and Health: Population-Based Research in the United States*, edited by C. G. Ellison and R. A. Hummer. New Brunswick, NJ: Rutgers University Press.

Ellison, Christopher G. and Jeffrey S. Levin. 1998. "The Religion-Health Connection: Evidence, Theory, and Future Directions." *Health Education and Behavior* 25:700–20.

Ellison, Christopher G. and Darren Sherkat. 1995. "Is Sociology the Core Discipline for the Scientific Study of Religion." *Social Forces* 73:1255–66.

Evans, William N. and Robert M. Schwab. 1995. "Finishing High School and Starting College: Do Catholic Schools Make a Difference?" *The Quarterly Journal of Economics* 110:941–74.

Ewing, Bradley T. 2000. "The Wage Effect of Being Raised in the Catholic Religion: Does Religion Matter?" *American Journal of Economics and Sociology* 59:419–32.

Featherman, David L. 1971. "The Socioeconomic Achievement of White Religio-Ethnic Subgroups." *American Sociological Review* 26:207–22.

Federal Reserve Board. 2009. "Household Debt Service and Financial Obligations Ratios." http://www.federalreserve.gov/releases/housedebt/.

Filsinger, Erik E. and Margaret R. Wilson. 1984. "Religiosity, Socioeconomic Rewards, and Family Development: Predictors of Marital Adjustment." *Journal of Marriage and the Family* 46:663–70.

Finke, Roger and Rodney Stark. 2005. *The Churching of America, 1776–2005: Winners and Losers in Our Religious Economy*. Rutgers, NJ: Rutgers University Press.

Fitzgerald, Scott T. and Jennifer Glass. 2008. "Can Early Family Formation Explain the Lower Educational Attainment of U.S. Conservative Protestants?" *Sociological Spectrum* 28:556–77.

Form, William. 2000. "Italian Protestants: Religion, Ethnicity, and Assimilation." *Journal for the Scientific Study of Religion* 39:307–320.

Frank, Robert. 2007. *Richistan: A Journey through the American Wealth Boom and the Lives of the New Rich*. New York: Three Rivers.

French, Eric. 2005. "The Effects of Health, Wealth, and Wages on Labour Supply and Retirement Behavior." *Review of Economic Studies* 72:395–427.

Gallagher, Sally K. and Christian Smith. 1999. "Symbolic Traditionalism and Pragmatic Egalitarianism: Contemporary Evangelicals, Families, and Gender." *Gender and Society* 13:211–33.

Gallup World Poll. November 8, 2010. "National Income and Happiness."

Garman, E. Thomas and Raymond E. Forgue. 2010. *Personal Finance*. Boston: Houghton Mifflin.

Giving USA Foundation. 2009. *Giving USA: 2008*. Glenview, IL: GUSA Press.

Glass, Jennifer and Jerry Jacobs. 2005. "Childhood Religious Conservatism and Adult Attainment among Black and White Women." *Social Forces* 83:555–79.

Glenn, Norval D. and Ruth Hyland. 1967. "Religious Preference and Worldly Success: Some Evidence from National Surveys." *American Sociological Review* 32:73–85.

Gokhale, Jagadeesh and Laurence J. Kotlikoff. 2000. "The Baby Boomers' Mega-Inheritance – Myth or Reality?" *Federal Reserve Bank of Cleveland Economic Commentary*.

Greeley, Andrew and Michael Hout. 2006. *The Truth about Conservative Christians: What They Think and What They Believe*. Chicago: University of Chicago.

Greeley, Andrew M. 1979. "The Sociology of American Catholics." *Annual Review of Sociology* 79:91–111.

———. 1989. "Protestant and Catholic: Is the Analogical Imagination Extinct?" *American Sociological Review* 54:485–502.

———. 2004. *The Catholic Revolution: New Wine, Old Wineskins, and the Second Vatican Council*. Berkeley: University of California Press.

Gregory, Frances and Irene Neu. 1962. "The American Industrial Elite in the 1870s." Pp. 193–211 in *Men in Business*, edited by W. Miller. Santa Barbara, CA: Greenwood Publishing Group.

Hackney, Charles and Glenn Sanders. 2003. "Religiosity and Mental Health: A Meta-Analysis of Recent Studies." *Journal for the Scientific Study of Religion* 42:43–55.

Halek, Martin and Joseph G. Eisenhauer. 2001. "Demography of Risk Aversion." *The Journal of Risk and Insurance* 68:1–24.

Hamington, Maurice. 1995. *Hail Mary? The Struggle for Ultimate Womanhood in Catholicism*. New York: Routledge.

Hammond, Judith A., Bettie S. Cole, and Scott H. Beck. 1993. "Religious Heritage and Teenage Marriage." *Review of Religious Research* 35:117–33.

Hauser, Robert M. and John Robert Warren. 1997. "Socioeconomic Indexes for Occupations: A Review, Update, and Critique." *Sociological Methodology* 27:177–298.

Hayashi, Takashi. 2005. "Intertemporal Substitution, Risk Aversion and Ambiguity Aversion." *Economic Theory* 25:933–56.

Haynie, Dana L. 2001. "Delinquent Peers Revisited: Does Network Structure Matter?" *American Journal of Sociology* 106:1013–57.

Heaton, Tim B. 2010. "Religion, Sexually Risky Behavior, and Reproductive Health: The Mormon Case." Pp. 368–84 in *Religion, Families, and Health: Population-Based Research in the United States*, edited by C. G. Ellison and R. A. Hummer. New Brunswick, NJ: Rutgers University Press.

Hechter, Michael. 1992. "Should Values Be Written out of the Social Scientist's Lexicon?" *Sociological Theory* 10:214–30.

———. 1993. "Values Research in the Social and Behavioral Sciences." Pp. 1–30 in *The Origin of Values*, edited by M. Hechter, L. Nadel, and R. Michod. New York: Aldine de Gruyter.

Hechter, Michael, Hyojoung Kim, and Justin Baer. 2005. "Prediction versus Explanation in the Measurement of Values." *European Sociological Review* 21:91–108.

Heyman, Isaac W. and Kathleen M. Eberstein 2010. "Jewish Identity and Self-Reported Health." Pp. 349–67 in *Religion, Families, and Health: Population-Based Research in the United States*, edited by C. G. Ellison and R. A. Hummer. New Brunswick, NJ: Rutgers University Press.

Hirschman, Elizabeth C. 1983. "Religious Affiliation and Consumption Processes: An Initial Paradigm." *Research in Marketing* 6:131–70.

Hitlin, Steven. 2003. "Values as the Core of Personal Identity: Drawing Links between Two Theories of Self." *Social Psychology Quarterly* 66:118–37.

Hitlin, Steven and Jane Allyn Piliavin. 2004. "Values: Reviving a Dormant Concept." *Annual Review of Sociology* 30:359–93.

Hoffer, Thomas, Andrew M. Greeley, and James S. Coleman. 1985. "Achievement Growth in Public and Catholic Schools." *Sociology of Education* 58:74–97.

Hoge, Dean R., Charles Zech, Patrick McNamara, and Michael J. Donahue. 1999. "Giving in Five Denominations." Pp. 3–10 in *Financing American Religion*, edited by M. Chaves and S. L. Miller. London: Sage Publications.

Hollinger, David A. 2004. "Rich, Powerful, and Smart: Jewish Overrepresentation Should Be Explained Instead of Avoided or Mystified." *The Jewish Quarterly Review* 94:595–602.

Houseman, Susan N. 2001a. "The Benefits Implication of Recent Trends in Flexible Staffing Arrangements." *Pension and Research Council Working Paper No. 2001–19*, The Wharton School, University of Pennsylvania.

———. 2001b. "Why Employers Use Flexible Staffing Arrangements: Evidence from an Establishment Survey." *Industrial and Labor Relations Review* 55:149–70.

Hout, Michael and Claude S. Fischer. 2002. "Why More Americans Have No Religious Preference: Politics and Generations." *American Sociological Review* 67:165–90.

Hout, Michael, Michael Greeley, and Melissa Wilde. 2001. "The Demographic Imperative in Religious Change in the United States." *American Journal of Sociology* 107:468–500.

Hout, Michael and William R. Morgan. 1975. "Race and Sex Variations in the Causes of the Expected Attainments of High School Seniors." *The American Journal of Sociology* 81:364–94.

Hummer, Robert A., Maureen R. Benjamins, Christopher G. Ellison, and Richard G. Rogers. 2010. "Religious Involvement and Mortality Risk among Pre-Retirement Aged U.S. Adults." Pp. 273–91 in *Religion, Families, and Health: Population-Based Research in the United States*, edited by C. G. Ellison and R. A. Hummer. New Brunswick, NJ: Rutgers University Press.

Hurst, Dawn S. and Frank L. Mott. 2006. "Secular Pay-Offs to Religious Origins: Gender Differences among American Jews." *Sociology of Religion* 67:439–63.

Hurst, Erik and James P. Ziliak. 2006. "Do Welfare Asset Limits Affect Household Saving? Evidence from Welfare Reform." *Journal of Human Resources* 41:46–71.

Iannaccone, Lawrence R. 1998. "An Introduction to the Economics of Religion." *Journal of Economic Literature* 36:1465–96.

Joas, Hans. 2000. *The Genesis of Values*. Cambridge: Polity.

———. 1976. "The Status Attainment Process: Socialization or Allocation?" *Social Forces* 55:368–81.

Johnson, Monica Kirkpatrick. 2001. "Job Values in the Young Adult Transition: Change and Stability with Age." *Social Psychology Quarterly* 64:297–317.

Johnson, Monica Kirkpatrick and Glen H. Elder, Jr. 2002. "Educational Pathways and Work Value Trajectories." *Sociological Perspectives* 45:113–38.

Jones, Charles F. and Elise F. Westoff. 1979. "The End of Catholic Fertility." *Demography* 16:209–18.

Juster, Thomas F. and Kathleen A. Kuester. 1991. "Differences in the Measurement of Wealth, Wealth Inequality and Wealth Composition Obtained from Alternative U.S. Wealth Surveys." *Review of Income and Wealth* 37:33–62.

Juster, Thomas F., James P. Smith, and Frank Stafford. 1999. "The Measurement and Structure of Household Wealth." *Labour Economics* 6:253–75.

Kadushin, Charles and Laurence Kotler-Berkowitz. 2006. "Informal Social Networks and Formal Organizational Memberships among American Jews: Findings from the National Jewish Population Survey 2000–01." *Sociology of Religion* 67:465–85.

Kalleberg, Arne L. 2000. "Nonstandard Employment Relations: Part-time, Temporary and Contract Work." *Annual Review of Sociology* 26:341–65.

Kalleberg, Arne L. and Jeremy Reynolds. 2000. "Work Attitudes and Nonstandard Work Arrangements in the United States, Japan and Europe." Pp. 423–73 in *Growth of Non-Standard Work Arrangements*, edited by S. Houseman and M. Osawa. Kalamazoo, MI: W.E. Upjohn Institute for Employment Research.

Kalmijn, Matthijs. 1991. "Shifting Boundaries: Trends in Religious and Educational Homogamy." *American Sociological Review* 56:786–800.

Keister, Lisa A. 2000a. "Race and Wealth Inequality: The Impact of Racial Differences in Asset Ownership on the Distribution of Household Wealth." *Social Science Research* 29:477–502.

———. 2000b. *Wealth in America*. New York: Cambridge University Press.

———. 2003a. "Religion and Wealth: The Role of Religious Affiliation and Participation in Early Adult Asset Accumulation." *Social Forces* 82:175–207.

———. 2003b. "Sharing the Wealth: The Effect of Siblings on Adults' Wealth Ownership." *Demography* 40:521–42.

———. 2005. *Getting Rich: America's New Rich and How They Got That Way*. Cambridge: Cambridge University Press.

———. 2007. "Upward Wealth Mobility: Exploring the Roman Catholic Advantage." *Social Forces* 85:1195–226.

———. 2008. "Conservative Protestants and Wealth: How Religion Perpetuates Asset Poverty." *American Journal of Sociology* 113:1237–71.

———. 2009. "Religion and Stratification: A Dynamic Social Balance Model." *Under review*.

———. In progress. "Is Church a Better Investment Than the Stock Market?" *Duke University Department of Sociology Working Paper*.

Keister, Lisa A. and Natalia Deeb-Sossa. 2001. "Are Baby Boomers Richer Than Their Parents? Intergenerational Patterns of Wealth Ownership in the United States." *Journal of Marriage and the Family* 63:569–79.

Kennelly, Karen. 1989. "*American Catholic Women: A Historical Exploration*." New York: Macmillan.

Kennickell, Arthur B. 2009. "Ponds and Streams: Wealth and Income in the U.S., 1989 to 2007." *Finance and Economics Discussion Series, Divisions of Research & Statistics and Monetary Affairs*. Washington, DC: Federal Reserve Board.

Kennickell, Arthur B., Martha Starr-McCluer, and Annika E. Sunden. 1997. "Family Finances in the U.S.: Recent Evidence from the Survey of Consumer Finances." *Federal Reserve Bulletin* January:1–24.

Kerckhoff, Alan C. 1993. *Diverging Pathways: Social Structure and Career Deflections*. Cambridge: Cambridge University Press.

Kim, Phillip H., Howard E. Aldrich, and Lisa A. Keister. 2004. "Household Income and Net Worth." Pp. 49–61 in *Handbook of Entrepreneurial Dynamics: The Process of Business Creation in Contemporary America*, edited by W. B. Gartner. Thousand Oaks, CA: Sage.

Kohn, Melvin L. 1959. "Social Class and Parental Values." *The American Journal of Sociology* 64:337–51.

———. 1969. *Class and Conformity*. Homewood, IL: Dorsey.

———. 1976. "Social Class and Parental Values: Another Confirmation of the Relationship." *American Sociological Review* 41:538–45.

Kohn, Melvin L. and Kazimierz M. Slomczynski. 2001. "Social Structure and Self-Direction: A Comparative Analysis of the United States and Poland." Pp. 65–92 in *Self in Society*, edited by A. Branaman. Malden, MA: Blackwell.

Kohn, Melvin L., Kazimierz M. Slomczynski, Krystyna Janicka, Valeri Khmelko, Bogden W. Mach, Vladimir Paniotto, Wojciech Zaborowski, Roberto Guitierrez, Cory Heyman. 1997. "Social Structure and Personality under Conditions of Radical Social Change: A Comparative Analysis of Poland and Ukraine." *American Sociological Review* 62:614–38.

Kohn, Melvin L., Wojciech Zaborowski, Krystyna Janicka, Bogdan W. Mach, Valeriy Khmelko, Kazimierz M. Slomczynski, Cory Heyman, and Bruce Podobnik. 2000. "Complexity of Activities and Personality under Conditions of Radical Social Change: A Comparative Analysis of Poland and Ukraine." *Social Psychology Quarterly* 63:187–207.

Kmec, Julie A. 1999. "Multiple Aspects of Work-Family Conflict." *Sociological Focus* 32:265–85.

Krause, Neal, Christopher E. Ellison, Benjamin A. Shaw, John P. Marcum, and Jason D. Boardman. 2001. "Church-Based Social Support and Religious Coping." *Journal for the Scientific Study of Religion* 40:637–56.

Kreider, Larry. 2002. *God's Perspective on Finances: How God Wants His People to Handle Money*. Ephrata, PA: House to House Publications.

Kuran, Timur. 2003. "The Islamic Commercial Crisis: Institutional Roots of Economic Underdevelopment in the Middle East." *Journal of Economic History* 63:414–46.

Laitner, John. 2001. "Secular Changes in Wealth Inequality and Inheritance." *Economic Journal* 111:691–721.

Lareau, Annette. 2000. *Home Advantage: Social Class and Parental Intervention in Elementary Education*. New York: Rowman & Littlefield Publishers.

———. 2002. "Invisible Inequality: Social Class and Childrearing in Black Families and White Families." *American Sociological Review* 67:747–76.

———. 2003. *Unequal Childhoods: Class, Race, and Family Life*. Berkeley: University of California Press.

Lawrence, Emily C. 1991. "Poverty and the Rate of Time Preference: Evidence from Panel Data." *Journal of Political Economy* 99:54–77.

Lee, Dwight R. 1996. "Why Is Flexible Employment Increasing?" *Journal of Labor Research* 17:543–53.

Lehrer, Evelyn L. 1995. "The Effect of Religion on the Labor Supply of Married Women." *Social Science Research* 24:281–301.

————. 1996a. "The Determinants of Marital Stability: A Comparative Analysis of First and Higher Order Marriages." Pp. 91–121 in *Research in Population Economics*, edited by T. P. Schultz. Greenwich, CT: JAI.

————. 1996b. "Religion as a Determinant of Fertility." *Journal of Population Economics* 9:173–96.

————. 1996c. "The Role of the Husband's Religion on the Economic and Demographic Behavior of Families." *Journal for the Scientific Study of Religion* 35:145–55.

————. 1998. "Religious Intermarriage in the United States: Determinants and Trends." *Social Science Research* 27:245–63.

————. 1999. "Religion as a Determinant of Educational Attainment: An Economic Perspective." *Social Science Research* 28:358–79.

————. 2000. "Married Women's Labor Supply Behavior in the 1990s: Differences by Life-cycle Stage." Pp. 227–52 in *The Ties That Bind: Perspectives on Marriage and Cohabitation*, vol. 80, edited by C. B. Linda Waite, Michelle Hindon, Elizabeth Thomson, and Arland Thornton. Hawthorne, NY: Aldine de Gruyter.

————. 2004a. "Religion as a Determinant of Economic and Demographic Behavior in the United States." *Population and Development Review* 30:707–26.

————. 2004b. "Religiosity as a Determinant of Educational Attainment: The Case of Conservative Protestant Women in the United States." *Review of Economics of the Household* 2:203–19.

————. 2004c. "The Role of Religion in Union Formation: An Economic Perspective." *Population Research and Policy Review* 23:161–85.

————. 2009. *Religion, Economics and Demography: The Effects of Religion on Education, Work, and the Family.* New York: Routledge.

————. 2010. "Religious Affiliation and Participation as Determinants of Women's Educational Attainment and Wages." Pp. 186–205 in *Religion, Families, and Health: Population-Based Research in the United States*, edited by C. G. Ellison and R. A. Hummer. New Brunswick, NJ: Rutgers University Press.

Lehrer, Evelyn and Carmel U. Chiswick. 1993. "Religion as a Determinant of Marital Stability." *Demography* 30:385–404.

Lenski, Gerhard. 1961. *The Religious Factor: A Sociological Study of Religion's Impact on Politics, Economics, and Family Life.* Garden City, NY: Doubleday.

Levin, Jeffrey S. 1994. *Religion in Aging and Health: Theoretical Foundations and Methodological Frontiers.* Thousand Oaks, CA: Sage.

Lieberson, Stanley and Donna K. Carter. 1979. "Making It in America: Differences between Eminent Blacks and White Ethnic Groups." *American Sociological Review* 44:347–66.

Lindsay, D. Michael. 2008. "Evangelicals in the Power Elite: Elite Cohesion Advancing a Movement." *American Sociological Review* 73:60–2.

Lupton, Joseph and James P. Smith. 2003. "Marriage, Assets, and Savings." Pp. 129–52 in *Marriage and the Economy: Theory and Evidence from Industrialized Societies*, edited by S. Grossbard-Shechtman. Cambridge: Cambridge University Press.

Maio, Greg R., James M. Olson, Mark Bernard, Michelle A. Luke. 2003. "Ideologies, Values, Attitudes, and Behavior." In *Handbook of Social Psychology*, edited by J. DeLamater. New York: Kluwer Academic.

Mantell, Ruth. 2009. "Home Prices Off Record 18% in Past Year, Case-Shiller Says." *MarketWatch.com*, http://www.marketwatch.com/story/home-prices-off-record-18-in-past-year-case-shiller-says.

Marcum, John P. 1981. "Explaining Fertility Differences among U.S. Protestants." *Social Forces* 60:532–43.

———. 1986. "Explaining Protestant Fertility: Belief, Commitment, and Homogamy." *Sociological Quarterly* 27:547–58.

Mathews, Shailer. 1896. "Christian Sociology V. Wealth." *American Journal of Sociology* 1:771–84.

Mauss, Armand L. 1984. "Sociological Perspectives on the Mormon Subculture." *Annual Review of Sociology* 10:437–60.

McDermott, Monica. 2002. "Trends in the Race and Ethnicity of Eminent Americans." *Sociological Forum* 17:137–60.

McQuillan, Kevin. 2004. "When Does Religion Influence Fertility?" *Population and Development Review* 30:532–43.

Mennino, Sue F. and April Brayfield. 2002. "Job-Family Trade-Offs: The Multidimensional Effects of Gender." *Work and Occupations* 29:226–56.

Mihelich, John and Debbie Storrs. 2003. "Higher Education and the Negotiated Process of Hegemony: Embedded Resistance among Mormon Women." *Gender and Society* 17:404–22.

Miller, Alan S. 2000. "Going to Hell in Asia: The Relationship between Risk and Religion in a Cross Cultural Setting." *Review of Religious Research* 42:5–18.

Miller, Alan S. and John P. Hoffmann. 1995. "Risk and Religion: An Exploration of Gender Differences in Religiosity." *Journal for the Scientific Study of Religion* 34:63–75.

Miller, Alan S. and Rodney Stark. 2002. "Gender and Religiousness: Can Socialization Explanation by Saved?" *American Journal of Sociology* 107:1399–423.

Mills, C. Wright. 1959. *The Power Elite*. New York: Oxford University Press.

Moody, James W. 2004. "The Structure of a Social Science Collaboration Network." *American Sociological Review* 69:213–38.

Mosher, William D., Linda B. Williams, and David P. Johnson. 1992. "Religion and Fertility in the United States: New Patterns." *Demography* 29:199–214.

National Philanthropic Trust. 2009. *A Chronological History of Philanthropy in the United States*. Jenkintown, PA: NPT Press.

Neal, Derek. 1997. "The Effect of Catholic Secondary Schooling on Educational Achievement." *Journal of Labor Economics* 15:98–123.

Nelson, Phillip J. and Kenneth V. Greene. 2003. *Signaling Goodness: Social Rules and Public Choices*. Ann Arbor: University of Michigan Press.

Nielsen, Lars Tyge. 2005. "Monotone Risk Aversion." *Economic Theory* 25:203–15.

Oats, Mary J. 1989. "Catholic Laywomen in the Labor Force, 1850–1950." Pp. 81–124 in *American Catholic Women*, edited by K. Kennelly. New York: MacMillan.

Oliver, Melvin and Thomas M. Shapiro. 1995. *Black Wealth/White Wealth*. New York: Routledge.

Ottoni-Wilhelm, Mark. 2010. "Giving to Organizations That Help People in Need: Differences across Denominational Identities." *Journal for the Scientific Study of Religion* 49:389–412.

Park, Jerry Z. and Joseph Baker. 2007. "What Would Jesus Buy: American Consumption of Religious and Spiritual Material Goods." *Journal for the Scientific Study of Religion* 46:501–17.

Park, Jerry Z. and Sam H. Reimer. 2002. "Revisiting the Social Sources of American Christianity 1972–1998." *Journal for the Scientific Study of Religion* 41:733–46.

Pearce, Lisa D. 2010. "Religion and the Timing of First Births in the United States." Pp. 19–39 in *Religion, Families, and Health: Population-Based Research in the United States*, edited by C. G. Ellison and R. A. Hummer. New Brunswick, NJ: Rutgers University Press.

Peek, Charles W., George D. Lowe, and L. Susan Williams. 1991. "Gender and God's Word: Another Look at Religious Fundamentalism and Sexism." *Social Forces* 69:1205–21.

Pope, Liston. 1948. "Religion and the Class Structure." *Annals of the American Academy of Political and Social Science* 256:84–91.

Regnerus, Mark. 2007. *Forbidden Fruit: Sex and Religion in the Lives of American Teenagers*. New York: Oxford University Press.

———. 2010. "Religion and Adolescent Sexual Behavior." Pp. 61–85 in *Religion, Families, and Health: Population-Based Research in the United States*, edited by C. G. Ellison and R. A. Hummer. New Brunswick, NJ: Rutgers University Press.

Regnerus, Mark D. and Christian Smith. 1998. "Selective Deprivatization among American Religious Traditions: The Reversal of the Great Reversal." *Social Forces* 76:1347–72.

———. 2005. "Selection Effects in Studies of Religious Influence." *Review of Religious Research* 47:23–50.

Regnerus, Mark D., Christian Smith, and David Sikkink. 1998. "Who Gives to the Poor? The Influence of Religious Tradition and Political Location on the Personal Generosity of Americans toward the Poor." *Journal for the Scientific Study of Religion* 37:481–93.

ReligionFacts. "Religion Facts: Just the Facts on Religion." Accessed October 28, 2010, at http://www.religionfacts.com/.

Reuters. 2008. "For Many U.S. Christians, It's God Before Mortgage." (September 21), p. 4.

———. 2009. "Many U.S. Christians Pay Tithe before Mortgage, Even in Crisis." (September 24), Reuters International.

Rogers, Richard G., Patrick M. Krueger, and Robert A. Hummer. 2010. "Religious Attendance and Cause-Specific Mortality in the United States." Pp. 292–320 in *Religion, Families, and Health: Population-Based Research in the United States*, edited by C. G. Ellison and R. A. Hummer. New Brunswick, NJ: Rutgers University Press.

Roof, Wade Clark and William McKinney. 1987. *American Mainline Religion: Its Changing Shape and Future*. New Brunswick, NJ: Rutgers University Press.

Sander, William. 1995. *The Catholic Family: Marriage, Children, and Human Capital*. Boulder, CO: Westview Press.

Sandefur, Gary D. and Thomas Wells. 1999. "Does Family Structure Really Influence Educational Attainment?" *Social Science Research* 28:331–57.

Schervish, Paul G. and Keith Whitaker. 2010. *Wealth and the Will of God: Discerning the Use of Riches in the Service of Ultimate Purpose*. Bloomington, IN: Indiana University Press.

Schnittker, Jason. 2008. "Happiness and Success: Genes, Families, and the Psychological Effects of Socioeconomic Position and Social Support." *American Journal of Sociology* 114:S233–59.

Schwartz, Shalom H. and Wolfgang Bilsky. 1987. "Toward a Theory of the Universal Content and Structure of Values." *Journal of Personality and Social Psychology* 58:878–91.

Shaefer, Richard T. and William W. Zellner. 2007. *Extraordinary Groups: An Examination of Unconventional Lifestyles*. New York: McMillan.

Sherkat, Darren E. 1991. "Leaving the Faith: Testing Theories of Religious Switching Using Survival Models." *Social Science Research* 20:171–87.

———. 2000. "That They Be Keepers of the Home: The Effect of Conservative Religion on Early and Late Transitions into Housewifery." *Review of Religious Research* 41:344–458.

———. 2004. "Religious Intermarriage in the United States: Trends, Patterns, and Predictors." *Social Science Research* 33:606–25.

———. 2006. "Religion and Economic Life." Pp. 658–61 in *International Encyclopedia of Economic Sociology*, edited by Jens Beckert and Milan Zafirovski. London: Routledge Press.

———. 2009. "Religion and Verbal Ability." *Social Science Research* 10:2–13.

Sherkat, Darren E. and Alfred Darnell. 1999. "The Effects of Parents' Fundamentalism on Children's Educational Attainment: Examining Differences by Gender and Children's Fundamentalism." *Journal for the Scientific Study of Religion* 38:23–35.

Sherkat, Darren E. and Christopher G. Ellison. 1999. "Recent Developments and Current Controversies in the Sociology of Religion." *Annual Review of Sociology* 25:363–394.

Sherkat, Darren and John Wilson. 1995. "Preferences, Constraints, and Choices in Religious Markets: An Examination of Religious Switching and Apostasy." *Social Forces* 73:993–1026.

Sikkink, David. 1999. "The Social Sources of Alienation from Public Schools." *Social Forces* 78:51–86.

Simmel, Georg. 1905. "A Contribution to the Sociology of Religion." *American Journal of Sociology* 11:359–76.

Singer, Judith D. 1998. "Using SAS PROC MIXED to Fit Multilevel Models, Hierarchical Models, and Individual Growth Models." *Journal of Educational and Behavioral Statistics* 24:323–55.

Sklare, Marshall. 1971. *America's Jews*. New York: Random House.

Smith, Christian. 2003a. "Religious Participation and Network Closure among American Adolescents." *Journal for the Scientific Study of Religion* 42:259–67.

——. 2003b. "Research Note: Religious Participation and Parental Moral Expectations and Supervision of American Youth." *Review of Religious Research* 44:414–24.

Smith, Christian and Robert Faris. 2005. "Socioeconomic Inequality in the American Religious System: An Update and Assessment." *Journal for the Scientific Study of Religion* 44:95–104.

Smith, David H. 2010. *Religious Giving: For Love of God.* Bloomington: Indiana University Press.

Smith, Tom W. 1990. "Classifying Protestant Denominations." *Review of Religious Research* 31:225–45.

——. 2002. "Religious Diversity in America: The Emergence of Muslims, Buddhists, Hindus, and Others." *Journal for the Scientific Study of Religion* 41:577–85.

Sombart, Werner. 1911. *The Jews and Modern Capitalism.* Translated by M. Epstein. New York: E. P. Dutton and Company.

Stark, Rodney. 2008. *What Americans Really Believe.* Waco, TX: Baylor University Press.

Stark, Rodney and William Bainbridge. 1987. *A Theory of Religion.* New York: Peter Lang.

Stark, Rodney and Roger Finke. 2000. *Acts of Faith: Explaining the Human Side of Religion.* Berkeley: University of California Press.

Steen, Todd P. 1996. "Religion and Earnings: Evidence from the NLS Youth Cohort." *International Journal of Social Economics* 23:47–58.

Steensland, Brian, Jerry Z. Park, Mark D. Regnerus, Lynn D. Robinson, W. Breadford Wilcox, Robert D. Woodberry. 2000. "The Measure of American Religion: Toward Improving the State of the Art." *Social Forces* 79:291–318.

Swidler, Ann. 1986. "Culture in Action: Symbols and Strategies." *American Sociological Review* 51:273–86.

Thibodeau, Richard, Edward J. O'Donnell, and with John C. O'Connor. 1997. *The Essential Catholic Handbook: A Summary of Beliefs, Practices, and Prayers.* Liguori, MI: Liguori Publications.

Thornton, Arland. 1985. "Changing Attitudes towards Separation and Divorce: Causes and Consequences." *American Journal of Sociology* 90:856–72.

Thumma, Scott. 2005. *Exploring the Megachurch Phenomena: Their Characteristics and Cultural Context.* Hartford, CT: Hartford Institute for Religion Research.

Thumma, Scott and Dave Travis. 2007. *Beyond Megachurch Myths: What We Can Learn from America's Largest Churches.* Hoboken, NJ: Jossey-Bass.

Tilly, Chris. 1996. *Half a Job: Bad and Good Jobs in a Changing Labor Market.* Philadelphia: Temple University Press.

Tolles, Frederick B. 1948. *Meeting House and Counting House.* Chapel Hill: University of North Carolina Press.

Tropman, John E. 1995. *The Catholic Ethic in American Society: An Exploration of Values.* San Francisco, CA: Jossey-Bass.

_____. 2002. *The Catholic Ethic and the Spirit of Community*. Washington, DC: Georgetown University Press.

Trust, National Philanthropic. 2009. *A Chronological History of Philanthropy in the United States*. Jenkintown, PA: NPT Press.

Vaisey, Stephen. 2009. "Motivation and Justification: A Dual Process Model of Culture in Action." *American Journal of Sociology* 114:1675–715.

Waite, Linda and Evelyn L. Lehrer. 2003. "The Benefits from Marriage and Religion in the United States: A Comparative Analysis." *Population and Development Review* 29:255–75.

Warren, John Robert and Robert Hauser. 1997. "Social Stratification across Three Generations: New Evidence from the Wisconsin Longitudinal Study." *American Sociological Review* 62:561–72.

Waxman, Chaim I. 1983. *America's Jews in Transition*. Philadelphia: Temple University Press.

_____. 2001. *Jewish Baby Boomers: A Communal Perspective*. Albany, NY: SUNY Press.

Weber, Max. 1930 [1905]. *The Protestant Ethic and the Spirit of Capitalism*. New York: Harper Collins.

Welch, Michael R., David Sikkink, and Matthew T. Loveland. 2007. "The Radius of Trust: Social Embeddedness and Trust in Strangers." *Social Forces* 86:23–46.

Wilcox, Bradford W. 1998. "Conservative Protestant Childrearing: Authoritarian or Authoritative?" *American Sociological Review* 63:796–809.

Wilder, Esther I. and William H. Walters. 1997. "American Jewish Household Income, 1969 and 1989." *Journal of Economic and Social Measurement* 23:197–212.

Willis, Paul. 1981. *Learning to Labor: How Working Class Kids Get Working Class Jobs*. New York: Columbia University Press.

Wilson, George. 2009. "Downward Mobility of Women from White-Collar Employment: Determinants and Timing by Race." *Sociological Forum* 24:382–401.

Wolfe, Alan. 1998. *Marginalized in the Middle*. Chicago: University of Chicago Press.

Wolff, Edward N. 1995. "The Rich Get Increasingly Richer: Latest Data on Household Wealth During the 1980s." Pp. 33–68 in *Research in Politics and Society*, vol. 5, edited by R. E. Ratcliff, M. L. Oliver, and T. M. Shapiro. Greenwich, CT: JAI Press.

_____. 1998. "Recent Trends in the Size Distribution of Household Wealth." *Journal of Economic Perspectives* 12:131–50.

_____. 2004. "Changes in Household Wealth in the 1980s and 1990s in the U.S." The Levy Economics Institute and New York University Working Paper.

Woodberry, Robert D. and Christian S. Smith. 1998. "Fundamentalism, et al.: Conservative Protestants in America." *Annual Review of Sociology* 24:25–56.

Wuthnow, Robert. 1994. *God and Mammon in America*. New York: Free Press.

_____. 2004. "The *Religious Factor* Revisited." *Sociological Theory* 22:205–18.

Wuthnow, Robert and Tracy L. Scott. 1997. "Protestants and Economic Behavior." Pp. 260–95 in *New Directions in American Religious History*, edited by H. S. Stout and D. G. Hart. New York: Oxford University Press.

Yamokoski, Alexis and Lisa A. Keister. 2005. "The Wealth of Single Women: Marital Status and Parenthood in the Asset Accumulation of Young Baby Boomers in the United States." *Feminist Economics* 12:167–94.

Zelizer, Viviana. 1978. "Human Values and the Market: The Case of Life Insurance and Death in 19th-Century America." *American Journal of Sociology* 84:591–610.

———. 1989. "The Social Meaning of Money: 'Special Monies'." *American Journal of Sociology* 95:342–77.

Zukin, Sharon and Jennifer Smith Maguire. 2004. "Consumers and Consumption." *Annual Review of Sociology* 30:173–97.

Zweigenhaft, Richard L. and G. William Domhoff. 1982. *Jews in the Protestant Establishment*. New York: Praeger Publishers.

———. 2006. *Diversity in the Power Elite: How It Happened, Why It Matters*. New York: Rowman & Littlefield.

Index